Endorsed by Authors, Experts, and Leaders

"After reading Spontaneous Tourism, you'll want to start exploring the world. This excellent book shows you why now is the time to go."
— JOEL WIDZER, AUTHOR OF *THE PENNY PINCHER'S PASSPORT TO LUXURY TRAVEL* AND CONTRIBUTOR TO MSNBC TRAVEL

"This is an encyclopedia of travel. From why to where to how, it is a goldmine of advice, resources and help."
— DAN POYNTER, AUTHOR OF *THE SELF-PUBLISHING MANUAL*

"Samans gives us the book I wish I had when I started to travel—all the basics plus some secrets for the world-traveled. A real tome!"
— CAROLYN HOWARD-JOHNSON, AUTHOR OF *THE FRUGAL BOOK PROMOTER*

Recommended by Busy People like You!

"This book helps you avoid some of the usual travel mistakes. It's a short cut to successful and enjoyable trips."
— ALEX NICKLAS, NATIONAL SALES MANAGER

"As a 20 year old, travel is such an abstract concept to me. I never realized how much thought and preparation goes into most trips! Spontaneous Tourism makes it much more tangible."
— JENNA AIELLO, FREELANCE PHOTOGRAPHER

"An experienced look at ways to explore the world both near and far. Definitely a book I will consult before my next trip. Well worth the investment."
— MICHAEL GREGORY, RESEARCH FACILITY SUPERVISOR

"A great book for anyone who has any desire to travel. Samans covers everything from the basics like catching a flight to advanced topics like frequent flyer programs in a straightforward and readable style."
— BRIAN ARCHIBALD, SOFTWARE DEVELOPER

"Thoughtful, engaging, and extremely informative. I'll put the travel tips and destination descriptions to use when I plan my next trip."
— MICHAEL WALLACE, GEOPHYSICIST

"Great advice from a world traveler and escape artist — tips and tricks for folks who live life on the fly."
— DAVID BOTTS, DIVEMASTER, SPEAKER, CRUISE VETERAN

SPONTANEOUS TOURISM

TOURISM

The Busy Person's Guide to Travel

JAMES C. SAMANS

CRYSTAL ORB

Spontaneous Tourism
The Busy Person's Guide to Travel

CrystalOrb LLC
2525 N 10th St. #811
Arlington, VA 22201
http://www.crystalorbllc.com

Copyright © 2008 James C. Samans

Edition ISBNs
　　Softcover　　978-0-9791897-0-8
　　Large Print　978-0-9791897-1-5
　　PDF　　　　978-0-9791897-2-2

**Library of Congress Number
LCCN 2001012345**

Edited by Carol Givner.
Cover and Layout by 1106 Design, LLC.

First Edition
Printed in the United States of America

**Publisher's Cataloging-in-Publication
(*Provided by Quality Books, Inc.*)**

Samans, James C.
　　Spontaneous tourism : the busy person's guide to
travel / James C. Samans. — 1st ed.
　　p. cm.
　　Includes bibliographical references and index.
　　ISBN-13: 978-0-9791897-0-8 (softcover)
　　ISBN-10: 0-9791897-0-5 (softcover)
　　ISBN-13: 978-0-9791897-1-5 (large print)
　　ISBN-10: 0-9791897-1-3 (large print)
　　[etc.]

　　1. Travel.　I. Title.

G151.S26 2007　　　　　910.2'02
　　　　　　　　　　　　QBI07-600121

Distributed by Midpoint Trade Books, Inc.

Quick Contents

vi

*"We do not remember days,
we remember moments."*

—Cesare Pavese

Detailed Contents

xix

About the Author

James C. Samans—the Spontaneous Tourist—travels more than 200,000 miles each year and holds elite status with United, Continental, AirTran, and Amtrak as well as the Hilton and Marriott hotel networks. He has been to every state in America and visited more than a dozen countries since 2004.

Jamie wrote this book to make travel more accessible to people with busy schedules. He can confidently say that you can take memorable trips in just a few days, because he regularly does it: Valentine's weekend in Paris, forty-eight hours in Singapore, Los Angeles to New York by train, a day trip to San Francisco from Washington, D.C. He's been to each of the domestic and international destinations he recommends to new travelers. All of the supplemental books he cites are books that he's read and found helpful.

Outside of his roles as an author and Spontaneous Tourist, Jamie works full time as an information security auditor in the Washington, D.C., metropolitan area and serves in the military as a reservist. He holds a Masters degree from the University of Maryland and resides in Arlington, Virginia.

You're welcome to email him with questions or comments at *author@spontaneoustourism.com*. He's also available upon request for discussions with book clubs and groups interested in travel.

Author's Disclaimer

Virtually all of the information provided in this book comes from the author's own firsthand experience and research. While every attempt has been made to ensure that this information is consistent and accurate, the travel industry is subject to almost constant change as a result of both competition and regulation.

Neither the author nor publisher shall in any way be held liable for monetary or other damages associated with the information provided in this book.

No travel provider or affiliate mentioned in this book provided any money, free or discounted services, or other compensation to gain a favorable representation or to be mentioned at all.

Acknowledgements

Who could ever imagine how many people are involved in creating a book?

Let me start by thanking **one**world, the Star Alliance, the National Passenger Rail Corporation (Amtrak), Greyhound Lines, Student Advantage LLC, and STA Travel for granting me permission to use their logos.

I'd like to thank Larry Tritten for licensing me his short story "Travels with Harry" to set the stage for everything that I had to say.

Thanks also to the many volunteers who served as peer reviewers for content throughout this book, helping to make sure it was as accurate as possible—Geoff Scott, Melanie Vaughan, Jim Cameron, Mark Moxon, Allison O'Dell, and Daniah Tajudeen.

The contributions of my editor, Carol Givner, are immeasurable. Michele DeFilippo of 1106 Design left me in awe with regard to both the quality and speed of her cover, interior layout, and typesetting work.

It's probably not possible to give enough credit to my girlfriend Gwen, who not only suggested the title for this book but also endured endless hours listening to me brainstorm and explain things about the book industry that she didn't care to know.

Of course, I'm very grateful for my cat-sitter, Deborah Head, who looked after my two kitties during the treks that I took around the world researching this book.

Special thanks to my dad, who unknowingly convinced me to go ahead with this project when he read and enjoyed an article on trains that I forwarded to his email; it was months later that he learned it was the first draft of Chapter 3.

Thanks to everyone who read a galley and decided to provide an endorsement, and to Mark Aguilera for helping me design an affordable direct marketing plan.

Finally, thanks to God, whose divine inspiration is the only possible explanation for a sudden wave of creative marketing ideas that came over me while visiting Puerto Rico in January.

Without all of them, the project I started would never have become the book that's in your hands today.

PART 1

Why You Should Go

The importance of travel, and why twenty-first century Americans in particular should be seeing as much of the world as possible.

"Experience is one thing you can't get for nothing."

—Oscar Wilde

CHAPTER 0

Travels with Harry

Author's Note: On one of my many flights in 2006, I came across a short story in United's Hemispheres Magazine that caught my attention. I was already writing this book and became convinced that it would be perfect as an opening. I contacted the author and licensed the rights to reprint it.

The main character in the story is the sort of person Spontaneous Tourism is meant to help, dreaming of travel but forever waiting for some future day—the sort you don't want to be. If you like, you can skip it and go ahead to the first chapter, but I encourage you to read it. It puts the rest of the book in perspective.

By Larry Tritten

Harry Daniels was a terrifically cosmopolitan person who had, however, never set foot outside of his country or even, with rare exception, his city. Reflecting on his failure to do so, he often likened himself to George Bailey in the movie *It's a Wonderful Life*. George Bailey had yearned to leave his small town of Bedford Falls, but whenever he'd been about to do so, a situation that called for a responsible decision to stay had prevented his leaving. In Harry's case, it wasn't responsibility that kept him but procrastination and indecision. When he was 20 he got a passport, which he carried in his shirt pocket in restaurants and bars, savoring the thrill of its exoticism while pondering his imminent trip to Europe … or somewhere. He ended up going to college instead, and the passport became a relic of personal memorabilia. In the meantime, Harry was a world traveler vicariously. He devoured spy novels set in the Bahamas, Dubrovnik, London, and Moscow and subscribed to magazines like *National Geographic* and *Arizona Highways*.

Out of college, Harry planned a trip to Hawai'i, but before he could leave, he got a job as a desk clerk in a big hotel and the trip was put on hold. At the hotel Harry found himself watching people show up from all parts of the country and world. He quietly served them while envying them all, and in the meantime he never got any farther from Chicago than Omaha, which he wasn't sure counted. But as a reader he was constantly traveling, and on the walls of his studio apartment there were posters of the golden-roofed Potala Palace in Lhasa, Tibet, a lush, palm-lined beach on one of the Maldives, and a luxury ocean liner pulling away from the dock with a storm of serpentine confetti coming down on the crowd seeing it off. Harry was a knockabout world traveler in his dreams. Which made him chronically wistful.

Then one day M. Bazzaz showed up.

A slight, sad-eyed man with the complexion of parchment, he arrived at the hotel wearing Travel Fox sneakers and a black suit worthy of a fundamentalist preacher or Transylvanian count and carrying a single small, dilapidated suitcase that might have belonged to a refugee. He checked into the hotel, paid cash for a room for a week, and stayed resolutely in it for a week, sending out twice a day for the Continental breakfast and meals of soup, cake, and pie. After the week was up, he was asked if he would be staying and said yes; he continued to order the meals but made no attempt to pay for them or the room. After two days of this, Harry was given the unpleasant task of going up to his room to set him straight.

Harry knocked on M. Bazzaz's door, not very firmly, since he felt a bit awkward.

After a few moments a voice said indistinctly, "Who is it?"

"Sir? I'm with the hotel."

"Ah."

"Sir?"

"Yes, eh?"

"Could I talk to you, please?"

The door opened and Bazzaz's eye morosely appeared. "Yes?"

"Can I come in?"

"Ah." The door opened all the way, reluctantly, Harry felt. Bazzaz crossed to the TV set and turned down Alex Trebek's voice. "Yes?" he said, without looking at Harry.

Harry looked around the room. There was only the small suitcase in one corner and, beside the bed on a stand, two books: *The Cake Bible* and *Fabulous Fruit Desserts*. He said, "The management asked me to see, if you're staying, uh—how …"

"To pay, eh?"

Harry smiled flatly, and nodded.

"Sir, I have no more money."

Harry raised his eyebrows.

"But I don't want to go."

Harry wondered what to say.

"I'm from a bottle, and this is much more comfortable."

"A … bottle?"

"Yes. Djinn."

Harry thought he'd said gin, but being well-read and veritably cosmopolitan, realized abruptly it was djinn, which was a variant of jinni. Genie.

"Genie?" he said.

"Yes, sir. Escaped. But, finding me, you can wish … not for much. No jewels, gold, power, long life. My powers are small. A trip is what you may get."

"A trip?"

"I have Bermuda, Shangri-la, Pittsburgh …"

Harry tugged at an earlobe. "Shangri-la? It isn't real."

"Try it."

Harry sighed.

"Los Angeles, sir? The sky like lilac, a nice Persian word. A moon like halvah. Women with hair the colors of copper and lemons, spiky and twisted."

Harry was enjoying visualizing such new-wave women but remembered suddenly the task at hand, which was suddenly twice as unpleasant. Bazzaz was a nut, to be sure, but a curiously likeable one—yet there was nothing he could do in favor of a guest who wanted to stay but couldn't afford to.

"If you want to stay but have no money, I don't think the management will allow that," Harry said, diverting the blame.

Bazzaz shrugged. "Well. Still, would you like the trip? Argentina, maybe? See Iguazu Falls, where 30 rivers meet and plunge over cliffs. Stand in the water mist; you are surrounded by the rainbows: lavender, blue, and yellow arches everywhere while the water thunders."

"That sounds great, but—"

"The Maldives, maybe? They are on your wall, yes? The ocean looks like emeralds illumined, the beaches—"

"How did you know that?" Harry said, startled.

"Djinns know."

Harry took a long breath and looked warily at Bazzaz, who then said, "And in your dresser there is … a collection. Flags of the World cards. From gum. 1970. You have all but Tunisia and Romania. Would you like to go to either?"

"There's no way you could know that," Harry said, staring at Bazzaz.

"Correct. Djinns know, though."

Harry paced to one end of the room, then back. "Wow!" he said.

"Big Apple?" Bazzaz suggested. "You will love Manhattan clubs. Neo-tomorrow décor. Glass ceilings, vinyl couches, neon floors. You may bathe in light."

"I—I'd love to go just about anywhere," Harry said. "Uh, except Omaha. So, what do you do?" he mused. "Snap your fingers and transport me?"

"Tickets. This is the 21st century, yes? I am like … what you call a travel agent."

"Suppose I chose Shangri-la," Harry said. "I'd get a ticket? On what airline?"

Bazzaz smiled. "That is a special. Choose it and see."

Harry stroked his chin thoughtfully. Winter was just around the corner in Chicago. "The Caribbean would be fine," he said.

"That is it?"

"Sure," he said impulsively, surprising himself. "A trip to the Caribbean, yeah."

"In your pocket."

"Huh?"

Bazzaz pointed to Harry's coat pocket. He felt the pocket and withdrew an envelope. Inside was a ticket to San Juan. Roundtrip, the date open.

"This is unbelievable," Harry said, which sounded both inadequate and trite, but certainly right on the money.

"Pleased?" Bazzaz asked.

"Dumfounded," Harry said.

"Maybe, then, tit for tat, you will make the management sympathetic with me."

Harry sat down on the bed and stared at the ticket, then looked at Bazzaz. "You don't have any money?"

"No, I have no job. Thence, no money."

7

"That's a problem," Harry said. "They'll want the money, and that's that." After a few moments, he said, "What about getting a job?"

Bazzaz smiled painfully. "I don't know. What can I do? I have only the experience of being bottled up for hundreds of years."

Harry was at a loss for encouraging words. He kept staring at the ticket, feeling altogether outlandish.

"Can you not help?" Bazzaz persisted.

"I'll do what I can," Harry said, knowing that it amounted to virtually nothing. He sat for a while in silence, then got up and said, "I'll go down and talk to them.… But …"

Bazzaz grimaced.

Downstairs, feeling dreamlike, Harry told the manager that Bazzaz was broke, and even as he sought something sympathetic to add, the manager was on his way upstairs, eyes narrowed. Harry waited behind the desk, unsettled by the whole matter. It occurred to him in a moment of bizarre consideration that he might let Bazzaz stay with him, but the notion promptly seemed ludicrous, partly because it sustained a reality that he would still possibly prefer to be a dream. Abruptly, he was called off to the hotel storeroom on another matter, and when he returned, the manager was leaning on the desk with a hard, self-satisfied expression.

"Another deadbeat bites the dust," he said.

"He's gone?" Harry asked.

"Did you see that suitcase?" the manager scoffed.

At home that night Harry put the ticket in the top drawer of his dresser, where he suspected it would disappear overnight. But in the morning it was still there. He tried to shut it out of his mind and didn't look again when he came home from work at the end of the day. The next morning it was still there.

The following day Harry called the airline to ask if there was a record of his reservation to San Juan. There was. During the next few days, several times Harry came to the brink of deciding to use the ticket and take a vacation, but he always hesitated. A couple of weeks passed, and Chicago's tough winter made its debut. Often each day Harry's mind would wander to thoughts of the Caribbean, of the azure waters and deep blue skies, stunning white beaches, and languorous palm trees of Martinique, Aruba, St. Croix, and Tobago, and he saw himself in the Sea Cliff hotel in the harbor of St. Thomas and at the Cinnamon Reef Beach Club on Anguilla behind a succession of yellow and pink fruit-flavored rum drinks.

Then one night Harry came home to find his apartment ransacked by thieves. His TV and VCR and stereo were gone, some of his clothes, the collection of expensive coffee-table books of photographs of faraway places, and the ticket was missing from the dresser drawer.

It seemed to Harry that it snowed continuously that winter. In the streets and against the buildings, snow fell silently like the soft settling of flakes in a stirred crystal paperweight. The days were dark, and the cold was always waiting when one left the comfort of warm rooms. But it was enlivening, too, in a way, and Harry usually took the opportunity provided by his lunch hour to leave the hotel and walk the streets to some restaurant blocks away. It was on one of these trips on a clear but livid day that, in passing a large frosted window, he glanced inside and something vaguely familiar caught his eye. Stepping back, he looked into a room whose walls were decorated with posters showing ocean liners and beaches and mountains. He stared at a man sitting at one of the three desks, eating his lunch from a brown paper bag. It was M. Bazzaz. Harry read the gold lettering on the window: ADVENTURER TRAVEL SERVICE. He stood there for a moment, musing, then opened the door and went inside. Bazzaz looked up at him as he sat in the chair beside his desk.

"Hello," Harry said.

Bazzaz put down the piece of German chocolate cake he was about to take a bite from. "Well," he said, and smiled. "Hello."

"You found a job," Harry said, pleased.

"Yes. I was good for something. A fount of stories to entice travelers …"

"Well, I'm glad it worked out. I couldn't do anything to stop—"

"No, no, please," Bazzaz said, smiling and holding up a hand. "It is all good now. And you? Took the trip?"

Harry told him what had happened, and Bazzaz made a glum sound and smacked his forehead with a palm. "Incredible!" Then, after a few seconds, he said, "Say, I'll bet you could use a vacation now. Eh? San Juan, was it?" He tapped a finger on the desk. "Get away from this cold. Bora Bora? Rio de Janeiro? Have Christmas on Christmas Island."

Harry said, "Well, I can't go now. But it sounds great."

"Ah." Bazzaz held up a finger. "Do yourself a favor. As we talk, just now, frogs prowl the ferns in the Amazon Basin and a butterfly the color of a lovely lady's eyeshadow lolls on a grand-grand kapok tree. You would love it. Why not watch the Christmas movies in a villa with an open-air living room on Jamaica, play golf among sugar cane and coconut trees? As we talk, in Costa Rica girls in pink swimsuits walk out of houses like white cakes to stand ankle deep in sand as warm as oven heat."

Listening to Bazzaz, Harry was borne away on a flying carpet of the imagination, even as he glanced through the frost-rimed window at the cold Chicago day.

Bazzaz went on in this vein, laying on lots of tropical imagery. After a while, as if coming out of a coma, Harry roused himself. He had to get back to the hotel, he said, but would Bazzaz consent to having lunch with him? Tomorrow?

The next day, throughout lunch, which for Bazzaz was mostly dessert (three kinds), Harry listened, spellbound, to more of the same kind of talk from his new friend. Bazzaz pursued Harry like a determined salesman. The lunch became a regular thing, at least once a week, and as the hounds of spring bore down on winter's traces, Bazzaz tapered off on the tropical imagery. As spring warmed, he was telling Harry about the white-misted blue towers of the Dolomites in Italy, the windows full of gold watches, crystal, and silk blouses, the gleaming bank windows along Zurich's Bahnhofstrasse, the dazzling reflected glow in the nighttime waters of the Seine made by the lamps along the Pont-Neuf. Harry felt that he was always on the verge of choosing a vacation, but in the face of so many fascinating tableaux, he never quite made up his mind. Someday, he told himself, he would take a trip, and then he would, of course, use the services of M. Bazzaz. Someday.

Larry Tritten is a veteran freelance writer (Scriptor horribilis) who has written for The New Yorker, Harper's, Vanity Fair, Playboy, and Cosmopolitan.

This story first appeared in the July 2006 issue of Hemispheres Magazine and has been reprinted with permission.

"Nothing is a waste of time if you use the experience wisely."

—Auguste Rodin

CHAPTER **1**

Travel Matters

Americans like to travel.

When asked what they'd do differently if they could live their lives again, people commonly say that they wish they'd traveled more. Travel is also one of the main goals that people have when they discuss their retirement plans.

You've picked up this book, so you're one of the people who'd like to travel. Most people don't actually end up *going* anywhere, though. One reason is that they're not sure where to begin. Without a handy reference guide like this one, the only way to figure it out would be to dive in and "learn by doing," making it more difficult for yourself and possibly making some mistakes.

Fortunately, by reading this book, you'll get a head start on travel, skip all of those "newbie" mistakes, and jump right to the advanced ones!

In the chapters that follow, we'll go over everything that you need to know to get out there and start seeing the world—transportation, lodging, paperwork, packing, and even some domestic and international destinations that are great for new travelers.

Before we do that, though, let's look at some reasons why so many people who want to travel never do—and what they're missing personally, socially, and professionally when they don't. Toward the end of the chapter, we'll talk about the concept of Spontaneous Tourism and how this philosophy can help you stop thinking about travel and start traveling.

Are you ready? Let's get started!

WHO SHOULD READ THIS BOOK?

Wait!

Before we go any further, let's take a moment to cover who should read this book. In some sense, the answer is "anyone," because the material we're going to cover here is factual and useful regardless of who you are or what you're doing. Even if you aren't part of the target audience, you'll learn a lot from what we'll cover. The people who will get the most out of this book, however, share a few common traits.

First, we're talking about travel for adults. Children are wonderful, but a family vacation is an entirely different experience, for a lot of reasons. The most obvious and cumbersome is the fact of a lot more luggage. Then there's the slower pace. You also lose a lot of flexibility, because children simply aren't allowed to go some places, won't enjoy certain kinds of travel, and aren't well suited to some lodging. On top of all of that, family trips also cost more.

> *Spontaneous Tourism* is actually a great book for parents to read. People with children sometimes forget that they need time for themselves too. Want to surprise that special someone with a weekend trip to Paris while the kids stay with their grandparents? This book will get you on the right track.

Also, this book was specifically written for an American audience. That's intentional, and it's not a matter of arrogance.

Americans are a lot less travel-savvy than people from the rest of the developed world. We have a unique national character and certain expectations, and to escape from our limited worldview, we need a reference guide targeted at overcoming those limits.

Does that mean non-Americans can't read this book? Of course not! It's a great reference for how travel works in general. Just keep in mind that when we cover domestic airlines and passenger rail, we'll spend most of our time on those systems as they exist in the United States, and when we talk about official paperwork like passports, we're talking about what's required for American travelers.

Before we do that, let's take a look at some of the reasons that we don't travel.

OBSTACLES TO TRAVEL

Some people don't want to travel—and that's fine. What's not fine is that there are lots of people like Harry from Chapter Zero who dream of exotic destinations but never get around to taking trips.

For the most part, these aren't lazy people. They're intelligent, motivated folks who are used to meeting the goals that they set for themselves. Many own their own homes and have jobs that pay well. A large number are college graduates, and some have even fit graduate school into their schedules.

Why, then, aren't they out seeing the world the way they say they want to see it? Are they lying to everyone? Are they lying to themselves?

Of course not. Obstacles get in the way. We all know people who have said that they would like to go somewhere, but they haven't been there yet. Why not, you ask? Oh, too busy, not enough money, someone would have to take care of the dog—there's a long list.

All of these reasons are valid. Travel certainly can be expensive, it does take time, and if you have a dog, your dog needs care while you're away. But these challenges can be overcome with good planning. When you hear these things, the core problem is American culture.

Culture

The United States is the wealthiest, most prosperous nation in the world. We have the highest standard of living and the largest economy. We have the strongest military. America is about success through superiority—doing it better than anyone else.

In fact, that's the problem!

The way that we define success places more emphasis on material possessions than it does on developing character and experience. Have a big house, a new car, and designer clothes. Get as much as you can as soon as you can, so everyone will know that you've made it. (Increasingly, we do it by borrowing, but that's a whole different story.)

Travel doesn't really fit in that mindset. Americans tend to view travel as a luxury that we'll pursue once we've satisfied all of our needs—loosely defined as having lots of stuff—but one that we can't let distract us along the way. Travel isn't a priority, and that's evident when we come up with excuses why not to do it.

Spending Habits

There's no way to travel without spending money. On the other hand, we spend a lot of money in the United States.

Think about how often you go out to eat, how much you spend on clothes, how much your car payment is each month. How much do you spend on gasoline each month for your car—and how much of the driving that you do is *really* necessary?

On top of that, America is a credit-centric society. Odds are that you already buy most of the things you have by using some form of credit—a credit card, mortgage, or auto loan. We'll spend money we don't have in order to buy more clothes, eat at restaurants, or go to the theatre, but when it comes to travel, we can't afford it. In most cases, we don't even bother to find out what it would cost before we decide that it's too expensive.

> The point isn't that you should be maxing out your credit cards buying airline tickets to Hawaii. It's that you need to admit to yourself that you *find* money for things that are important—and so far, travel hasn't been one of them.

There may not be a cheap way to see a particular destination on a particular day, but two things are guaranteed. First, on any given day, there are places you haven't seen that are cheap to see. Second, whatever place you'd like to see, there will be discounted travel opportunities in the future. Pay attention to special fares and deals. Accumulate rewards over time by joining frequent travel programs. You can make any trip affordable if your timing is flexible.

Priorities

We're busy people. Americans spend a lot of time working, and we tend to take our work home with us. The widespread use of cell phones and wireless email keeps us in touch with everyone even when we're on vacation. We even answer our phones while we're having dinner.

Our connectivity may or may not make us more productive—there's some indication that it might actually keep us from getting work done in a lot of cases—but it's unhealthy either way. People need to get away from work and do something else. Travel provides an opportunity to do that.

You can fit travel into any schedule. We've been conditioned to think that a trip is worth the effort only if we're able to spend a significant amount of time at a destination. That's ridiculous. If it were true, no one would take business trips to see distant clients, and no one would travel on Thanksgiving.

Change your mindset. Understand and accept that the only measure of whether a trip was worthwhile is what you saw, did, and experienced while you were there. Flying for twelve hours to spend a weekend in Paris is not a bad use of your time if you have a great time in Paris.

Think of travel time as free time where no one can disturb you. No cell phones ringing, no emails to answer, none of those potential time-wasters that fill a typical day. Make your travel time productive time, and instead of being time wasted, it will be time reclaimed and well spent.

When you start thinking this way, all sorts of travel becomes possible. If you were going to spend Friday working on a presentation in the office, bring it with you to do while you're en route to a fabulous destination. When you arrive, you'll have just finished a day of work and be ready for some fun.

Independence

It's amazing. Even with all of our communications technology, Americans are becoming less social. We spend more time on computers and phones than we do talking with people, and we let work keep us from seeing family and friends.

We also tend to be very individualistic in the United States. Our culture puts a big emphasis on being independent. We idolize the "self-made" person who's gotten where he or she is without any help.

That means that when we need someone to help out—for example, to let the dog out while we're away for the weekend—we don't feel comfortable asking. It also means that when we do ask, our friends and family members are more likely to refuse, because they value their personal space as well and don't want to be bothered.

If you have pets or need someone to take care of things while you're gone, the best thing to do is to hire someone. By offering to pay, you convert the situation from a plea for help to an opportunity for profit, so you're more likely to get a positive response. We certainly do love home-based business.

Attitude

People in other countries tend to think of Americans as arrogant people, and that opinion isn't always unjustified. We're taught at an early age that we live in the world's greatest country. It's a belief that we take to heart, but what does it mean?

Without traveling, we don't have any way to actually compare life in America to life anywhere else. All we're sure of is that we're great. In our competitive minds that means that everyone else isn't great. Why don't they all want to be Americans and enjoy the wonderful lives that we have? Since we're the best and brightest, how could our nation's actions not always be the best possible actions?

The same attitudes trickle down to the regional and state levels as well. Depending on where you live, you might assume that people from West Virginia are unsophisticated, New Yorkers are snobby, or Texans are cavalier. Hopefully, as you're reading this, you're seeing the flaw in that way of thinking.

Our country has done some amazing things, but it doesn't mean that everyone else is inferior. It doesn't mean that they're better than us either. Their ways of doing things could be just as good as ours. Even people who recognize our success in the world still have pride in their own countries.

19

TRAVEL IS A SELF-IMPROVEMENT COURSE

It's hard to maintain an attitude of cultural superiority when you travel. Over time, you can't help seeing that in a lot of cases other countries are doing their own thing, and that it works fine for them. That wears away our tendency to think that we have the "one true way" to do everything.

> Once you start traveling, you'll quickly see that your perspective on the world is much broader than the perspectives of people you know who haven't been anywhere. In some cases, that might lead to some arguments when you disagree with what they know is the right way to do something, but it can only help them, you, and America itself in the long run.

Take people one at a time, and don't be quick to dismiss their cultures as less worthwhile than yours. When you leave on a trip, whether it's to another state or another country, understand in advance that things where you're going won't be quite the way that you're used to them back home. Accept that, enjoy it, and embrace it.

We live in a world of diverse cultures and ideas, and that's not a bad thing. You're welcome to oppose ideas that you think are wrong, but make informed decisions.

Language

English is spoken in all fifty of the United States as well as its territories (though not exclusively). There are quite a few other English-speaking countries in the world as well, including some that you might not realize, such as Singapore.

Lots of people around the world also learn English as a second or third language, because it's very useful when dealing with people from English-speaking countries. The fact is, though, that English is not spoken everywhere.

Fortunately, there are some ways to reduce the language barrier.

> The first time that you find yourself in a country whose main language isn't English, you'll immediately appreciate why you should have paid more attention in French, Spanish, German, or whatever language class you took!

Learn!

Americans have a harder time than most people when it comes to language because we, as a general rule, do such a poor job of learning other languages. Schools usually mandate two or more years of a foreign language. We try, but the kind of immersive practice that's common in Europe isn't so easy in the U.S. because the value is unclear. It isn't until our first trips overseas that we discover how valuable it is to know another language.

Your best bet when traveling overseas is always to learn at least a little of the language before you go. Pick up a course catalog for your local community college, and you may be surprised to see how many language courses are offered. Drop by the bookstore and you'll find language courses on audio CDs, which are perfect to use while you're commuting to school or work, or even on the plane.

21

DON'T BE THE "UGLY AMERICAN"

One of the biggest mistakes that Americans make is assuming that because a lot of people overseas speak English, they can merely show up and expect not to have any problems. Some even become hostile when the people they encounter don't understand them.

You've got to overcome the sense that someone who can't speak your language is less intelligent than you are. One language is as good as another. It's a matter of luck that you were taught to speak English rather than something else at an early age, and it's just as tough for someone else to learn English as it is for you to learn their language.

Always *try* to speak to someone in his or her own language whenever possible. If you aren't able to get your point across, ask if he or she speaks English in the form of an apology, which it should be. You're the one who can't communicate.

Another way to learn language is through the use of interactive computer software. The most elaborate packages cost hundreds of dollars and can get you close to fluency. Travelers who aren't looking to spend a fortune, though, will be fine with the $10–15 software programs that focus on travel language.

Look for Similarities

All languages have some degree of commonality, but certain languages are quite closely related. The Romance languages, for example—Spanish, French, Italian, and Portuguese among them—have similar structures and many common or related words.

If you know one language within a given family, you'll find that you can understand some of what's being said in another of the family's languages. It's easiest to use this ability when reading, because the information is presented directly and you have a lot of time to process it. Spoken languages are harder to understand because of accents, pronunciation, and the speed at which they're spoken.

English is a hybrid—to paraphrase H. Beam Piper, it's the result of Norman soldiers trying to pick up Saxon barmaids in the ninth century. It's also relatively difficult to master, so those of us who learned it as children should be very grateful. The upside is that as you travel, you'll find that you can recognize some words from both families.

> Most of the travel-related nouns we use come from the Romance side, so you might be a little lost in German-speaking countries. For instance, you'll probably recognize "l'aéroport" as the French word for airport, but it's not quite as obvious that "flughaven" is the German word.

Bring a Travel Dictionary

It's incredibly useful to have a travel dictionary whenever you visit a country that doesn't use English as its main language, which would be most of them. These handy references come in pocket sizes and have translations and pronunciations for common travel words and phrases—not enough to pretend you're a native speaker, but enough to get by while you're visiting.

Increasingly popular are electronic translators, which allow you to type or speak a word in a foreign language and get back its English meaning. The cheapest of these can be bought for under $20 and are the size of a pocket calculator.

More advanced models are available as well, but electronic translators are usually limited to the most widely used languages. For specific dialects or languages that don't use a Roman-style alphabet, your best bet is still a paper dictionary.

BENEFITS OF TRAVEL

Travel costs money, takes time, and might require you to learn a new language, but it's not without its rewards. In fact, it's one of the most rewarding things that you can do.

Let's talk about the three ways that travel helps you.

Professional Development

In case you haven't heard, the world has recently been enveloped in a phenomenon called *globalization*. It's the reason that a lot of American jobs have been outsourced to foreign labor. It's also the reason that a lot of foreign markets have been buying more from American companies.

Globalization is the integration of the world's economies into a single interacting system. It's not finished, but things are changing. Technology is connecting us in ways that we've never been connected before. Taxes on imports and exports are being reduced. In some cases, such as the European Union, national borders themselves are losing significance.

A number of worthwhile books have been written on this subject, including Tom Friedman's bestseller, *The World is Flat.* Every day, more jobs are taking on an international flavor, as workers from around the world are brought in to form teams. The Internet makes a lot of this possible. Sometimes team members work together for months and never actually meet.

So, what does this mean for you?

Simply put, as jobs move onto the global stage, employees who have an international perspective are better able to adapt. By traveling abroad, you're gaining insight into foreign cultures, and that makes it easier for you to work on diverse teams. Knowing other languages gives you more flexibility with your career.

Domestic travel helps as well. Many large companies, and even some smaller ones, have offices in several places around the country. Your customers may also be in different states. If you've been there, that's a shared experience to bring up in conversation.

Even the simple logistics of coordinating and making flights shows a lot of personal responsibility and can impress an employer. Across the board, travel reinforces behaviors and attitudes that twenty-first century employers want to see in their employees.

NOT JUST FOR THE CORPORATE WORLD

Maybe you own or plan to start your own business, or perhaps you're an aspiring actor or musician. Travel plays a role in these kinds of careers, too. It's extremely useful to see how people think, act, and live in other places. That's why so many schools offer study abroad programs for their students.

Cultural insight translates into advantage. Mention your travels in business plans and work them into essays for graduate school applications. The broader your view of the world, the better equipped you are for *any* career. Anyone asking about you from a business perspective knows that.

Good Citizenship

Your responsibilities don't end when you leave work. There's a lot of personal responsibility that goes into being an American citizen. You have a say in the running of the world's strongest nation.

It's tempting to dismiss whatever goes on around the world as being not our problem. What you need to understand is that every action undertaken by our nation does, in fact, affect us. Whenever the United States makes a foreign policy decision, we cause changes in the world beyond our borders. Each of these actions has consequences.

Whichever side we support gains an advantage, meaning that the other side isn't happy with the United States. Because we're American citizens, their anger is directed at us, which can translate into acts that impact our lives economically or even physically. We can't afford to be unaware.

Think for Yourself

It's natural for Americans to rally around the flag and support our leaders in time of crisis. What we need to ask ourselves, though, is whether the stand that they've taken—that we're being asked to take—is the right one.

Travel helps to undermine the arrogance that tells us we're right simply because we're Americans. When we see the broader world first-hand, we discover that not everything is quite the way that we anticipate, or even the way that the news reports it. In some cases, we may feel compelled to disagree with what our leaders are telling us. In others, what we know from experience tells us that we need to stand firm despite international pressure.

What's important isn't which side we take on a particular issue but that we understand why we're taking that side, that we're not merely being lulled into obedience by patriotic music, marketing hype, and claims that opposition is anti-American. Nothing could be farther from the truth.

Understand Others

The United States traces its earliest origins to diversity. Our system of government is strongest when people are well informed, are willing to fully debate issues before deciding what to do, and

25

understand the implications of their decisions. When we don't understand what's going on, we allow things to be done that may not be in our interest.

Political polarization tends to be the enemy of democracy, allowing people to concentrate enormous power in the name of serving an often-slim majority. Travel helps us gain a better understanding of how other people think. If we can learn why they believe what they believe, we may be able to persuade them to change their minds, or at least predict how they'll react. That helps us to overcome the divisions that tend to arise along lines of wealth, race, and gender.

Travel is also helpful when it comes to solving social problems. Too often, debates on solutions devolve into all-or-nothing arguments that a particular course of action would result in the complete destruction of society. Why not look at what people in other countries are actually doing and see what results they're having? If it works, we might try it. If not, we have saved time and effort by avoiding a failed idea.

Good Times

What is it that you're working for, if all that it leads to is more work? Travel gives you another option, a way to get out and do something fun without feeling as if you spent money with nothing to show for it.

There's food to be sampled, drinks to be had, and great photo opportunities. You'll see and do new things, meet new people, and come back with stories to tell. It's even a little contagious— once you get into it, you'll find yourself trying to convince friends that they should be traveling, too.

Having a blast might not sound as lofty as things like succeeding in the global economy or being a good citizen. As time goes by, though, it's that crazy weekend trip to London that you'll remember, not the time that you stayed home and watched a movie.

RECAP

Travel is enormously important. In fact, it has more effect on a person's view of the world than most other things that he or she might spend time doing.

Most Americans say that they'd like to travel, but their lives are busy, and if they don't make traveling a priority, they won't end up doing it. Things like cost, time, and other obligations are legitimate concerns but more often than not reflect that travel isn't a priority in their lives.

Friends and relatives can help with some of the conflicts that arise when you want to take a trip. Don't be afraid to ask them for help! If you feel genuinely bad about imposing on others, offer to pay them so that it's a job rather than a favor.

Make an effort to overcome cultural superiority, especially when you travel outside of the United States. Americans come from a wonderfully rich and powerful country, but that doesn't mean that the ways that other people do things are inferior or that we know everything. In fact, seeing firsthand that people in other states and countries do things differently but with good results is part of why travel is so beneficial. It changes our world-views and helps us to see things from a broader perspective.

Language can be a significant barrier for Americans, because we typically do such a bad job of learning languages. In part, we're spoiled by the fact that English is so widely spoken around the world. Don't let that fool you into thinking that everyone speaks English. Above all, don't think that they're under some obligation to speak English just because you do.

Work hard to break the subconscious feeling that someone who doesn't speak your language is less intelligent than you. One language is pretty much as good as another, and when you're in their country, you're the one who can't communicate. Bring a travel dictionary or electronic translator, study the basics with audio classes or language software, and do the best you can.

Travel might seem like a lot of work, but it also has a wide range of benefits. Americans, in particular, need to travel because of our nation's preeminent role in the world. As professionals, we're facing competition from an increasingly global economy. Those who understand international business will be equipped to succeed, while those who have a more limited perspective may well be in trouble.

As citizens, too, we have an obligation to see the world from a broader perspective. The United States holds enormous power in the world, and the actions of our country affect millions of lives beyond our borders. Whenever America supports one side in a dispute, it changes the balance of power in that area, and the losers hold us as a whole responsible.

When we travel, we gain firsthand knowledge of the world around us. We're less swayed by patriotic music, flag-waving, and political doubletalk, and we can confidently disagree when we think the decisions being made are the wrong ones. We also gain the confidence to support our government when we agree with its actions, even if others disagree.

Finally, travel is a lot of fun. When you take trips, you're making memories that will last for a lifetime.

TIPS FOR MAKING TRAVEL FIT

- Treat travel as an investment in your life, not a frivolous expense.
- Distinguish between obstacles and excuses. You can schedule around obstacles, but excuses will come up every time you try to plan a trip. Live with obstacles, overcome excuses.
- Start saving before you have a destination, so you can jump on a special deal when you see it. You don't need a specific destination in mind!
- A great way to commit yourself to making travel a priority is to get your passport, so you'll already have it when an opportunity arises. We'll cover passports in detail in Chapter 7.
- Don't assume that travel necessarily means flying. In the next several chapters, we'll go over the different benefits of traveling by air, rail, road, and sea. If a plane is too expensive, consider taking the bus.
- If your job involves reviewing resumes, writing documents, programming, or anything else that can be brought with you, you can use your travel time as productive work hours. Some employers may allow you to claim these hours on a timesheet, which helps to reduce the cost of your trip.
- Bring your laptop on long trips. It's useful for watching movies, doing work, playing games, and even listening to music. An external battery pack gives you enough power for all but the longest flights.
- Most busy people subscribe to magazines or newspapers that they rarely find time to read. Bring your reading backlog on the trip and catch up en route.

"Time is the longest distance between two places."

—Tennessee Williams

PART 2

How You Can Get There

Five classic ways to get from place to place, the
pros and cons of each, and an idea of what to
expect from the one you pick.

31

A QUICK COMPARISON OF THE WAYS TO TRAVEL

- **Flying** is fast but you need to be at the airport early, and last-minute fares to a specific destination may be pricey.
- **Trains** are relaxing and let you see the scenery but often experience delays over long distances.
- **Driving** offers maximum flexibility but is more expensive than it seems and can be exhausting.
- **Buses** make sense when you need the lowest cost, but you'll be sacrificing comfort.
- **Cruises** give you the ultimate luxury experience but have no flexibility in their itineraries.

CHAPTER **2**

Flying

When most people think of traveling, they think of flying. Planes are usually the fastest way to travel and may be the only realistic way to get to some destinations. Technology has made planes safer, and competition has made airfares much less expensive than they were just a decade ago. All of these factors make airlines a popular choice for the Spontaneous Tourist.

Deciding that you're going to fly, though, is just the beginning. There are a lot of things to take into account before you buy tickets! Which airline makes the most sense? Where do you want to shop for low fares? Is price always the only consideration? Let's find out.

MEET THE AIRLINES

The United States has more than a dozen national carriers and a large number of regional airlines. Safety is enforced by the Federal Aviation Administration (FAA) and is pretty much the same across the board. Comfort, seating practices, and service can vary widely, though.

The domestic market for commercial air travel is split between two types of airlines—legacy and low-cost—with regional carriers playing a supporting role. There are also foreign carriers who provide service out of the United States and can be divided along similar lines.

Legacy Carriers

The United States deregulated airfares, schedules, and routes in 1978. Prior to that time, airlines operated under strict regulations imposed by the government. Afterward, they were given much greater latitude over management decisions and were free to thrive (and fail) as the market directed. The airlines that predate deregulation are today known as "legacy" carriers.

Legacy carriers typically use small planes to bring passengers to the carriers' regional "hubs," which are then connected by larger planes. Virtually all international travel is provided by legacy carriers. These airlines are also known for providing multiple classes of service, which we'll talk more about later.

Since deregulation, some carriers have merged and others have been absorbed in bankruptcy. The seven that remain today are American Airlines (AMR), United Airlines (UAL), U.S. Airways, Delta Air Lines, Northwest Airlines, Continental Airlines, and Alaska Airlines.

> At one point, the legacy airlines were called "major airlines," but that's an outdated term because it's based on revenues. These days, many of the low-cost carriers have revenues comparable to the legacy airlines.

Many other countries have also deregulated air travel in recent years, leaving former national carriers like British Airways, Air France, and Lufthansa in a situation comparable to U.S. legacy carriers. Some of these airlines have joined alliances (p. 46), while others are unaffiliated. You'll find an extensive list of foreign airlines in Appendix B.

Low-Cost Carriers

Deregulation ushered in a new age of competition in the airline industry, prompting a change in the playing field. With fares falling, investors discovered that there was an enormous market for vacation travel to popular destinations. New airlines that sprung up to serve these markets shunned the hub-and-spoke networks built and serviced by legacy carriers in favor of concentrating on point-to-point routes with high passenger volume.

Even some legacy airlines have embraced the low-cost model. United created its subsidiary Ted to offer flights between major cities at rates lower than standard United fares. U.S. Airways merged with a low-cost carrier (America West) as part of its emergence from bankruptcy to integrate a low-cost mentality into its operations.

35

Most low-cost carriers offer only one class of service for passengers and limit their service to large or especially profitable airports, such as major cities and popular vacation destinations. In some cases, though passengers are guaranteed to have a seat on the plane, specific seats are assigned only within 24 hours of departure.

LOW-COST LUXURY

Not all low-cost carriers limit themselves to one class of seating. AirTran is one that went against the grain to offer Business Class seating. For as little as $35 per flight segment, flyers get larger seats, more leg room, and free drinks.

In the competitive world of low-cost fares, this decision helped to differentiate the airline from its rivals and lure business travelers away from the legacy carriers. Since then, other carriers like Spirit Air and ATA have added upgraded service.

Being low-cost doesn't mean being unfriendly. In fact, for several years, many of the low-cost carriers have ranked above the legacy airlines for overall customer satisfaction. Part of that success stems from the overall job satisfaction of employees, who haven't had to endure the pay cuts at legacy airlines. The low-cost market is also thriving overseas. New airlines in Europe and Asia are offering fares much lower than the former national carriers and often lower than the cost of a bus ticket. Refer to Appendix B for a list of foreign low-cost carriers.

Regional Carriers

Aside from the legacy airlines and their low-cost competitors, there are also regional carriers such as Mesa, American Eagle, and ExpressJet. These carriers are relatively unknown to travelers but actually carry a significant portion of the nation's regional air traffic.

The regional airlines operate under contract to the legacy airlines under names like United Express and U.S. Airways Express, helping to move people from small "spoke" airports to regional hubs. You may not realize they even exist, but without the efforts of the regional carriers, legacy airlines would be hard-pressed to maintain service across their networks.

Regional carriers play a similar role overseas. Not all countries have major airports. Larger airlines are able to provide service using local carriers.

BUYING LOYALTY

So, you've got a lot of choices when it comes to air travel. As a Spontaneous Tourist, which airline makes the most sense for you? That depends on where you're going—not just today, but next week, next month, and even next year. It also depends on what's most important to you.

Let's look at some of the ways in which airlines try to buy your loyalty.

Classes of Service

You may be perfectly happy sitting in a narrow seat with a little bit of leg room, munching on tiny pretzels washed down with soda served in a plastic cup. On airlines, that's called Coach (or Economy) seating, and it's standard fare—literally!

The cheapest Coach tickets are non-refundable, meaning you'll pay a penalty if your plans change. Airlines also offer unrestricted tickets, which cost considerably more but can be changed or refunded without penalty, and a variety of fare categories in between. These affect price, but they all give you the same seat.

Flying First Class

You step into the plane and a flight attendant takes your jacket. As you sink into a wide, comfortable seat and stretch your legs out in front of you, the attendant reappears.

"Would you like something to drink?"

The other passengers—the ones flying *Coach*—are just beginning to board while you're sipping orange juice. Since you're sharing the overhead bin with only one other person, there's plenty of room for your carry-on luggage.

Shortly after takeoff, the flight attendant brings you a fresh cocktail to accompany the warm mixed nuts that you're enjoying and asks you by name which of several entrees you would like for dinner. A white tablecloth is placed over the table to set it for the meal, which arrives on china to be enjoyed with real flatware.

Of course, the first class experience varies by airline and length of flight. The most consistent advantage of domestic First Class service is a larger, more comfortable seat. The scenario described above applies to international flights as well as most long-haul domestic trips—those lasting three hours or more.

After more than a decade of ruthless cost cutting that saw the paring back of virtually all services and amenities, there are signs of a revival for premium air travel. New airlines like MAXjet and

L'avion are setting the bar high with planes that have only premium-class seating. If these airlines are successful, legacy carriers will need to upgrade their offerings to retain customers.

EXTRA LEG ROOM FOR LESS

Passengers in Coach frequently cite lack of leg room as a source of frustration. Premium seating offers more leg room, but the cost is out of reach for many people.

United Airlines offers a compromise with Economy Plus seating. Positioned toward the front of the main cabin on United and Ted aircraft (as well as some United Express flights), Economy Plus seats are the same width as regular Economy seats but have up to five extra inches of leg room.

Mileage Plus members are given free access to Economy Plus seating once reaching Premier status (the lowest tier). Other flyers may purchase an annual "Economy Plus Access" package or buy an upgrade at the time of check-in based on availability.

International Classes of Service

Overseas flights are very different from what you'll experience on domestic trips. Even in Coach, you'll get meals—a rare offer these days when traveling stateside—and premium classes of service retain a lot of the treatment that has been cut on flights within the United States.

There are three reasons why this is the case.

- **Bigger planes.** It takes a lot of fuel to fly across an ocean, so it's cheaper to make the trip with more people on the plane. With more people to serve for such a long time, airlines can't afford to make the kind of cuts in their staffing and supply stockpiles that they have for shorter flights.
- **Less competition.** The wide-body aircraft used on overseas flights are very expensive to purchase and maintain, so low-cost carriers tend to focus their attention on the domestic

market. The legacy carriers do compete with one another, but they're smart enough to do that by boosting their service rather than cutting their prices.

- **Stronger customer focus.** On long flights, a few unhappy passengers can make the trip miserable for everyone. Since airlines make quite a bit more money on international flights than domestic ones, they want to impress their passengers and keep their loyalty, so they put more effort into providing good service.

Knowing that people will pay more for comfort on a long flight, the airlines offer three different classes of service on international flights. The highest class, usually called First Class, includes amenities like fresh flowers and seats that fold into flat beds.

Prices for international First Class seats, though, can cost as much as $10,000. To bridge the gap, airlines also have a mid-range offering (usually called Business Class) that's comparable to what used to be found in domestic First Class.

GOING TO LONDON?

Flying from the East Coast to London in Business Class with a legacy carrier could easily set you back $4000 or more. That's less than First Class, but it's still too much for most people.

MAXjet *(www.maxjet.com)* set out to change that. The airline flies just two routes, taking passengers from Washington-Dulles or New York-JFK to London's Stansted Airport. All 102 seats per flight are Business Class, and prices start around $800.

Rated as being at least as good as Business Class with a legacy carrier, the MAXjet experience includes gourmet meals, fine wines, and airport lounge access with the price of the ticket. MAXjet and other all-premium class airlines are listed in Appendix B.

Frequent Flyer Programs

On May 1, 1981, American Airlines launched AAdvantage, a program designed to build loyalty among regular American flyers by allowing them to earn credits for each flight and use them for free travel. The idea was popular and today, virtually all airlines have a frequent flyer program.

Signing up for frequent flyer memberships is free. Don't go running out to sign up for all of them just yet, though. There are a few things that you need to know first—like how miles are earned, what you can get for them, and the best way to go about getting them. When you're ready, information on each airline's program is provided in Appendix B.

Earning Miles

Each airline makes its own rules for its frequent flyer program. The legacy carriers' programs are very similar to one another, awarding passengers one mile credit for each mile of actual flying. Some of the low-cost carriers also follow this model, while others use a completely different system based on points.

Each program's miles need to be considered in the context of what they'll get you under the rules of their sponsoring carrier—for example, 100 TrueBlue points will get you a free ticket to anywhere JetBlue goes in the United States, but the same ticket from United might take as many as 50,000 Mileage Plus miles.

> Carriers that offer elite status to frequent flyers use miles to award status tiers as well as giving passengers the chance to trade them for awards. These may not be the same miles, though. We'll cover how to qualify for elite status a bit later.

In addition to "base" miles (those that are actually flown), airlines frequently offer opportunities to earn "bonus" miles. Specific offers vary by airline, but you might get bonus miles for checking in online, using an airline-sponsored credit card (more on this later), or shopping at a partner's Web site. There may also be special mileage bonuses for passengers with elite status, which we'll soon discuss.

Redeeming Miles for Tickets

Add your base and bonus miles together, and that's your total redeemable mileage. But what do you do with them once you have them?

The most common use for frequent flyer miles is to trade them for free tickets. At one time, there was no difference between a free ticket and a paid ticket—they were good at any time for any seat. Most low-cost carriers' free tickets still work this way, but the legacy carriers now offer two different types of award fares. Standard award tickets (names vary by carrier) give you unrestricted use, but they cost a lot of miles, usually around 50,000 for a domestic roundtrip.

You only need to use half as many miles to get a discount award ticket, but there are only a certain (low) number of seats set aside on each flight for discount awards. Finding one that leaves from your preferred airport and goes where you want to go can take some patience, so the question is, would you rather spend more miles or be more flexible?

> Discount award fares exist for First Class seats, too, and fewer people think to ask for them, so these seats tend to be easier to get. On average, you'll spend more miles for a discounted First Class ticket than a discounted Coach fare, but you'll still save miles versus a standard Coach fare.

Redeeming Miles for Upgrades

If your airline offers more than one class of service, you may be able to use your miles to upgrade to a higher class. How many miles you'll spend for an upgrade varies by carrier and is also based partly on the distance and partly on the fare code of the ticket—the farther that you're going, the more miles you'll have to spend to get an upgrade, but you won't spend as many to upgrade from a full-fare ticket as one that's heavily discounted.

Upgrades aren't always available, but it's not as hard to get one as you might think. Many airlines offer complimentary last-minute upgrades for their elite members, so people tend to save their miles in the hopes of being upgraded at the airport. You can use miles to upgrade at the time of ticketing, though, so you'll already be confirmed in the higher class of service when you arrive!

THE SCOOP ON INTERNATIONAL UPGRADES

Airlines set tighter restrictions on upgrades for international flights than apply in the domestic market. Full-fare (Class Y) tickets are always upgradeable, and refundable fares usually are, too, but most of the deeply discounted fares advertised as specials can't be upgraded.

Also, be aware that most airlines limit international upgrades to one class of service—if you have a Coach ticket, you can upgrade to Business Class, but you'd need to buy a Business Class fare to upgrade to First Class.

Elite Status

Airlines depend on their customers to stay profitable (or failing that, to stay in business at all). They know that they can't always promise the absolute lowest fare to any destination you might want, though, so they do their best to keep their fares competitive and use superior service to offset the difference.

The problem is that cuts in service are one of the most common ways that airlines try to reduce costs when they run into financial trouble. Any drop in service means the risk of losing some passengers to competing airlines, so with competition so fierce, how can an airline hope to retain the loyalty of its customers? The answer is what airlines call "elite status."

Airlines grant elite status to flyers based on how often they fly and what kinds of fares they purchase. Within the basic elite structure, they then set up "status tiers"—Continental, for example, uses Silver, Gold, and Platinum—and publish the minimum standards that passengers need to meet each year for each tier.

Qualifying for Elite Status

You'll remember that when we first talked about frequent flyer miles, we drew a line between "base" miles earned for actual flying and "bonus" miles that could be earned from things like using an affiliate credit card. Both types add up to give you your total redeemable mileage.

For purposes of earning elite status, though, airlines don't take bonus miles into account. They want to know how much you actually fly with them, because that's how they make money. It's these miles—the base miles you earn—that qualify you for elite status.

Recently, airlines have added a new twist to this formula. Recognizing that they make more money from customers who buy more expensive tickets, some airlines have added elite mileage bonuses based on fare class (i.e. full-fare or paid First Class seats). These bonuses are different from bonus miles and do count toward elite qualification.

Airlines also occasionally offer special promotions that specifically give passengers the chance to earn elite-qualifying miles. These promotions tend to appear toward the end of each calendar year to help current elite members qualify for the next year.

43

CHANGING AIRLINES

Airlines want your business. If you're an elite member with one airline and want to start flying with another instead, mail or fax them a copy of your elite member card and ask them to give you equal status in their program. They're usually happy to oblige (once; then you have to earn it).

Benefits of Elite Status

Elite status tiers allow airlines to separate the customers they can't afford to lose from those who bring in less money. They can then lavish special privileges and extra attention on elite members while reducing services for other passengers—and cutting the costs that go with them.

Even at the lowest tier, you'll get access to shorter check-in lines. Many airports also offer special screening lines for elite members. As your tier level increases, you'll be given preference for upgrades over flyers with lesser status. At the highest level, most fees will be waived, and you'll have access to dedicated reservations agents to help you make or change itineraries.

> Frequent travel programs are a broad topic. Travelers wanting to learn strategies for receiving upgrades and other benefits should refer to Joel Widzer's *The Penny Pincher's Passport to Luxury Travel: The Art of Cultivating Preferred Customer Status.* Another excellent source of information is *Mileage Pro: The Insider's Guide to Frequent Flyer Programs* by Randy Petersen and Tim Winship.

Alliances

Deregulation brought about massive changes in the U.S. airline industry as new airlines began to compete with legacy carriers for their passengers on domestic routes. International routes, however, have remained largely protected from new entries because the planes are so expensive.

Do you want a Credit Card?

Airlines offer bonus miles for almost everything you can imagine, from staying in a hotel to renting a car to buying groceries.

Increasingly, they're also offering something else: a branded MasterCard or Visa credit card that promises to let you earn miles for everyday purchases. You'll find these cards available from legacy and low-cost carriers alike.

Is it a good deal?

Well, that depends on your personal shopping habits. These cards really do let you earn miles for purchases—usually a mile per dollar spent, and some offer two miles for every dollar used with their sponsoring airline to purchase tickets. That can add up fast.

Unfortunately, there's a downside. They've got annual fees—usually $75 or more—and the interest rates that they offer tend to be around prime plus 9.9%, which comes out to 17% or more.

So, the question is, what sort of spender are you? If you tend to equate available credit with cash in your pocket, don't get lured in by the promise of miles. You don't want to carry a balance on an airline card, period.

On the other hand, if you're disciplined with your money, an airline card is a great way to consolidate your spending and rack up thousands of miles each year.

Compare a $75 annual fee with the free upgrade the miles get you en route to Tokyo, and it's an easy decision. Just pay that balance in full, each and every month.

Consequently, while prices *have* fallen considerably on overseas travel (especially during slow seasons, such as going to Europe during the cold months), legacy carriers nonetheless count on their profitable overseas routes to shore up their domestic operations. Foreign major carriers, facing their own low-cost competitors, have a similar interest in overseas routes. Alliances address these overlapping business interests.

There are three major airline alliances in existence today—Star Alliance, **one**world, and SkyTeam—and all of the legacy carriers except for Alaska Air belong to one of them. (Currently, no low-cost carrier belongs to one of the major alliances.)

What do alliances mean for you? Flexibility. You can fly with any member airline but earn mileage with your home airline of choice—for example, a United Mileage Plus member who flies with allied airline Lufthansa will receive Mileage Plus credit for the flight (including elite qualifying miles). Alliance members also acknowledge one another's status tiers for perks like upgrades and faster check-in.

In addition to the major alliances, airlines often have reciprocal agreements with one another to share mileage credit. For example, United Mileage Plus members can earn miles for their flights on Aloha Air, but U.S. Airways flyers cannot do so—even though U.S. Airways flyers can earn miles on United as part of the Star Alliance—because Aloha Air's partnership with United is reciprocal and not part of the broader alliance agreement. Alliance membership and partnerships are annotated for each airline in Appendix B.

NO ALLIES, LOTS OF PARTNERS

Alaska Airlines isn't part of any alliance, but it has put together its own network of partnerships. American, Continental, Northwest, Delta, British Airways, Qantas, Air France, and even Amtrak are on the list. Learn more about their frequent flyer program at *www.alaskaair.com/mileageplan*.

Star Alliance

United and U.S. Airways are the domestic members of the Star Alliance, the largest of the three worldwide air alliances. Travel within North America is augmented by Air Canada.

The 18-member Star Alliance is very strong in Europe, counting among its members Lufthansa, Austrian, BMI (British Midlands), Scandinavian, TAP Portugal, Swiss, Spanair, and LOT Polish Airlines. Most of these airlines also provide service to Russia.

The Asian market is also strong, with Japan-based All Nippon Air (ANA), Thai Airways, Singapore Airlines, and Korea's Asiana Airlines adding their routes to the service map. Air China has accepted an invitation to join the alliance, and Shanghai Airlines will soon follow with the goal of creating a dual-hub system in China.

Air New Zealand serves the Australian market. Brazilian airline Varig and recent addition South African Airways provide additional service within South America and Africa, respectively.

one*world*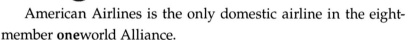

American Airlines is the only domestic airline in the eight-member **one**world Alliance.

Although **one**world is the smallest of the alliances in terms of carriers, the size is deceptive given the enormous scope of American and its allies. British Airways provides European service in conjunction with Iberia, Finnair, and Ireland-based Aer Lingus (although that carrier has announced that it will leave **one**world in 2007 to pursue a low-cost business model).

If you plan to travel around South America, **one**world is unmatched, with Chilean carrier LAN supplementing American's strong presence. Principle Australian carrier Qantas provides unparalleled service to and within Australia, while China and surrounding destinations are covered by Hong Kong-based Cathay

Pacific. Japan Airlines and Dragonair, scheduled to join **one**world in 2007, will further enhance the alliance's Asian market, while Royal Jordanian offers expanded routes in the Middle East.

SkyTeam

Counting among its ten members three domestic carriers—Continental, Delta, and Northwest Airlines—SkyTeam gives its members the most flexibility to reach out-of-the-way domestic destinations with its member carriers. AeroMexico provides expanded South American coverage, while European service is provided by Alitalia, KLM, Air France, and CSA Czech Airlines. Air France also provides expanded access to Africa.

Connections throughout Asia are made through Korean Air, which also provides the two SkyTeam destinations in Australia. Aeroflot-Russian Airlines' membership gives SkyTeam the distinction of having the most extensive service of the three alliances throughout Russia. Service to Australia is more limited.

Airline Lounges

Some airlines maintain private lounges in major airports to provide an alternative to waiting in the terminal. The specific amenities of these lounges vary both by carrier and by airport, but the standard is a quiet, business atmosphere where you can relax before a flight.

In most lounges, complimentary snacks and soft drinks are provided, and alcoholic beverages. There are newspapers, telephones and fax machines, and television. Wireless Internet access may be available in some locations.

With a few exceptions, access to an airline lounges is limited to members. Depending on your tier status with a given airline, you may be entitled to purchase a discounted one-time pass. Some airlines also extend complimentary access to their lounges for passengers flying Business or First Class.

Annual membership fees are usually over $300—but you may also be able to purchase a membership with miles.

Airlines that are members of the same alliance may grant reciprocal access to members of their allies' lounges. Sometimes, a special class of membership is needed, so be sure to do your homework! The lounges associated with each airline are listed in Appendix B.

Price

"Which one's the cheapest?"

More than one ticket has been chosen solely on the basis of price. Farefinder web sites like Expedia, Travelocity, and Priceline make it easy to compare prices among airlines, while Kayak takes it a step further by comparing prices between the farefinders. Just plug in your origin and destination, when you want to leave, and when you want to return, and you'll get a range of different fares from which to choose. If your travel plans are flexible, you can even see if an earlier or later date will be cheaper.

If price is your only consideration, travel sites are a great way to go. Be careful, though, if your plans change. Tickets bought through travel sites may be subject to heavy penalties if your schedule changes. You also won't be able to upgrade these types of tickets in most cases.

Direct Booking

If you have an airline preference, you can also find a lot of great deals by visiting your favorite airline's Web site directly. Most domestic airlines now offer a "low fare guarantee," that you won't find a lower fare from that carrier posted anywhere else. Airlines started offering these guarantees to compete with the travel sites, and they work! If you find a cheaper published fare for the flight somewhere else, send proof, and you'll get a credit for the difference.

> On Orbitz, you can look for all of the flights operated by a particular alliance. Once you know which flight you want, you can still go to that airline and book directly.

Promotional Offers

Most airlines offer discounts on a regular basis. Sometimes, these are seasonal—for example, flights to Florida are expensive in the winter but very cheap during the summer, because people don't feel the need to go somewhere warm when it's already warm where they live. Other promotions are designed to boost popularity, such as when a new route is introduced.

You can find the latest promotions offered by a given airline on its Web site. In particular, the legacy carriers tend to offer promotions for a specific period of time and given certain restrictions, such as buying 14 days in advance and traveling on a Tuesday, Wednesday, or Thursday. Depending on the specifics, Spontaneous Tourists may be able to grab a fare to somewhere like Hawaii or Australia for less than a third of the usual cost.

READ THE FINE PRINT!

Heavily discounted fares are almost always non-refundable. There may also be a *minimum stay* requirement, meaning a certain number of days must pass between your departure and your return flight. Minimum stays can range from a weekend to seven days. If you don't meet the requirements, you'll be quoted a regular fare.

Internet Fares

Airlines don't like to fly with empty seats. Every seat unsold is money wasted, because the plane is going to its destination one way or another. Legacy carriers are particularly vulnerable to this problem because of their elaborate hub-and-spoke networks. To fill empty seats, many airlines offer special last-minute prices published as Internet fares.

Each airline's Internet fare list has a different name, like E-Fares or E-Savers, but otherwise they're more or less the same. These lists tend to be published mid-week for departures that same weekend (though some carriers do publish Internet fares for the following week as well), and the fares can be less than 25% of the usual price—perfect for Spontaneous Tourism!

Your odds of getting a good Internet fare selection are best if you live near a major airport, ideally a hub for the airline offering the fare. Low-cost carriers have a limited number of discounted fares and may not publish them weekly. Legacy carriers, though, publish them almost every week, and the list usually includes international as well as domestic destinations.

> Travel dates for Internet fares are pretty much set in stone. Most require that you leave on a Saturday. Some mandate a Monday or Tuesday return flight, while others allows Sunday returns. If you travel on a different day, you won't get the fare.

CHOOSING AN AIRLINE

We've covered a lot of different things about airlines in this chapter—frequent flyer programs, alliances, upgrades, and prices, to name a few. There aren't any absolute rules when it comes to choosing an airline, but these are all things that you should take into account. There are other considerations, too.

Your point of origin plays a big role in deciding which airlines make the most sense. Certainly, you'll want to choose one that serves whichever airport is closest to you. In a major city, you may have your pick of every airline, but smaller markets are served by fewer carriers. For legacy carriers in particular, consider

51

which airlines have their hubs at your airport of choice. You'll find many more flights out of a hub, and they'll be cheaper.

Also, think about where you're going. If you'll be flying overseas, you'll want to build a relationship with at least one legacy carrier. Choose an airline whose alliance can get you to most of the places that you want to go, and be sure to use an alliance member when you make your flight arrangements. (Actually, consider non-alliance partners in making this decision, too—just be sure that the airline you're flying with will get you elite-qualifying miles with your home airline.)

> Some people sign up for every frequent flyer program and end up with a handful of miles in a dozen or more programs—too few with any one program to get anything.
>
> It's better to focus on one or two frequent flyer programs so you can quickly build up miles to use for travel and upgrades.

What about the Low-Cost Carriers?

Some people use a legacy carrier's alliance for all of their travel abroad but prefer to use a low-cost carrier for their vacations and other trips within the United States. Whether or not this makes sense depends a lot on how much you travel.

Many of the low-cost carriers are profitable, while the legacy airlines are struggling with obsolete technology and high business costs leftover from the days of regulation. Southwest Airlines has more domestic flights on a given day than most of its older competitors, while JetBlue—which earned "major airline" status when it exceeded $1 billion in revenue in 2006—is on the forefront of innovation.

Low-cost airlines are often painted by the legacy airlines as unreliable companies that might disappear overnight. That's unfair. Certainly, some airlines fail—Independence Air, for example, got off to a good start but fell victim to high fuel prices and vanished in early 2006. Even JetBlue fell victim to scheduling problems in early 2007 that resulted in hundreds of flights being cancelled. On the other hand, it shouldn't be a comfort to know that the legacy carriers have more experience dealing with bankruptcy than their rivals!

LUXURY IN COACH CLASS

Low-cost carriers usually have one class of service, but it's not always fair to compare it to Coach on a legacy carrier.

JetBlue's comfortable leather seats feature individual televisions with DirecTV for every passenger. A recent study by J.D. Powers and Associates rated the airline first in customer satisfaction, and they're at the vanguard of an effort to add wireless Internet access to U.S. planes (already offered by many foreign carriers).

Yet, as much as the low-cost carriers deserve applause for making vacation travel more affordable and stopping the endless cuts in service that we have seen from the legacy airlines over the last twenty years, there are some downsides.

The route maps of these newer airlines are not as extensive as their established competitors. (Most don't allow you to earn credit for flights with other airlines.) You also need to be sure that you understand how their frequent flyer programs work.

Aloha Air and Hawaiian Airlines operate similarly to the legacy carriers and have partnerships established that allow you to earn miles when you travel with them. Midwest Airlines passengers can earn miles when flying with Northwest, while Frontier and AirTran have a reciprocal agreement that lets their frequent flyers earn credit for flying on either airline.

Point-based programs like JetBlue's TrueBlue and Southwest's Rapid Rewards are very different from their mileage-based counterparts. When you fly with these carriers, you'll earn points toward free tickets, but each point credited expires one year after the date that it was earned, and there's often no way to extend the life of unused points. Other low-cost carriers use a two-year expiration window, but there's still no way to keep the points from expiring. (Mileage-based programs, in contrast, usually reset the expiration clock whenever miles are earned or redeemed.)

At first glance, that doesn't seem so bad, because the total number of credits you need to earn an award is much lower than with a legacy carrier. The problem is, if you're an occasional traveler, you may never qualify for a free ticket, because they keep expiring. Not only that, but if you do get enough credits for an award, *that* will expire one year from issue, too!

You should consider frequent flyer programs among other criteria when looking to form a relationship with an airline. In the end, though, it comes down to what makes the most sense for your particular situation. All of the low-cost carriers are ranked high for customer service and overall satisfaction, so if you can build a relationship with one, why not?

THE AIRPORT EXPERIENCE

Regardless of which airline you're flying, some things don't change. One thing that doesn't is that everyone has to get from the airport entrance to the gate—and that means jumping a few hurdles!

Check-In

Before you get into the security line, you'll need to check in for your flight. A lot of airlines give you the option to check-in on the Internet and print your boarding pass at home. This saves them money and saves you time, and there may even be incentives like extra airline miles if you do it. Some airlines even let you check in online if you're checking baggage.

Amazingly, a huge number of people don't like to check in online. Reasons given include not liking the flimsy printer-paper boarding pass, concerns that an online check-in will result in extra screening (and delays), or wanting to request last-minute upgrades or seat assignments. It's personal preference.

If you don't check in online, many airlines also give you the opportunity to check in and print a boarding pass from self-service kiosks. These give you "real" boarding passes on card-stock paper, the same kind you'd get from the counter, so more people use them than print from home.

Passengers who want or need to check in with a ticket agent may have a longer wait. Carriers that offer elite status for their frequent fliers often have special check-in lines for their preferred customers or passengers with premium tickets. There may still be lines, but they'll be shorter—one of the most visible benefits of frequent flyer status.

Checking Baggage

It's much faster to get your boarding pass if you only have carry-on bags. Spontaneous Tourists are encouraged to pack light and carry everything on, but that's not always possible. In particular, be sure to check *www.tsatraveltips.us* so you know what items are forbidden in carry-on bags. As of this printing, a rule called 3-1-1 allows you to bring a single one-quart zip-top plastic bag, with gels and liquids not larger than 3 oz. each, through security. Anything larger, except for medicines and a few other special items, needs to be in your checked luggage.

If you need to check luggage, plan to be at the airport at least a half-hour earlier than would be the case without baggage. The lines can be very long at the counter. Elite status lines help, but on busy days, there may still be a long delay.

You can save time by going to the curbside luggage check stand if one's available. You'll pay a few bucks and maybe a tip, but once you've gotten rid of your baggage, you can go to the self-service kiosk to get your boarding pass. That extra time might be what you need to catch a flight if you're running late.

WHAT HAPPENS TO CHECKED BAGS?

When a bag is checked, it goes through special security screening. From there, the bags are routed to the appropriate plane and packed in the cargo hold.

Modern commercial aircraft fly at very high altitudes. You don't feel the effects because the passenger cabins are pressurized and climate controlled, but cargo holds aren't. Don't pack anything delicate—or living—in checked baggage. Airlines have special pressurized holds for pets and other delicate cargo.

If you're changing from one airline to another as part of a multi-flight series, you may be able to get your checked baggage routed to your next flight automatically. Check with your airlines to see if they have an "interline baggage agreement."

Security Screening

Once you have your boarding pass, you'll advance to the next hurdle of an airport—the security screening line. In the United States, passenger screening is done by the Transportation Security Administration (TSA), which is part of the Department of Homeland Security. We'll cover the U.S. process in particular, but the general practice is fairly consistent even in other countries since so many airlines fly to the United States.

Finding the Screening Line

It sounds silly, but getting into the right screening line isn't always straightforward. Be sure that the line you're in goes to the terminal or gate where your flight will be departing—at McCarran Airport in Las Vegas, for example, there are two different lines, and each goes to a different terminal. If you pick the wrong one and get through security (it happens), you'll have to leave and start over at the back of the right line.

Increasingly, airlines are also putting up the money to operate special screening lines exclusively for their preferred customers—travelers with First Class tickets and those with elite status in frequent flyer programs. As this trend continues, it will make elite status that much more valuable. If you're *not* an elite member, though, be sure you don't end up in this line, or they'll turn you away.

Pre-Screening

Prior to reaching the security scanning equipment, you'll be asked to present your boarding pass and a government-issued photo I.D. card. The purposes of this check are to verify that you're the owner of the boarding pass *and* to see if you've been selected for additional random screening, something that's indicated on the pass when it's printed.

Hand over your I.D. and boarding pass, and it will be reviewed and stamped or otherwise marked before being handed back to you. At this point, you can put your I.D. away, but keep your boarding pass in hand.

Getting Ready

Now it's time to get ready to go through the scanning equipment. Take off any metal items that you're wearing. Remove your coat and shoes. If the buckle on your belt is metal, you'll have to take that off, too. You can put all of this into one of the plastic bins or into your carry-on bag.

Laptop computers and video cameras need to be removed from their cases and placed in their own *separate* plastic bins—

you can't put other things in with them (for reasons that aren't clear). Your bag can go directly on the screening machine belt. Make sure everything's gone in before you walk away.

Going Through

Once your bags and other items have gone into the screening machine, wait at the line until you're asked to go through. Walk through the scanner and present your boarding pass to the screener. He or she will review it and, assuming you didn't set off an alarm, allow you to pass.

> Everyone, including little children and people in wheelchairs but not incapable of standing, has to *walk* through the screening equipment alone. Use of a cane or other assistance isn't allowed.
>
> Why TSA doesn't provide known-safe wooden canes—or why it would matter if someone else provided assistance since the machine would still be scanning both people—is a mystery.

If you set off the detectors, you'll be asked if you've forgotten anything, be allowed to take it off, and try again. Eventually, if you can't find what's setting off the machine, you'll be taken aside for additional screening.

Additional Screening

If you're selected for additional screening, you'll be asked to stand on a marked surface with your arms out. At this point, someone of the same gender as you will use the back of his or her hand to frisk you and run a metal detector wand over your body.

After that, you'll be allowed to collect your bags and proceed. The process can be a hassle, but it's for your own safety.

Bag Checks

If your bag shows something suspicious during the X-ray process, the screener will request a "bag check." TSA personnel will ask you to observe while your bag is opened. (You aren't allowed to touch your bag during this process, but they want you to know that nothing is being stolen.)

X-ray scans are tricky, and it's not uncommon for something harmless to set off concern. It's also possible that you have a prohibited item that you forgot to remove. Common examples are pocket knives, lighters, and sharp nail files. In August 2006, new restrictions were also put in place for liquids and gels such as toothpaste (see p. 55). If something can't be taken through, you'll have the choice of mailing it home or leaving it behind.

Getting to the Plane

So you've made it through security, and now you need to get to your plane. All planes leave from assigned *gates*, and you'll find the gate for your plane printed on your boarding pass (unless you printed it at home, in which case you'll need to check a departure board).

Beyond that, each airport is set up differently. A large airport will usually have several different *concourses*, identified by letter, with different airlines assigned to gates at each concourse. (The reason for this system is that airlines actually lease the gates at airports to which they provide service.) Smaller airports may have only one concourse.

How you get from the screening area, which is usually in the main passenger terminal, to the gate for your plane depends on the airport's size and layout. You might have to walk, or there may be "people mover" belts to stand on. Some airports have train systems to go from the terminal to the various concourses. Then there are airports that have other ways of transporting you, like mobile lounges. You never know.

At the Gate

When you reach the gate, your first priority is to make sure that the plane hasn't left. Assuming it hasn't, see how much time that you have before it starts boarding.

It's entirely possible to miss a plane—let's say, you were running late, had to wait to check a bag, got picked for extra screening, and got lost en route to the concourse. You get there and the plane is just pulling away from the gate. Once the door is closed, it stays closed until the flight arrives at its destination. You'll have to talk to the agent, and see what can be done.

Food for the Flight

First Class passengers get meals on any flight long enough to serve them. With just one exception noted below, though, domestic airlines don't serve meals to passengers flying Coach—and that includes flights to Hawaii.

Fortunately, most of the legacy carriers have food available for purchase in Coach, including some fresh food items on longer flights (usually in the $5–7 range). In general, low-cost carriers don't sell meals, but they typically have better snacks—JetBlue, for instance, now offers ramen noodle cups on longer flights. Whether cash or credit cards are accepted varies by airline.

Another option is to buy food in the terminal and bring it with you onboard the plane. Many airports have a wide array of restaurants that can prepare your food to go, so you can enjoy a tasty meal on the plane. (You aren't allowed to bring food from outside of security, though.)

IN MEMORY OF A GOLDEN AGE

Continental Airlines has endured the same hard times as other airlines. To face those challenges, it's had to make tough choices and cut costs, but there's one cut that it hasn't made. Continental is the *only* domestic airline that serves meals in all classes of service.

There was a time when this was standard. Today, it's a bold move that makes this carrier stand out among all of its competitors, legacy and low-cost alike.

Check for Upgrades

If you were waitlisted for an upgrade, there's no need to bother the airline staff at the gate, but do listen for your name to be called. Passengers need to check in by 30 minutes before the departure time, and if someone who had a premium seat didn't show, the airline will start giving those seats to waitlisted passengers in order of priority.

Should you be called, bring your boarding pass up with you, and it will be replaced with one that has your upgraded seat assignment. (It's really exciting the first few times this happens.)

Wait

There's not a whole lot else you can do while waiting for a flight to board. Maybe you have a book or magazine to read (or can get one from a newsstand or bookstore on the concourse). If you've got a laptop computer, you could play a game.

Bottom line, though, is that you have the wait. Usually, it's not a long wait, but if the flight is delayed, especially due to weather or some other long-term situation, it's possible you'll be waiting for hours. This situation is exactly why some people decide to join airline lounges. It can be much more comfortable—and quieter—to sit and wait in an airline lounge than at the gate. But then, it costs money to join. It's a matter of priorities.

Boarding

The gate agent will let you know when it's time to board. Smaller flights may board all at once, while larger planes typically board according to class of service, elite status, and seating row.

Most boarding in the continental United States is through a covered tunnel called a "jet way" that links right to the cabin door. In some cases, though—smaller domestic airports, some very large airports overseas, or commuter flights—boarding may still involve walking out onto the tarmac (ground) and climbing up stairs. Ask for help if you need it.

RECAP

Flying is usually the fastest way to get somewhere. You have the choice of flying a legacy carrier or one of the low-cost airlines, which focus on popular destinations and major cities.

Most low-cost carriers offer only one class of service. On a legacy airline, you may have the opportunity to purchase or upgrade to a higher class of service, including First or Business Class. Frequent flyer programs allow flyers to earn credits that can be used to earn free tickets or upgrade a purchased ticket (usually by one class of service). Depending on how many miles you fly each year, you may also qualify for elite status, which gives you special privileges.

There are three major airline alliances, and six of the seven legacy carriers belong to one of them. Alliances allow a frequent flyer to earn miles with his or her preferred airline even while flying a partner airline. It is best to join the frequent flyer program of only one airline in each alliance.

Finding the best fare price for airline tickets requires research. Travel sites find the lowest fares but sell tickets that are not upgradeable. Most airlines offer low-fare guarantees for fares booked on their own sites.

Which airline you should fly depends on where you're going. Choose the alliance that makes the most sense for your international travel plans, and use carriers in that alliance whenever you go overseas to earn a lot of miles and qualify for elite status. Use your home carrier whenever possible to get the most perks.

Be sure to leave enough time to go through the whole airport process, from check-in through arrival at the gate. During busy times of day, security screening can take a very long time, so plan accordingly.

Looking Ahead at the Airline Industry

The last few years have been rough on the airline industry. Fuel prices keep rising, but strong competition has kept fare increases in check. Most of the legacy carriers are either in or teetering on the edge of bankruptcy.

In late 2006, U.S. Airways made an unwelcome bid to merge with bankrupt carrier Delta. Just weeks later, rumors emerged that United was in talks with Continental about a defensive merger if the U.S. Airways-Delta deal went through. U.S. Airways withdrew its bid in February 2007, but analysts foresee a wave of consolidation ahead for the industry.

Spontaneous Tourists watching these events unfold should be optimistic. There's a good chance that consolidation will give domestic airlines the cash flows they need to rebuild their crumbling levels of service, and there are so many airlines at this point that competition isn't likely to suffer.

Meanwhile, keep an eye out for possible changes in U.S. law that would allow foreign carriers to operate flights within the United States, which would push prices even lower. As always, the lowest priced fares will come with the fewest frills and most restrictions.

TIPS FOR FLYING

- When you're booking award travel, remember that discounted First Class awards may require fewer miles than standard awards in Coach class.
- Arrive at the airport at least one hour before domestic flights or 90 minutes when flying internationally. This is a bare minimum!
- You're usually allowed no more than two pieces of checked luggage, one carry-on bag, and one "personal item," like a purse or laptop case.
- Most airlines won't let you check luggage within 45 minutes of departure.
- International flights include meals in all classes of service. On longer domestic flights, most legacy carriers sell food in Coach, while low-cost carriers provide snacks.
- Alcoholic beverages are typically free for passengers in Coach on transpacific (but not transatlantic) flights.
- Some airlines charge for headphones, and when they are free, they may not be very good, so consider bringing your own.
- Power plugs are usually not available in Coach.
- Premium seats include power plugs on international flights, but you may need a power inverter.
- On some airlines, you are allowed to use your cell phone while the plane is taxiing to the gate.

CHAPTER 3

Trains

The first transcontinental railroad in the United States was completed on May 10, 1869, at Promontory Summit, Utah. A golden spike was used to commemorate the completion of the track, which ushered in a new age of transportation in America.

Over 150 years later, rail travel continues to play a role in American transportation. Between October 2004 and September 2005, over 25 million people rode on trains operated by Amtrak. Many more used regional rail to commute to and from work.

Around the world, trains have an even more extensive role. Canada, Western Europe, and Australia all have highly developed and efficient passenger rail systems. Many countries in other parts of the world also have widespread rail infrastructure.

Let's consider why trains are appealing, and then we'll cover some of your options for using passenger rail for Spontaneous Tourism.

WHY TRAVEL BY TRAIN?

For all of their popularity with commuters, American trains no longer capture the excitement that they once did. We tend to be a nation of airlines, people rushing to get from place to place as quickly as possible. Even high-speed trains are 75% slower than planes, and over long trips (like going from New York to Los Angeles), that means three *days* instead of six *hours*.

So, why travel by rail? Because traveling by train isn't about getting there as fast as possible. It's about sitting back, relaxing, and taking in the experience. When you fly, you see clouds. From the train's large windows and expansive observation cars, you see the countryside. The train is not just a way to get to a destination. The trip is part of the fun.

Relaxation

When you're on a train, you have no need to rush around, and none of the pressure that defines the lives of many Americans. The train is on its way, and it will be there when it arrives. Nothing you can do will change that, so you can relax.

You won't hear a lot of people on their cell phones. Train travelers spend time talking with friends who are accompanying them, not people hundreds of miles away. Usually, there's no Internet access, so your email will have to wait. But then, it *can* wait, can't it?

Get a drink. Play some cards (very popular on trains). Reconnect with someone you've known for a while but never seem to have the time to *really* talk to anymore. Look out the window and watch the scenery as it goes by.

Meeting People

People on planes often keep to themselves. A good portion of train travelers, however, like to meet new people when they travel, and the length of a trip makes that easier.

On domestic trains, you'll probably encounter a lot of foreign tourists. That's because rail plays a *much* stronger role in travel in other parts of the world. European, Australian, or Asian tourists visiting the United States find it entirely natural to fly into a coastal city and travel inland by train.

Also, a lot of people are simply fans of train travel and make a point of taking cross-country or long-distance trips on an annual or more frequent basis. For these travelers, the destination may not even be important. It's all about the journey.

DOMESTIC RAIL

Rail is a regulated industry in the United States. The National Passenger Rail Corporation, popularly known as Amtrak, was created by Congress in 1970 and has been responsible for providing all interstate passenger train service since it began operations on May 1, 1971.

The United States has rail infrastructure in all states. Amtrak offers passenger service to more than 500 destinations in 46 states (the other four having only freight service). This capability is supplemented by commuter rail systems operated by Amtrak within certain states.

With the exception of the area between Washington, D.C., and Boston, known as the Northeast Corridor, passenger trains share freight tracks. In fact, nearly 70% of the rail infrastructure used by Amtrak is leased from the freight companies.

Routes

Because trains move in straight lines along established tracks, they have the flexibility to stop at a number of places along the way. Amtrak routes are therefore referred to by names rather than origin and destination (as would be the case with an airline flight).

For example, the Coast Starlight travels from Seattle to Los Angeles and provides service to a large number of points along the West Coast. The Southwest Chief originates in Los Angeles

67

and goes to Chicago by way of Arizona, New Mexico, and Missouri. Many of the route names have historic significance from the early days of American rail travel, long before Amtrak came into existence.

A complete listing of routes and destinations can be found on the Amtrak Web site, *www.amtrak.com*, but most of these can be grouped by type of service. Let's look at some of Amtrak's regional offerings.

The Northeast Corridor

Between Washington, D.C. and Boston, Amtrak owns and maintains dedicated passenger train tracks and an electric power infrastructure that makes its trains faster, smoother, and more reliable. Travel on the Northeast Corridor is designed to cater to business travelers and commuters more than Spontaneous Tourists, but you'll certainly be welcome.

The commuter focus means you'll find lots of available trains along the Corridor with service running approximately every hour from the early morning through the late night. (Trains move overnight, of course, but generally don't leave after 10:00 p.m. or before 4:00 a.m.)

You'll find a café car on most Corridor trains but probably not a dining car. Sleeper cars are also uncommon. Business Class seating is usually available on these trains for an additional fee.

Acela: High-Speed Service in the Northeast

The Acela Express, Amtrak's high-speed rail offering, began service on December 11, 2000. Taking advantage of the electric infrastructure on the Corridor, the Acela hits speeds of up to 150 mph and can get you from New York City to Washington, D.C., in a little more than three hours.

An upscale train designed for business travelers who value time more than money, the Acela offers Business Class as its basic service level, with First Class seating available for those who want the extra pampering. All seats have power outlets, and four-seat conference tables are available.

You'll pay for the prestige of riding the Acela, which costs double the price of a ticket for the same itinerary on a regular train, but the experience is impressive.

East to Chicago

Moving away from the Northeast Corridor requires a shift to diesel engines operating without a dedicated infrastructure, because Amtrak shares those freight tracks. Though each route goes its own way, Chicago is the destination for all northwest-bound trains heading away from the Corridor. The Windy City is a major convergence point between East and West for Amtrak service.

> My experience is that despite the lovely scenery, the routes connecting New York and Pennsylvania to Chicago are less impressive than most other routes. It may be because these trains are a connection between the commuter-focused Northeast and the vacation-oriented Midwest.
>
> Whatever the reason, it's easier to enjoy the trip if you're heading away from the East Coast to start a west-bound journey. If you've just come off a Superliner, don't be surprised if you feel disappointed.

The American West

Leaving Chicago on a westbound train, or heading toward it on one of the eastbound routes, you'll experience Amtrak from an entirely different perspective. All trains west of the Mississippi are two-level Superliners. Passenger cars have expanded luggage and seating on both levels. You'll find the café area located on the bottom level of an enormous observation car with huge viewing windows for enjoying the scenery.

Sleeper cars are always included on these trains—you'll be on them for two days if you're going all the way to the West Coast—and the accommodations are very nice. You'll also find a formal dining car where you can enjoy three scheduled meals a day.

BATHING ON THE TRAIN

One of the most common questions about traveling by train is how you keep clean. Less than twenty years ago, west-bound Amtrak service had showers on the lower levels of passenger cars. Today, those are gone, replaced by extra seats. (If you wonder why, be sure to read the section on "Politics" later in this chapter.)

Sleeper cars on all routes still include these showers, for the exclusive use of passengers traveling with berths. Larger compartments, such as the Deluxe Bedroom, actually include an in-room shower. For the rest of us, it's advisable to bring at least a washcloth.

The West Coast

From Seattle to Los Angeles, Amtrak's Coast Starlight route shows you some of the most beautiful scenery to be found in the United States. First Class passengers can take advantage of the exclusive Pacific Parlor Car for a complimentary afternoon wine tasting. Feature films are shown in the lower-level movie theatre, and games for children can be found in the Kiddie Car.

Along the coast of southern California, the Pacific Surfrider connects San Luis Obispo to San Diego. Popular with commuters and travelers alike, you can bring your bike or surfboard or enjoy your trip even more with an upgrade to Business Class seating.

Bring Your Car: The Auto Train

Catering to the enormous influx of tourists who travel from the Northeast to Florida every year and want to bring their cars along, Amtrak offers Auto Train service between Lorton, Virginia, and Sanford, Florida. In addition to the cost of the passenger ticket, you'll pay around $180 more to bring your car on the Auto Train (or around $350 more for a van or SUV).

On the way, you'll enjoy complimentary meals regardless of your class of service. Amtrak also offers portable media players for use on the Auto Train. Probably the most family-oriented of Amtrak trains, the Auto Train features Superliner cars and a variety of sleeper berths.

Accommodations

Most Amtrak routes feature reserved seating, which does not necessarily mean that you'll be assigned a specific seat, but rather that a seat will be available for you on the train. The seats are very large and comfortable compared to those found on airplanes with a considerable amount of leg room.

A Coach seat can recline 45 degrees and has a movable leg rest and foot rests on the seat in front of you. Sleeping in a Coach seat on Amtrak is much easier than doing the same on an airplane. You'll also have a tray table. (Power outlets may be provided, but it varies, so don't count on it.)

In addition to the comfortable basic Coach seating, Amtrak offers a wide variety of services for its passengers. Not all services are available on all routes, but you'll know at the time you book your trip what you'll have on your particular train, including some of the following.

Café Car

In the café car, also called the lounge, you'll find a tasty assortment of snacks and beverages for sale. You can buy wine, beer, and liquor as well as coffee, tea, and soft drinks. You can also get Amtrak logo merchandise, such as playing cards and blankets.

The café car is a comfortable place to eat, enjoy the scenery, and play cards or other games. You'll be able to keep your table as

71

long as you're eating or drinking something you bought. There's limited space, though, so patrons come first.

> The café car has prices comparable to a movie theatre. It's convenient to buy cold drinks and hot food, but bring some snacks with you and supplement them with what you can buy onboard. (For health reasons, Amtrak can't refrigerate anything for you.)
>
> As for alcoholic beverages, you can bring your own only if you are traveling in a sleeper berth and keep them inside.

Dining Car

Longer distance trips include a formal dining car that offers scheduled meal service for breakfast, lunch, and dinner. Ordering is done from a menu with prices and quality comparable to a mid-tier restaurant. For breakfast and lunch, passengers are free to arrive when they like within service hours. Dinner, which is more popular among travelers, is set according to reservation. Seating is always four to a table.

On long trips, always plan with the cost of food in mind. The price of a train trip can be much higher if you eat every meal in the dining car—unless, of course, the meals are free, as they are for First Class passengers.

Business Class

Amtrak offers Business Class seating on select routes along the Northeast Corridor and along the Pacific coast. The cost difference to upgrade from Coach on a standard train is generally very reasonable—as little as $20. The amenities that you get are limited but can make sense depending on your situation.

The key difference is that when you travel Business Class, you'll get access to a power outlet, perfect for connecting a laptop or charging a cell phone. Beverages from the café car are also complimentary for Business Class passengers. (Free drinks are *not* included on the Acela, however, where Business Class is the minimum class of service.)

In general, Business Class cars have fewer passengers and tend to be quieter. Depending on the circumstances, that can be worth the upgrade.

First Class

Amtrak offers First Class accommodations on Acela Express trains. In a First Class car on the Acela, you'll have a more spacious seating layout and personal service from in-car attendants, with complimentary beverages and hot meals ordered from a menu and served on china.

Amtrak also considers all passengers who book sleeping car reservations on non-Acela trains to be First Class. Meals in the dining car for these passengers are complimentary.

> Meals are an important consideration in deciding whether or not to reserve a sleeper berth on a long trip. The cost of meals may offset the higher ticket price.

Prior to boarding, First Class passengers have access to any ClubAcela or Metropolitan Lounge facilities available at the station (see p. 75).

Sleeper Berths

As comfortable as Coach seating is on an Amtrak train, over long distances it can be much easier to sleep when lying down flat, with fresh sheets and a pillow. Berths come in a variety of styles, from simple Roomettes to elaborate Deluxe Bedrooms that include in-compartment showers. Prices vary based on the length of the route and other considerations, such as the seasonal occupancy rate.

During the day, you'll have comfortable seats in your compartment that provide the same exceptional views, more privacy, and your own power outlets (a genuine luxury on the train). Berths include turn-down service in the evenings and are about the size of an extra-long twin mattress. Moreover, because all berths are considered First Class accommodations, you'll enjoy complimentary meals and other amenities.

There are a limited number of berths on any train, and they tend to be filled well in advance of the normal seats. If you absolutely must have a certain type of berth, plan to make your reservations a month or more in advance. The more flexible you are, the later you can wait.

SPACE-AVAILABLE BERTHS

As with airline seating in First Class, Amtrak strives to fill all of its berths on a given trip. That means that if you don't have a berth when you board but there's one available, you can purchase the upgrade at a greatly reduced rate.

When this works, it works great. Keep in mind, though, that there are hundreds of people on the train, and there may be just a few (or no) unoccupied berths. That Coach seat you purchased may very well be where you stay.

Guest Rewards

The Amtrak Guest Rewards program is operated along the same lines as an airline frequent flyer program, awarding passengers two points for every dollar spent on Amtrak travel (special bonuses apply for Acela tickets) as well as points for purchasing products or services from affiliated vendors. Points can be used for upgrades or free tickets.

Like the airlines, Amtrak has its own credit card that can be used to earn points, and a number of hotels offer Guest Rewards point accumulation as part of their own affiliate programs. Two tiers of recognition exist within Guest Rewards, Select and Select Plus, which provide additional benefits, including point bonuses and access to lounge facilities.

Complete details on Amtrak Guest Rewards can be found online at *www.amtrakguestrewards.com.*

> Amtrak links point accumulation to dollars spent rather than distance traveled. This structure makes Guest Rewards more valuable to business commuters than to those who travel farther and less frequently, like Spontaneous Tourists. Points still add up over time, however, so be sure to sign up.

ClubAcela

Amtrak operates ClubAcela facilities at its busiest Northeast Corridor stations. Outside of the Northeast Corridor, select Amtrak stations offer comparable *Metropolitan Lounges.* First Class passengers have unlimited access, as do Select Plus tier members of Guest Rewards. Select tier members and passengers flying with Continental in certain circumstances are granted limited access. Other passengers simply can't use the lounges.

Similar to the lounges operated by airlines, Amtrak's lounges offer patrons complimentary snacks and beverages, reading materials, and a comfortable place to relax prior to boarding. Internet, phone, and fax services are complimentary where available.

Discounts

Amtrak offers discounts to members of the American Automobile Association (AAA), students, military personnel and veterans, seniors, and members of the National Association Rail Passengers (NARP).

Military discounts are available for active troops and veterans (10% for active personnel, 15% for veterans). To get these discounts, current military personnel can show a standard military I.D., but veterans must have a Veterans Advantage card *(www.veteransadvantage.com).*

For the 15% student discount, a school I.D. is *not* acceptable—students need to have either a Student Advantage card *(www.studentadvantage.com)* or an International Student Identification Card (ISIC), available through STA Travel *(www.statravel.com).*

> Student Advantage cards are commonly honored throughout the United States for a variety of discounts, but for overseas travel, you'll want to have an ISIC.

To qualify for any discount, you'll need to have suitable identification. In most cases, booking must be completed three days in advance, and certain types of tickets (such as Acela First Class) may not be eligible.

Challenges with Domestic Rail

Traveling by train provides an alternative to flying and can be a lot of fun. It's also a great way to see parts of America that are otherwise hard to see. There are a few challenges, however, of which you should be aware whenever you plan a train trip.

Timetables

The first and foremost use for rail in the U.S. is transporting freight. Outside of the Northeast Corridor (where Amtrak owns and maintains most passenger rail tracks), freight trains generally have priority. Trains are also subject to delays caused by weather or debris affecting tracks.

For travelers, this means that a degree of flexibility is required, particularly when traveling long distances. A train can't depart until it has arrived, so a delay en route to a station means a delayed departure for leaving that station. When this occurs, it can mean delays of up to a few hours. Some routes, like the Florida-based Silver Meteor and Silver Star, are late more often than not.

Amtrak provides scheduling updates via an advanced automated system. This system, built around a persona called "Julie," can be reached by calling 1-800-USA-RAIL and is extremely reliable.

Overbooking

Booking is electronic, and it's extremely rare for a train to be oversold. If a train is canceled because of mechanical problems or bad weather, however, the passengers booked on that trip will be added to one of the next available trains.

If it gets bad enough—such as if a large number of trains are canceled due to a hurricane—it's possible that trains will be sent out with standing room only. This is by far the exception, but it can happen. Be aware.

THE VALUE OF AN UPGRADE

In February 2006, when I returned from an overseas trip to find the Northeast buried in snow and all domestic flights grounded, I decided to take a train from Philadelphia back to Washington, D.C.

I'd never even heard of Amtrak's Business Class offering until that night. When I bought my ticket, I noticed it was only a $20 difference and decided to give it a try. That's how I found myself in a quiet section off the café car, sleeping comfortably while people were standing in the aisles of the Coach cars.

Politics

Like all rail systems in the developed world, Amtrak is subsidized by appropriations from the government. Unlike the rail systems of other developed nations, however, Amtrak does not enjoy the full and consistent backing of its patron. In fact, at any given time, it might be accurately depicted as fighting for existence.

Exerting constant pressure to privatize rail, politicians regularly insist or even mandate that Amtrak become self-sufficient and stop relying on government subsidies. The fact that no passenger rail network in the world has achieved this goal does little to undermine the politics, and Amtrak struggles to get what it needs every year when Congress debates the budget.

As a Spontaneous Tourist, you'll witness the impact firsthand. Amtrak provides a high level of service but suffers from shortages of items and staffing on some trips. Many dining cars have scaled back service to pre-cooked meals or limited entrée selections. Efforts to expand high-speed rail are stifled, and accommodations aren't all they could be. (Safety is never compromised.)

Clearly, passenger rail is not a money-maker. It's a losing proposition because trains specifically provide service to places that aren't profitable so people can get to and from those places. (That's why Amtrak was created. The freight companies that had previously operated passenger rail reported no profit in decades.)

Without government subsidies, nationwide passenger rail would go away and be replaced by service on profitable routes only. The real question, therefore, is whether we as Americans think there's value in being able to travel around our country by train.

Deciding the answer is up to you.

RAIL AROUND THE WORLD

Trains are common in many parts of the world. Most developed nations have extensive passenger rail service. Without exception, these services are treated as symbols of national prestige and receive considerably more attention than Amtrak. Rising stars like China place enormous emphasis on the availability of trains as a mark of sophistication and prosperity.

In developing nations, rail infrastructure may be limited or of poor quality. Trains are an extremely efficient means of transporting raw materials and finished goods. To devote the resources needed to transform a freight system into one that caters to personal comfort is a considerable undertaking.

Governments struggling to balance different priorities may not maintain proper safety and maintenance standards. Train derailments, uncommon when rails are well maintained and proper safeguards are in place, are extremely serious when they do occur. Moreover, mechanical problems can result in significant travel delays.

Spontaneous Tourists should consult a country-specific guidebook or other reliable reference material and plan longer itineraries when considering train travel in developing nations.

Canada

Nationwide passenger trains in Canada are operated by VIA Rail Canada *(www.viarail.ca)*, which provides service to more than 450 destinations with multiple classes of service. Comfort Class is the Canadian equivalent of Amtrak's Coach seating. Sleeper accommodations are available on most long-distance routes, and VIA 1 cars provide First Class customers with three-course meals and complimentary beverages. Additional services vary by route, including a "Romance-by-Rail" private suite package for couples.

Spontaneous Tourists can take advantage of the North America Rail Pass to get unlimited use of Amtrak and VIA Rail Canada trains for a full 30 days. Off-season pricing is considerably cheaper.

Europe

Throughout Western Europe, you'll find clean, fast trains that can take you most places you want to go at prices that are a bit higher than you'd pay for an equal-distance domestic trip. France's TGV *(Train à Grande Vitesse,* or "High Speed Train") is particularly impressive, attaining speeds of up to 186 mph. Since its debut in 1981, the TGV has expanded its service to 70 destinations in 13 regions.

In addition to basic tickets, travelers can choose from single-nation and multinational passes, including a Eurail pass for unlimited travel across 18 countries as well as regional passes for travel in Eastern Europe, the Balkans, and Scandinavia. Americans can take advantage of discount pricing by purchasing rail passes in advance through Rail Europe *(www.raileurope.com)*.

Most European trains offer multiple classes of service. The price of upgrading to First Class is generally reasonable, but the difference in service is very noticeable. Sleeper berths are available on many overnight trains, as well as innovative convertible seats in Coach compartments that allow passengers to stretch out and lie flat.

International Train Travel in Europe

The relative size of European nations compared to the United States and the high quality of the various interoperable train systems makes it convenient and relatively fast to explore Europe by rail.

Moving between member nations of the European Union is essentially transparent. Certain scenarios in Eastern Europe, however, may require a train traveling from one country to another to pass through a third nation for which a travel visa is required (such as Belarus). Ensure prior to your departure that you have any travel documents that will be needed.

Russia

Trains in Russia are slow but inexpensive and generally reliable as a means of traversing the enormous countryside. Private and state-run trains exist within the Russian rail system. The private trains are better equipped and more expensive, and two classes of seating are typically offered. Foreigners usually prefer *coupe*—private cabins with two or four berths—over *platzkart*, which is open and crams six berths into the same space that otherwise would hold four.

Japan

Rail service in Japan is operated by an array of different providers under the umbrella of Japan Railways *(www.japan-rail.com)*. Japan has an extremely developed rail infrastructure, including the *shinkansen* ("Bullet Train"). Introduced in 1964 as the world's first high-speed train, the *shinkansen* now provides service on the main island on Honshu as well as a connection between Yatsushiro and Kagoshima on Kyushu. Since its debut, the technology used in the *shinkansen* has formed the basis for other high-speed trains throughout Asia.

Spontaneous Tourists should be warned that experiencing the *shinkansen* is expensive even by pricey Tokyo standards. Fortunately, for those willing to explore at a slightly slower pace, Japan Railways offers a variety of more affordable options, including discounted rail passes exclusively to tourists for periods of seven, 14, or 21 days.

Australia

Great South Railways *(www.gsr.com.au)* offers service connecting six major Australian cities. The size of Australia means that train travel requires a significant commitment of time. Making the long journey from, say, Sydney to Perth by train provides an easy opportunity to see the harsh interior of the continent up close.

Depending on your schedule, you may want to take advantage of a rail pass. Travelers with a lot of time can get passes good for six months for much less than $1000—and the rest of us can get good deals, too.

Asia

You'll find first-rate trains in South Korea operated by national provider Korail *(www.korail.go.kr)*. Foreign travelers can take advantage of the KR Pass to make full use of the Korean rail system, with less than $200 getting you a 10-day unlimited pass.

China also has an expanding rail infrastructure. In recent years, the Chinese government has made train service a priority, most recently testing a magnetic levitation train of its own design with plans to eventually reach 280 mph. At the moment, however, Spontaneous Tourists will encounter a widespread rail network that has more in common with Russia's service than Korea's or Japan's. Foreigners taking Chinese rail will want to choose "soft" over "hard" seats and should be prepared to accept that the Chinese train system was designed to meet the travel needs—and standards—of the native population.

Service throughout smaller Asian nations varies. Taiwan was scheduled to complete a *shinkansen*-type high-speed train in 2006. Vietnam and Thailand have impressive, modern train services, while Cambodia relies primarily on buses.

Mexico

With the exception of a few small, well-run luxury routes that connect popular destinations, the Mexican passenger rail system has essentially ceased to exist since it was privatized in the 1990s. Amtrak provides service to several border towns, but no direct service exists between the U.S. and Mexico.

Central and South America

The availability and quality of trains throughout Central and South America varies by country. Chile *(www.efe.cl)* has an efficient national train service. Argentina and Ecuador, on the other hand, have virtually abandoned their once-extensive rail networks in favor of buses.

For travelers looking for spectacular scenery, the Panama Canal Railway Company's route is something special.

For around $25, passengers can enjoy the famous Canal and its lush surroundings from the comfort of luxurious wood-paneled and air-conditioned cars while traveling between Panama City and Colon. Visit *www.panarail.com* to learn more.

Africa

Although an extensive rail infrastructure was built in Africa during colonial times, it is obsolete and generally in poor repair. In Zimbabwe, for example, trains are exceedingly slow, while much of Ethiopia's rail network has ceased operating. Service may be intermittent. Have alternate travel in mind in the event that a train does not appear when expected.

A handful of nations, including South Africa, Tunisia, and Egypt, have made investments in upgrading their railways. Trains in these nations operate reliably with comfortable accommodations.

RECAP

Passenger rail in the United States is provided by Amtrak, which offers service to over 500 destinations across 46 states. Accommodations include café and dining cars, sleeper berths, and multiple classes of service. Trains west of the Mississippi River feature two-level Superliner cars. Amtrak also operates the Acela Express high-speed train between Washington, D.C., and Boston, as well as the family-oriented Auto Train between Virginia and Florida.

Overbooking is rare, but trains require some flexibility, especially over long distances and when traveling on tracks owned and operated by freight companies, which is the case almost everywhere outside of the Northeast Corridor. Amtrak also faces continuous political opposition and routinely is forced to reduce amenities to remain solvent.

Amtrak offers discounts to seniors, military personnel, veterans, students, and members of AAA or NARP. Discounts are either 10% or 15% off ticket prices and identification and advance booking are required.

Trains are very popular throughout the developed world, where they are considered symbols of national prestige. Canada's rail network connects to Amtrak, and travelers can take advantage of a North American Rail Pass to use both networks for up to 30 days. Similar passes are available to travelers in Europe, Japan, Australia, and some Asian nations. Russia has an extensive if slow train system, and China has placed a high priority on modernizing its rail capabilities. There is no direct rail connectivity between Mexico and the United States. Passenger rail service in Central and South America, Asia, and Africa varies by country.

Looking Ahead at the Rail Industry

The twenty-first century has been hard on Amtrak, thanks in large part to a presidential administration that made no secret of wanting to break up the company in favor of private regional service. Technical challenges have impacted the much-anticipated Acela high-speed service, and funding shortfalls have taken their toll on service levels.

We can probably assume that high-speed rail will continue to expand along the busy Northeast Corridor and that demand will remain strong for specialized services like the Pacific Surfliner and Auto Train routes. Spontaneous Tourists wanting to travel cross-country by train, though, may want to book their tickets sooner rather than later.

TIPS FOR RAIL TRAVEL

Domestic Rail

- Sign up for Guest Rewards before taking an Amtrak trip. The points will add up over time.
- When you consider Amtrak sleeper berths, remember that the prices include meals, which might otherwise cost you up to $40 per day.
- For overnight trips without a berth, bring a blanket and pillow to be more comfortable.
- If it looks like the train will be crowded, see if an upgrade is available.
- Bring your own snacks instead of buying them in the café car. You'll save money.
- Don't overestimate the speed of trains. Long trips take a long time.
- Bring playing cards or even board games. It's a great way to pass the time.
- Remember that traveling by train is more than transportation. It's part of the trip.

Trains Abroad

- Do lots of research! One great resource is *www.webtravel guide.com/railguide*.
- If you're traveling by train in developing nations, expect and plan for delays.
- You can save a lot of money on overseas train travel using rail passes, but you have to buy them before you leave.

*"Thanks to the Interstate Highway System,
it is now possible to travel from coast
to coast without seeing anything."*
—Charles Kuralt

CHAPTER 4

The Open Road

Even though America was built by railroad, and the airlines certainly cater to our inclination to use our time as efficiently as possible, the highway holds a special place in our hearts and minds.

One reason mass transit is so underdeveloped in the United States is that even when it's made available, we still find reasons not to use it. The metric system didn't take hold in the United States, because our brains think in miles. And why walk when we can hop in the car to drive a tenth of a mile? Short distances, long distances—as a nation, we *love* to drive, and we do it constantly.

So, what does the road offer Spontaneous Tourists? Let's look at America's affinity for highways in a (relatively) objective fashion and find out.

THE FREEDOM OF DRIVING

Ask a dozen people what's so great about driving, and you'll get at least one who mentions *freedom*. It's true. Trains have tracks, and planes are on a schedule, but when you can drive, you can go anywhere! (Well, almost anywhere.)

Freedom is important to Americans. Beyond the concept, the word itself is ingrained into how we see ourselves, our country, and our place in the world. Freedom is our claim to fame, the foundation on which we build. It's everything. So, the thinking is, if cars are part of our freedom, then they, too, are part of what makes us great.

The act of packing a bag, throwing it into the trunk, and hitting the open road isn't just a vacation, or even an adventure. It's a journey into the American psyche.

Road Trips

A huge number of Americans take road trips—long-distance treks by automobile—every year, and a lot more plan or wish to do the same. A road trip is the ultimate adventure, glorified in novels and movies alike, the embodiment of our national character. No one can hold you back when you have a car.

Indeed, travel by car provides enormous flexibility. With no schedule, you stop where you want to stop. You see what you want to see. It's a liberating experience.

Those are the upsides. Driving has its place. It's impossible to get to some places without driving there, especially outside of major cities. Even a trip that relies on a form of long-range mass transit like a train or plane has a good chance of benefiting from a car at the destination.

Unfortunately, there are downsides—lots of them.

Driving Dilemmas

When you decide to take that first road trip to some distant place, it probably doesn't occur to you just what you're getting into. You own the car, so travel is essentially free, right? You have absolute control over the trip. What could possibly go wrong?

Gasoline

The price of gasoline—which, if you're driving abroad, may be called *petrol*—rises and falls in response to market conditions, such as supply, demand, and whether or not the President is feeling well. The trend is hard to predict, and prices can vary widely by region.

Within the United States, gasoline spiked to more than $3.00 per gallon during 2006 before dropping to a relatively stable cost of around $2.20. Gasoline outside of the United States is enormously more expensive, reaching nearly £1.00 per liter in Britain—which, since we Americans don't think in metric, you may not realize is more than $5.00 per gallon.

If you're traveling with a lot of people, maybe you think you'll all pile into that SUV you own or have borrowed from someone and get going. Before you accept everyone's word that you'll split the gas cost, consider how many miles you're going and how many miles that behemoth gets per gallon. Not so cheap.

Tolls

Governments build roads, bridges, and tunnels as public services and pay for them with tax dollars. Due to the gap between taxation and spending, many of these projects are also supported by tolls that you pay whenever you use them.

Depending on where you're going, you may have a relatively toll-free experience, or you may find yourself stopping almost constantly. The invention of wireless payment methods like EZ-Pass has made paying tolls effortless, but don't forget that you're still *paying* them. $3.00 here and $5.00 there can add up.

> If you know the area, you may be able to circumvent a toll by taking an alternate route. If this makes sense, great—but be careful you aren't driving so far that you're spending more on gas than the toll!

Mileage

Gas and tolls are direct costs, meaning you pay for them as they come up. Mileage, on the other hand, is an indirect cost. Automobiles have a finite lifespan that can be approximated for a given brand based on age and mileage. In other words, every mile that you drive shortens the remaining life of your car.

Driving back and forth to work or school, local trips—these add up. But get in the car and drive the 3000 miles from New York City to Los Angeles, and you've just made a really big dent in your car's life.

Proper maintenance, like oil changes every 3000 miles and following the manufacturer-recommended schedules for more elaborate service, can extend and maximize the life of your vehicle. Don't forget, however, that the lifespan remains finite. Do you want to waste three months' driving life in one week? Think about it.

OTHER PEOPLE'S CARS

Investors often talk about using Other People's Money (OPM) to buy investments, leaving the buyer's money free to do other things. The same idea can be applied to road trips.

If you're set on the idea of taking a road trip, consider renting a car rather than using your own. Sure, you'll pay for the gas and tolls anyway, and you'll have to deal with all of the other hassles of driving, but when it's done, you can simply hand the car back.

Of course, be sure that the car you rent comes with unlimited mileage (most do), and that you're either covered by your own insurance or that you purchase a supplemental policy from the rental agency.

Oh, and be sure that you don't take the car somewhere you're not allowed—for example, U.S. rental companies generally don't mind you driving to Canada, but Mexico is off-limits without written permission. Breaking the rules leaves you liable for the cost of the car.

Fatigue

The upside of driving is that you can go wherever you want, but the downside is that you have to drive yourself there. Driving hour after hour takes a serious toll on your alertness and ability to respond to events around you. You'll get tired and lose concentration.

Music and varying temperature help, but only up to a point. Drink coffee or tea if you like, but don't depend on it. Caffeine isn't a replacement for rest.

You can manage driving fatigue by switching drivers and taking rest breaks. Long road trips alone are definitely not recommended. When you stop to eat, plan to get out of the car and walk around. Do some simple stretches and exercise.

> When planning a road trip, remember to consider the cost of food. The longer the trip, the more food you'll need.

After a while, a two-person driving rotation will leave both people too exhausted to be effective. If one person sleeps while the other drives, the driver is driving alone. If you have three or more people, you may be able to trade off indefinitely, but it's still a good idea to stop for sleep every day.

Pollution

Hundreds of millions of people drive cars each day around the world. Whatever your position on global warming, obviously cars pollute the environment—look at the smog in big cities. The decision is up to you, but be honest with yourself.

Getting Lost

Okay. You've thought about mileage, gas prices, and the tedium of driving for days on end, and you *still* want to take a road trip. So be it—but remember to get directions before you leave. Maps are critical to taking long trips. Planning a route can save you hours of backtracking and piles of money. Not knowing where you are also makes it very difficult to call for help if something goes wrong.

A road atlas costs about $20 and pays for itself with one trip. Be sure to get one.

Car Trouble

Make sure that you have a plan in the event that your car breaks down on the side of the road. It can happen with a rental just as easily as with your own vehicle. While regular maintenance helps prevent problems, sometimes they occur anyway.

For long trips, bring maintenance supplies. Besides having a spare tire, wheel wrench, and car jack, you should also bring spare bottles of oil, transmission and power steering fluids, and coolant. Oh, and it might seem obvious, but check to make sure that your spare tire isn't flat before you leave. It happens.

If you have to stop, pull far off the road before getting out of your car. On a highway, try to get to a protected pull-off or exit even if it means driving on your wheel rim—a significant number of people are struck each year while working on their cars along the side of the road.

Having a cell phone is a good idea, but keep in mind that they don't work everywhere, especially if you have a digital-only phone. It may take time for help to arrive. Stay in your car if possible, especially in bad weather. If you have to walk to a service station, go back the way that you came unless you know how far it is to a station ahead of you.

These tips can't guarantee that you won't have trouble with your car, but following them will at least help you stay safe while you deal with the situation. That's what counts.

AAA: A Driver's Best Friend

The American Automotive Association (AAA) was founded over 100 years ago with the goal of benefiting drivers. Best known for its roadside assistance services, AAA offers an impressive array of other benefits to its members.

For $59 a year, you get not only roadside assistance but discounts on hotel rooms, no-haggle prices on new cars, and reduced-rate insurance. You also get a few benefits that don't involve driving, like special discounts on Amtrak train tickets.

One of the most innovative benefits that AAA offers its members is the TripTik. Members have always been able to obtain complimentary maps, but TripTiks go a step beyond basic maps to provide point-to-point driving directions for each part of your journey as well as things to see along the way.

Of course, the roadside assistance that AAA offers remains the Association's signature benefit. Members have access to a toll-free number from which an agent can dispatch a tow truck or other service vehicle. Covered services include:

- Towing
- Dead batteries
- Flat tires
- Running out of gas
- Locksmith services

If you're planning a long road trip, you should have a AAA membership. Visit their Web site at *www.aaa.com* for more information.

93

TRAVELING BY BUS

Let's be honest—traveling by bus isn't the most glamorous way to get from place to place. It's slow, you'll probably have a lot of stops (but can't necessarily count on the schedule), and your friends won't be nearly as impressed with your upcoming bus trip as they'd be if you decided to drive.

Taking the bus, however, is a great compromise between the freedom of planning road trips and the hassles of taking them. Very few places can't be reached by bus, and someone else is driving. Not only that, but the driver knows how to get there, and you're not responsible for the gas *or* the maintenance costs.

Taken together, these factors help to explain why driving turns out to be almost as expensive as flying, but traveling by bus is about the cheapest way to get around—ideal for Spontaneous Tourism on a budget.

Bus service in the United States is technically a competitive industry, but Greyhound Lines consolidated much of the market with its 1997 purchase of Carolina Trailways, after which most carriers entered into cooperative schedules. We'll look at the Chinatown Bus network—an actual competitor to the bus giant. Most of what is discussed in this section, however, reflects Greyhound's status as the de facto national bus carrier in the United States.

Ticketing

If you want to take the bus, you'll need a ticket, just as you would for the train or an airline. Greyhound provides ticket sales at most of its service locations—not all of which are actual "stations"—and also allows customers to purchase tickets and check schedules online at *www.greyhound.com*.

> You'll pay a non-refundable $11 gift fee if someone else buys your ticket online.

Fares vary based on the distance being traveled and the popularity of the route. All routes go between major cities, but it's very inexpensive to stop a bus. You'll find that there are thousands of places that you can reach, including many that you *can't* get to by air or rail.

Discounts and E-Fares

Greyhound has long offered discounts on tickets for military personnel, AAA members, students, seniors, and a number of other groups. E-fares are a more recent addition to the discount market. These are reduced-rate tickets between major cities on the East and West Coasts that are available only to customers who shop for tickets online. In the East, the focal point is New York City, and in the West, it's Los Angeles.

Since E-fares are good for one-way or round-trip travel in either direction, you can get around pretty cheaply. At the time of printing, for example, an express bus ticket E-fare from New York to Washington, D.C., was $23 each way. Compare that to the cost of flying!

BLURRING THE LINE

The rise of low-cost airlines had a big impact on bus services, which suddenly found themselves competing with cheap flights. Independence Air, in particular, threw the market into a flux by offering tickets from its hub in Washington, D.C., to destinations like New York City for $59—or less!

Fuel prices took their toll—Independence Air ceased operations in early 2006, and reality has tempered the ambitions of other low-cost airlines, but ever since, bus providers have had to cooperate to offer rock-bottom fares. Their new competitors are in the skies.

Road Rewards

A bus version of the frequent flyer programs run by airlines, Road Rewards allows passengers to earn points for riding

Greyhound. The points earned for a given trip are based on the length of travel. Rewards range from free companion fare to free tickets anywhere in the Greyhound network.

Signing up is free, but points expire every twelve months. Visit *www.greyhound.com/roadrewards* to learn more about the program.

Discovery Pass

When you purchase a Discovery Pass, you get unlimited use of Greyhound and affiliated bus services in the United States and Canada until it expires. Spontaneous Tourists can take advantage of this flexibility to see as much as they have time for, leaving when they're ready without the hassle of purchasing individual tickets. You can find out more at *www.discoverypass.com*.

Getting Ready

Once you've bought your ticket, you're ready to take the bus. If you're new to the bus, though, here's an idea of what to expect.

Departure Points

Greyhound buses arrive and depart from various points around the United States according to a schedule, but not all of those points are equal.

Stations in large cities may have fast food at the station so passengers can grab a bite to eat. In smaller cities, you'll probably find vending machines instead. Small towns tend to have bus stops at gas stations or convenience stores.

Luggage

You'll also be able to store large bags in luggage compartments underneath the bus, where they're protected from the weather. There are also overhead luggage racks for carry-on bags, but everyone needs to share these, so don't overdo it.

Delays

Buses run on a schedule, and drivers do their best to follow it. At the same time, remember that buses use the highways, so they're subject to delays like road construction, accidents, and heavier-than-expected traffic. From time to time, buses might also break down, and depending on where it happens, it can take a while to get a replacement bus.

When a bus is delayed reaching a station for any reason, the entire schedule is delayed. Some of the delay might be made up along the way to the next stop, but that's not always possible. Be flexible and patient. The bus will eventually arrive.

Overbooking

Seating is first-come, first-serve, and the number of tickets sold is not limited. (Greyhound *does* add buses when a route appears to be particularly popular—subject to availability.)

What this means for Spontaneous Tourists is simple. Arrive early, and when the line starts to form, be as close to the front as possible. Fortunately, when the bus stops at a rest area, you'll have priority re-boarding if you were already onboard.

Onboard Accommodations

Greyhound buses are air-conditioned and clean. The seats are comfortably padded with footrests and individual reading lights, and they lean back about 20 degrees so you can relax. Leg room is comparable to Coach seating on an airplane. A bathroom compartment can be found at the back of the bus. All in all, Greyhound operates comfortable buses.

Unfortunately, buses can't really be that comfortable over long distances, any more than Coach seating on an airplane can. You can get up and stretch a bit, but there's not much room. Too much air conditioning can make it cold. The longer that you're on the bus, the longer the distance you're traveling, the more uncomfortable you're going to find the entire experience.

> Unlike trains, buses are *not* part of the fun. They're just transportation.

Remember that you're taking the bus to get somewhere. Think about what you'll do when you get there, and what you'd like to see. Keeping a positive attitude is important when you're on the bus for a long time.

Make the best of it. Bring a blanket in case you get cold. Have a pillow and a sleep mask if you plan to sleep. Music or earplugs can help with noise. If you have a laptop computer and headphones, maybe this is a good time to get some work done or play a video game. Remember that book you wanted to read? A bus trip presents you with a lot of free time, so you might as well put it to good use.

Food

No food is sold on the bus, but you can bring your own snacks and drinks. You'll certainly want to bring water.

On longer trips, the bus will stop every three or four hours along the way, and you'll have the chance to pick up a quick meal. Even if you aren't going to eat, these breaks are a welcome opportunity to get off the bus and stretch.

Safety

Riding the bus is generally safe if you follow basic travel advice. Keep an eye on your carry-on bags, and take them with you when you get off the bus for a break. Try to use small bills ($20 or under) to pay for food rather than larger bills or credit cards.

A fact of bus travel is that stations tend to be located in lower-income areas. These places are not necessarily dangerous, but you invite problems if you appear nervous or wave around a lot of money. Looking like you belong somewhere is the best way to be left alone.

The Chinatown Bus

Many people have heard of the "Chinatown bus," but few know much about it other than that it's supposed to be a very cheap way to travel. Let's try to separate the fact from the fiction.

First, this bus service really does connect Chinatowns along the East and West Coasts. Secondly, these buses are indeed cheap, as in $35 for a round trip between New York City and Washington, D.C., which you'll recall was a $46 ticket at the time of this printing even with Greyhound's best E-fare.

Now, here's where it gets tricky. No single company operates Chinatown bus service. There also aren't any stations, and the buses leave from general areas rather than specific spots.

The good news is that the Internet has made Chinatown buses much easier to understand. A number of carriers have their own Web sites with scheduling information, which gives you a good chance of being able to catch a bus. Some of the most popular companies on the East Coast include—

- New Century Travel *(www.2000coach.com)*
- Today's Bus *(www.today-bus.com)*
- Apex Bus *(www.apexbus.com)*
- Washington Deluxe *(www.washny.com)*
- Dragon Coach *(www.ebusticket.com)*

> Some companies let you buy your ticket online, but there's not much point. They're easy to buy when you find the bus.

So, what's it like to take the Chinatown bus? Air conditioning and comfortable seats are the norm. Aside from the hectic boarding process, it's not much different from Greyhound—except there usually aren't stops along the way for food.

Buses in Other Countries

Around the world, buses are popular as a form of transportation. Wealthy countries use bus service to supplement their trains, while developing nations may opt for buses to avoid the cost of passenger rail.

If you'll be taking the bus overseas, consult a guidebook. The safety tips already given for domestic bus travel apply overseas as well.

Conditions on buses generally reflect the wealth of the usual passengers. In Europe, you'll find buses similar to those found in the United States—comfortable, clean, and air-conditioned with fairly consistent schedules. Take a bus in sub-Saharan Africa or rural China, on the other hand, and you may find yourself standing, breathing dusty air for hours on end as you lumber down a dirt track. Then again, be especially careful taking luxury tourist buses in third-world countries, because these buses may be appealing targets for robbers.

RECAP

Driving is ingrained in the American mindset as an expression of our freedom. Everyone loves the idea of taking a long road trip. Unfortunately, road trips have a long list of disadvantages, including the cost of gas and tolls, the impact of mileage on a car, driver fatigue, and the potential for getting lost or breaking down.

If you're set on driving, get a map, check your spare tire, switch drivers every few hours, and take breaks to eat and rest. AAA offers roadside assistance and free maps and directions as well as discounts on hotel rooms, so you may want to consider joining.

An alternative to driving is taking the bus. American bus service is provided in large part by Greyhound, which also owns Carolina Trailways. The bus is not a glamorous way to travel, and although the seats are comfortable, long bus rides are not fun. You can go a long way for very little money, however.

In cities that participate, the unofficial "Chinatown bus" is the absolute cheapest way to travel, connecting cities at ticket prices of around $20 each way. These buses are safe and on a par with Greyhound accommodations, but they operate in an ad-hoc fashion that requires some flexibility.

Buses are found all over the world and generally reflect the safety and comfort standards of their host nations. Third world buses tend to be crowded, slow, and unreliable. Luxury tourist buses in these countries, though, may be targets for robbers.

Looking Ahead at America's Roads

There's little doubt that demand for driving will continue to be strong throughout the coming decades. For all their expense, road trips are part of the American psyche. With growing evidence of environmental damage, political instability, and advances in technology, though, we may be on the verge of witnessing a major shift in the type of vehicles that we take on those trips.

Hybrids have gained in popularity and are expected to thrive for several years, but they are an interim solution. In the long term, America and the rest of the world will migrate away from the gasoline-driven internal combustion engine in favor of new fuels like ethanol, biodiesel, hydrogen, and pure electric. Consumers will not accept these technologies unless they deliver performance on par with gasoline, so look for them to phase in slowly over the next few decades.

The beauty of buses is their resilience in the face of change. While new fuels will eventually revolutionize the vehicles themselves, Spontaneous Tourists with tight budgets can count on Greyhound and other providers to be there with low-cost fares and extensive networks for the foreseeable future. Abroad, developing nations will find it easier to operate luxury motor coaches than to build and maintain elaborate next-generation rail lines. The roadways of Planet Earth have a bright future.

TIPS ON THE ROAD

- Bring cash when you take long trips. Credit cards aren't accepted everywhere, especially in small towns or outside of the United States.
- Keep a few low-value bills in your pocket to avoid drawing attention to your wallet.
- Cell phones that support analog roaming have the best chance of getting a signal in rural America.
- Outside of the United States, don't be surprised if your cell phone doesn't work at all. (GSM phones might, but PCS and CDMA phones definitely won't.)
- Shelter at bus stops varies, so have an umbrella or poncho in case it rains.
- If you're taking the bus in a developing country, be sure that your bags are rainproof. Luggage is usually put on the roof.
- Arrive at the bus station about an hour before the scheduled departure.
- Allow at least half an hour for any transfers or connections in case the bus is late.
- Remember to keep a positive attitude and always stay flexible when you take the bus.

CHAPTER 5

Cruises

Most people don't think of cruises as a way to travel, simply because they're so luxurious that they're seen as a destination unto themselves. True, there's little more important on a cruise ship than passenger comfort, but most cruises do take you somewhere, whether that means they stop at ports along the way or actually end at a different place than they began.

In fact, cruises are a great way to see things that you might not see any other way. Visit islands that are out of reach to commercial airlines. Explore ancient ruins hours from major cities while the ship is anchored off the coast. Dive around reefs without having to charter your own boat, and when you're done, come back aboard for some of the finest dining anywhere in the world and a good night's sleep in a comfortable bed.

Welcome to the world of cruises.

WHY *NOT* CRUISE?

For too many people, cruises are a pipe dream that they'll never pursue. Worse, their reluctance is probably because they're misinformed. They think that cruises cost a fortune, or they harbor exaggerated fears of seasickness—a valid but highly overstated concern on today's enormous vessels—and food poisoning (not unheard of on a ship, but no more common at sea than in any other restaurant or cafeteria setting).

If they manage to get past these objections, time becomes the next obstacle for would-be cruise passengers. Lacking several weeks to invest at sea, they instead decide to stay at home and do nothing. They wait, for some day in the distant future, when the stars will align and grant them approval to go.

The truth is that you don't need weeks to enjoy a cruise, and you don't need thousands of dollars to afford one. Maybe you're a little timid because you don't know what you're getting into, and that makes sense. Cruising is quite different from, say, flying. When you finish reading this chapter, though, you'll have the answers you need.

Commit to trying it at least once. By the time you get back from your first cruise, you'll wonder why you waited so long!

CRUISE CONCEPTS

Okay, so you've been convinced that you should take a cruise. You've crossed over from would-be cruiser to *will*-be cruiser. Here are some basic cruise concepts that will help you plan your trip.

Types of Cruises

Most people who've never been on a cruise (and some who have) tend to assume that cruises mean tropical islands, but there are quite a few types of cruises you might take. Read through the descriptions and you might be surprised at how many different ways you can enjoy traveling on the water.

Caribbean

This is your stereotypical cruise. It probably departs from Florida or somewhere in the Gulf of Mexico (Puerto Rico is another possibility) and travels around the Caribbean, maybe stopping in the Bahamas, at Aruba, or another tropical island.

The weather will be warm, and activities focus on being outside in the sun—snorkeling, swimming, sunbathing. Cruise lengths for a Caribbean itinerary start at three days.

Mediterranean

In terms of weather, taking a cruise in the Mediterranean is very similar to taking one in the Caribbean. Instead of tropical islands, though, your ports of call will be nations in Europe and North Africa. Italy and Greece, in particular, tend to be popular places to stop on any Mediterranean itinerary.

You can get a three-day itinerary on a Mediterranean cruise. Unless you live in Europe, however, remember that you have to factor in travel time across the ocean. Plan to spend at least a day traveling each way.

Alaskan

Cruises to Alaska are extremely popular and offer a very different experience from what you'd find on a tropical itinerary. It's not always cold. During the summer it's usually in the 70s or higher. Cruises don't run much later than the end of September, when it's not nearly as warm. Cruises that go to the Arctic Circle, of course, can be chilly any time of year.

When you take an Alaskan cruise, the trip is more about coastal scenery than ports of call although you may stop in Juneau, Vancouver, or a few other ports along the way. Three-day and four-day itineraries are available, but these are limited to the lower parts of Alaska. Seeing the northern tier takes longer, usually about a week.

Transoceanic

Once the only way to travel from Europe to North America, transatlantic cruises have been supplanted by air travel as a mode of transportation, but they still operate as a very unique and interesting way to cross the ocean. Most transatlantic cruises run between New York and ports in the United Kingdom. You can expect to take a full week to make the voyage and fly back.

Like its Atlantic counterpart, a transpacific cruise is mostly time spent at sea. Some itineraries do include ports of call, which may provide an opportunity to visit places like Guam or Tahiti.

Sailing across the Pacific Ocean takes a long time. A cruise to Australia or Asia is an option only for those who can set aside two to four weeks, assuming you get on the plane to fly back as soon as you disembark. Given the long timeline, transpacific cruises really don't conform to the usual model for Spontaneous Tourism.

Transcanal

Ships travel through the Panama Canal every day, but most of them are cargo vessels. Travelers looking for something different can experience the Canal firsthand on a cruise that travels through it to ferry passengers from one side of North America to the other—a process that takes a full week.

Hawaiian

Did you know that you can take a cruise around the Hawaiian Islands? Fly to the island of your choice, and spend as few as three days (or as long as a week) sailing between and visiting the eight islands that make up America's fiftieth state.

> Under the Jones Act, passed in the 1920s, any ship that sails directly from one U.S. port to another must sail under the American flag. A recent law allows foreign-built ships to change flags while providing inter-island service in the Hawaiian Islands.

Riverboat

For a completely different experience, you might try a riverboat cruise. You can take a cruise on the Mississippi, Nile, or along any of more than a dozen other major rivers around the world. Most are run by small, specialized companies, and itineraries and lengths of trips vary by company.

A riverboat is much smaller than an oceangoing vessel, so you'll enjoy a more intimate experience. These also tend to be more exclusive (simply because fewer people look into them), so you can expect exceptional personal service.

Cruise to Nowhere

Earlier in this chapter, we briefly mentioned that there are cruises to nowhere. It's true! Cruise ships are fun places to be, even without a destination. Board, head out to sea for a fun day of dining and entertainment, and then return to port. It's a great way to spend a weekend.

Most major cruise ports offer Cruises to Nowhere. Two or three days are usual for these fun-filled excursions, but they even run the occasional overnight itinerary. Ironically, these tend to cost *more*, maybe because they attract people who can spare money more easily than time.

Antarctic

In ranking the world's most exclusive destinations, the world's seventh and only unsettled continent ranks just behind orbit. No commercial airlines will take you there, but there are cruise itineraries that can, ranging from luxury ships to icebreakers.

Of course, Antarctica isn't close to America or anything else. You'll have to plan a much longer itinerary to visit this mysterious place than you would for most other trips—at least two weeks. Bragging rights, though, are virtually guaranteed.

You can learn more at *www.polarcruises.com*.

Major Cruise Lines

There are dozens of cruise lines around the world. They aren't necessarily independent companies. Carnival, for example, owns Holland-America. They operate as separate lines, because the party atmosphere on a Carnival ship is very different from the old-world elegance for which Holland-America is famous.

Since each cruise line is essentially unique, the best way to get a feel for a particular line is to visit its Web site. Here's a table showing some of the most popular cruise lines and their Web sites. Additional information can be found in Appendix C.

Cruise Line	Web Site
Carnival	*www.carnival.com*
Princess	*www.princess.com*
Norwegian	*www.ncl.com*
Royal Caribbean	*www.royalcaribbean.com*
Holland-America	*www.hollandamerica.com*
Disney	*www.disneycruise.com*
Regent Seven Seas	*www.rssc.com*
Cunard	*www.cunard.com*

Specialty Cruises

In addition to the large-scale voyages operated by the major cruise lines, lots of smaller companies operate specialty cruises. Cruises on the Rhine, trips on luxury sailboats, and "Semester at Sea" educational programs are all operated as specialty cruises. As with the major cruise lines, itineraries vary.

Traveling on Freighters

Most of the enormous cargo vessels that carry the world's materials and finished goods between continents were built to accommodate large crews. Over the years, however, advances in technology have reduced the number of people needed to crew the ships, which means that some of the staterooms once used by officers are empty.

Cruise Terminology

When you're planning a cruise, here are some terms you may encounter.

Aft: To the rear of the ship.

Captain: The officer in command of the ship. Modern ship captains have few social duties, these now being performed by Cruise Directors.

Cruise Director: The person in charge of all cruise-related activities and social functions.

Disembarkation: Leaving the ship for good.

Double Occupancy: The rate that *each* person pays if there are a total of two; generally *not* available to a single passenger.

Embarkation: Boarding the ship for the first time.

Going Ashore: Leaving the ship with the intention of returning to continue the voyage.

Nautical Mile: A unit of measure for distance traveled at sea. One nautical mile is equal to 1.15 standard miles or 1,852 meters.

Port: A point of embarkation, or when used as a direction, to the left-hand side of the ship.

Single Supplement: The surcharge imposed by a cruise line if a single passenger books a stateroom alone; meant to offset the lost revenue from not having a second passenger.

Starboard: To the right-hand side of the ship.

Stateroom: A cabin equipped with the comforts appropriate for a passenger or officer.

Stern: The rear of the ship as a location; not to be confused with "aft," which is a direction.

You can book passage on a freighter for less than a typical cruise would cost on a per-day basis. The fare includes meals, which you'll share with the officers and crew in the ship's mess. It's not gourmet cuisine, but they eat well. During the day, the crew has duties, so you'll have to entertain yourself. Amenities vary by ship, but there may be fitness equipment or a saltwater pool for swimming.

Understand that cargo vessels are extremely slow, and they go where they need to go for commercial reasons. On some occasions, a ship will be diverted to a new port while it's en route, and depending on the situation, it can take over a month to cross the ocean. Most Spontaneous Tourists probably won't be able to spare the time.

THE CRUISE EXPERIENCE DECODED

As we've covered previously, cruising is a mystery to a lot of people. Since people like to know what they're getting into, not knowing what to expect on a cruise is a big turn-off that keeps them from giving it a try.

In this section, we'll go through the entire cruise process, from the time that you start looking to the time that you get home. Along the way, we'll cover a lot of specific topics that you might have wondered about, so you can feel a bit more confident about booking your first sea adventure.

Ready? Let's get started!

> The information in this section applies to the sea and ocean cruises offered by most major cruise lines. Specialty and riverboat cruises run by smaller operators may do things differently, and specifics vary by cruise line. Always ask for detailed information when you prepare for a cruise.

Planning

Before you can leave, you have a lot to do. Start by deciding *how long* you can afford to be gone, *how much* you can afford to pay, and *where* you'd like to go. These three factors will help you narrow your options.

Next, consider what you're looking for in terms of atmosphere—wild party is on one side and elegant luxury is on the other, with a few steps in between. This will help you decide which cruise lines you want to consider.

Armed with this knowledge, you're ready to look for a cruise that fits.

Finding the Right Cruise

Going online will help you research available cruises. In addition to some cruise-specific sites, most of the legacy airlines have cruise departments, and you can earn frequent flyer miles for using them. Plug in the information you've decided, such as how long you can be gone and where you'd like to go, and you'll get a list of cruises that might work.

In addition, each cruise line has its own Web site. Once a cruise catches your eye, you should look it up on the cruise line's site to get more details. In particular, the cruise lines have extensive information on each ship in their fleets that you can consider in narrowing your choices.

Cruising is also one area where working with a travel agent can be a big help. The ticketing process can be a little complicated, and the experience is determined by the line and even the ship that you take. A good travel agent can find a cruise in your price range that you'll enjoy.

Prices and Staterooms

From a cruise Web site, you'll be able to see what the cheapest prices are for each cruise, as well as zooming in to see how those prices break down by type of stateroom. Larger rooms with better views are, of course, more expensive, but they're not necessarily worth the price. Here are some reasons.

- **No class distinction**. Today's cruises are one-class. Booking an interior stateroom on a lower deck gets you the same privileges as someone who has a large suite with a balcony on a higher deck—dining, entertainment, use of the fitness center, and even 24-hour room service.

- **Stability**. Most people realize that ships roll back and forth on the sea and that it gets worse in rough weather, but you may not realize that it gets worse higher up and toward the outside of the ship. The most stable places are those on low decks in the center of the ship. If seasickness is a worry, the least expensive cabin is the most appealing!

- **Wasted luxury**. How much time do you think that you'll spend in your stateroom, anyway? Even the smallest stateroom is quite comfortable in terms of amenities, and most of what you want to do is outside of your room. If you plan to be there to change and sleep, you can save quite a lot of money by foregoing the balcony and enjoying the spectacular views from the common-area lounges.

My personal feeling is that the only stateroom luxury worth paying for is a porthole, because natural light makes most people happier. Whatever your preference, keep in mind that prices are usually listed as "double occupancy." That means that the price applies per person *if two people book*. If you're going to be traveling alone, you'll pay a higher rate—called the "single supplement"—to cover the lost profit from leaving the space empty.

MAKE A NEW FRIEND!

If you're planning to take a cruise alone, you do have an alternative to paying the single supplement: ask the cruise line to assign you a roommate. If they have another single passenger of the same gender for the same size room, you'll be paired up.

Oh, and if they don't find someone? You'll still get the double-occupancy rate for the cabin, and you'll have it all to yourself. What a deal!

Booking

Once you know what you want, it's time to book your tickets. Actually buying the tickets is fairly straightforward. You contact your agent, verify the itinerary, and provide payment information. Unless you live in the same city as the cruise's port of embarkation, you'll want plane tickets to get you there and back again.

Airfare

Most cruise agents can arrange for airfare to and from the city of embarkation, as well as transfers from the airport to the port and back again. Taking them up on that deal makes sense if you prefer that one person handle everything. Ports may be half an hour or more away from the airport, which leaves you to either pay for an expensive taxi or figure out the local bus system. On your first cruise in particular, it can be a relief to have the transfer service pre-arranged.

Transfer service also provides a form of insurance. If the cruise line makes your flight arrangements, they have to get you to the ship regardless of when you arrive or refund your money and take you home. The same applies to getting you to the airport in time for your return flight. Some cruise lines also retrieve the checked baggage of cruise passengers from the baggage claim area and have it transported directly to the ship. When you make your own flight arrangements, you don't automatically get either benefit. On the other hand, it's not uncommon for the airline and flight itinerary selected to be more expensive than you can get on your own.

One way around this dilemma is to make your own flight arrangements and purchase the transfer service as an add-on once you've booked your flights. It usually costs less than $50 for round-trip transfers.

> As you get more experienced, you may prefer to handle your own transfers to save money. It's especially appealing to do it yourself in cities you know or where you have friends who can help.

Getting Ready

Your cruise documents will arrive anywhere from a few days to a few weeks from the date that you buy the tickets. Usually, they're delivered using one of the express services, and they always require your signature. These are tickets, not boarding passes. If you lose them, it takes some effort to get them replaced.

Once you receive the documents, read over everything carefully. You will need to fill out some forms, including official immigration paperwork for any cruise that involves leaving the United States. You'll also find your itinerary, flight information for reservations made through the cruise line, and vouchers for the transfer service if you purchased it.

If anything doesn't look right, contact the cruise line immediately. Either way, you've still got a few other things to consider between the day that you booked your cruise and the day that you leave.

Official Documents

Any cruise that involves international travel is likely to require a passport. Depending on the countries visited, you may also need to arrange for one or more visas. At a minimum, you're going to need to bring a government-issued photo identification card, such as a driver's license.

A photo I.D. and copy of your birth certificate or naturalization paperwork may be acceptable for cruises traveling to and from Canada or Mexico. That's changing, however, and by 2008, you'll need to have a passport for any travel outside of the United States.

For more information on passports and visas, see Chapter 7.

Cruise Insurance

When we talk about cruise insurance, it's not medical or liability that we're after, because the ship has facilities to deal with that sort of thing. The issue is what happens if you have to cancel your plans.

Unlike airline tickets, which usually charge a relatively minor fee to rebook an itinerary on a non-refundable fare, cruise tickets may not be redeemable for any other cruise unless the itinerary changes because of the cruise line. The company might waive that rule for, say, a verifiable death of an immediate relative, but last-minute challenges at work won't cut it. (It makes sense, because a cruise is transportation and accommodations rolled into one. There's a lot that goes into a ticket.)

Cruise insurance will reimburse you for the cost of the cruise if you have to cancel for some reason. How much it costs depends on who offers it, and whether you want it depends on the cost of the cruise. For a three-day or seven-day cruise, it's probably overkill. If you're planning a 28-day transoceanic cruise to Australia, though, the odds are in favor of a conflict.

Packing

When you pack for a cruise, it's more like a traditional vacation than Spontaneous Tourism. You'll be unpacking everything in what amounts to a safely guarded hotel room, so you can bring whatever you like without worrying about carrying it around with you. Clothing for the ship and for any trips ashore, as well as bathing suits and even things like laptop computers, may be on your packing list.

Even so, why bring things that you really won't need? You'll find some good general packing advice in Chapter 6, which you can adapt to fit your particular cruise itinerary.

DRESSING FOR DINNER

Some cruise lines, including Holland-America, plan formal evenings into their schedules as part of the fun. On these occasions, it's preferred that you have formalwear (tuxedos for gentlemen, gowns for ladies) to dress for dinner and the evening activities that follow.

If you don't own formal attire, you can arrange in advance to rent it from the cruise line. You can also get away with semi-formal clothing (suits for gentlemen, cocktail dresses for ladies) in just about all cases—though anything that doesn't include a coat and tie is really out of the question.

Embarkation

Assuming that you caught your flight on time, made it to the destination airport, and either used the transfer service provided by the cruise line or made your own way to the port, the next step is embarkation—going through the check-in and boarding process. Most cruises involve leaving their country of origin, so there's a little more that happens during this process than people who are used to domestic air travel might expect.

Security Screening

In today's world, hostile intentions have to be assumed. Embarkation begins with security screening similar to what you'd find at the airport (though a lot more friendly), including x-ray inspection of your carry-on luggage and walking through a metal detector.

Customs

In some cases, you may have to go through Customs prior to checking in for the cruise. The purpose for this is a little vague but seems to be a form of pre-processing to help the Customs personnel where you'll be arriving verify that you traveled to your destination by ship. Assuming that you have your cruise tickets with you, it goes very quickly.

Check-In

During check-in, you present your tickets along with any other forms that needed to be filled out (such as a health questionnaire), and the cruise line staff confirms your stateroom. If you didn't get a specific room assignment when you booked, you'll be assigned a room from the list of what's available.

Cruises love building a loyal customer base, so it's quite common to be upgraded to a better stateroom if one is vacant. If you wanted an interior lower-deck cabin for a reason, however, you can always refuse the upgrade. Once you have your room key, it's time to board the ship.

> On some ships, you may be able to register a credit card for direct billing of shipboard expenses. If this is offered, it's much more convenient than carrying cash.

Boarding

Walking up the gangway to board a ship is a special kind of thrill, especially on your first voyage. It's a sort of mental break from the rest of the world. Other than that, it works pretty much like you'd expect—walk to the open hatch, enter the ship, and then track down your stateroom. There, you'll probably be greeted by your cabin steward, who will handle things like tidying your room and any laundry services you request.

Prior to Departure

Depending on when you board, you may have some time to unpack and get acquainted with the ship. It's also quite common for cruise ships to have a buffet waiting for newly embarked passengers, so if you're hungry or just want to mingle with other people, it's worth dropping by.

Usually about half an hour before departure, there'll be an announcement concerning the mandatory lifeboat drill. Pay attention to where you'll need to report and when—it's maritime law that everyone participate. Besides, in the event of an emergency, you *really* want to know what to do.

Bon Voyage!

Once the lifeboat drill is done, it's time to "weigh anchor and set sail." Tradition calls for you to join the other passengers on the decks, waving farewell to the people who are inevitably waving from the dock. Yes, this still happens today, and whether you know someone or not, it's fun to do!

Life at Sea

With the shores a fading memory, the cruise has officially begun. As we mentioned earlier, cruising is not only a form of transportation from one place to another (even if the destination is the same place you started) but also your lodging, meals, and entertainment rolled into one. Pampering is the rule instead of the exception, and you'll be delighted with what's offered.

Specific amenities vary not only by cruise line but by ship. Almost all modern cruise ships have pools, hot tubs, and fitness centers (particularly important, given the amount of food that's served). Movie theatres, lounges, bars, and open deck space to lounge or walk are also typical. Mid-sized cruise ships with 1200–1500 passengers may have art galleries, full-service spas, and standard-size basketball and racquetball courts. Some of the really large ships cater to as many as 4000 passengers and even have their own bowling alleys!

Games are played throughout the day and night. Cruises also offer first-rate entertainment, comparable to what you'd find in Las Vegas, with dancers, comedians, and musicians, and at least one nightclub. Live music is played in most of the ship's lounges. Do whatever you like. You'll have lots of choices.

Eating Onboard

Food is the centerpiece of the cruise experience. Breakfast starts early and ends late. Lunch spans four or five hours, and if you get hungry, you can enjoy all-day and midnight buffets. Choose table service dining if you like, or opt for a casual, self-serve cafeteria. On the off-chance that you're hungry outside of the usual mealtimes, you can even order from a 24-hour room service menu—and it's all free, included in the price of your ticket.

Some cruise lines mix a few formal nights into longer itineraries. Not every cruise line does it, but having a chance to wear a tuxedo or gown can really add to the fun. They also may offer more than one dinner seating, depending on how many passengers will be dining.

In general, you'll be given your dinner seating time and table when you first arrive at your stateroom. Dining with others is a great way to make new friends, and cruise lines usually try to set singles together and couples with other couples. Of course, you might find that you don't get along with some of your companions. No need to be miserable. If that happens, talk with the dining room manager for a discreet relocation.

ADDITIONAL CHARGES MAY APPLY

While all of your food in the dining rooms and cafeterias is included, some things cost extra. On most cruises, for instance, you pay per-glass for alcoholic beverages, including wines with dinner. Carbonated soft drinks may also cost a nominal fee, so many passengers take the opportunity to enjoy the fresh fruit juices and iced tea that are freely provided.

It's increasingly common for cruise ships to also offer one or more restaurants that have a charge beyond your ticket price. These range from specialty coffee bars to exclusive, private dining in an extremely formal setting (typically geared toward couples who want a romantic evening alone).

You can be quite happy never paying to eat at these restaurants, because the standard food is extremely high-quality. Even if you do, though, you'll find that it's far less costly than an equivalent restaurant on land—the cruise line subsidizes the cost with the money that covers your included meal.

Shore Excursions

As great as life is on the sea, it's the stops along the way that make taking a cruise a mode of transportation. Every port of call offers you an opportunity to go ashore, either on your own or as part of an organized tour called a shore excursion. Both approaches have merit.

If you go by yourself, you won't be tethered to the group. You can see what you want when you want, and you can really experience the local culture. On the other hand, if you don't have any idea what you're doing, you might get lost, waste time wandering in circles, or miss great sights that the group got to see. In certain cases, it can even be a little dangerous to just wander off, although if you demonstrate common sense as a traveler you'll be fine.

Your cruise ship will have a desk or office dedicated to helping you select and sign up for shore excursions. Space is limited, so you'll want to find out what's being offered as early as possible and reserve any spots you want on the tours. If something interests you, and you can afford it, try it! Cruise lines make a point of offering excursions that passengers will enjoy.

Shore excursions aren't free, but they're also not mandatory. In fact, you don't have to go ashore at all; if you prefer, you're welcome to stay aboard and continue to enjoy what the ship has to offer.

Plenty of people do just that. Spontaneous Tourism, however, isn't about staying in the hotel. If you're going to travel, you need to step off the ship and see the world around you. If the tour is too pricey, take the opportunity to wander a bit.

Don't Miss the Boat

Before the ship comes into a port, the captain or cruise director will announce the scheduled departure time and when passengers need to be back on board, which is usually half an hour before the ship will set sail. Make a point of remembering these times! It's extremely rare for a passenger to actually be left behind, but there's a considerably greater risk that the entire ship will have to wait for you, and that's neither fair to everyone else nor likely to make you a lot of friends among the crew.

Disembarkation

All good things come to an end, and cruises are no exception to that rule. Depending on how many passengers are disembarking at a particular port, leaving the ship can get hectic. The captain or cruise director will start making announcements with regard to disembarking passengers long before the ship arrives in port, so you'll know what you need to do and where you need to be to make things go smoothly.

Baggage

You may be asked to tag whatever luggage you don't plan to hand-carry and leave it outside of your stateroom the night before. Whatever bags you mark will be picked up and taken off the ship for you to collect later, which is much more convenient than having to lug everything off yourself.

Of course, you'll want to keep clothing and hygiene items with you for the morning. Expensive or delicate items also belong in your carry-on bag. Depending on the cruise, you may or may not actually go through formal Customs screening, but if you've been outside of the country, you'll have to complete a declarations form.

Tipping

If there are people whose efforts made your cruise a memorable time—your cabin steward, for instance—it may be appropriate to give them gratuities before you depart (assuming that you haven't already done so). Use cash, and either present the gift directly or leave it in an envelope with the recipient's name marked.

It's increasingly popular for cruise lines to add a "service charge" to your onboard account in place of individual gratuities. If your ship does this, it will be noted in your cruise materials and also on your bill. The intent is to make the process more convenient for you.

Some people prefer to have the service fee removed and continue the practice of rewarding exceptional service with personal gratuities. If that's your preference, the ship can accommodate you. You can also request that a higher or lower amount be charged.

Leaving the Ship

Disembarking is usually done according to some order, such as the number of your stateroom or a special code assigned on your luggage tags. The goal is to keep the gangway from becoming too crowded or making people wait for long periods of time.

Find a comfortable spot, such as a lounge or café, to wait until you're called, then proceed to the gangway where you will record your departure. On ships that don't have formal Customs staff waiting, that will be where you turn in your declarations form as well.

Once that's taken care of, walk down the gangway and follow the directions to collect your luggage. If you're using the transfer service, there will be additional signs or other guidance to get you to the buses. Otherwise, you're on your own.

Welcome ashore!

RECAP

Most people don't think of cruises as a way to travel, but they can be a great way to visit several places in a short amount of time. Too often, though, people assume that they need several weeks to take a cruise, or that it will cost thousands of dollars. That's just not true.

You can choose from many different types of cruises. Besides the typical Caribbean itinerary, cruises travel around the Mediterranean, along the Canadian and Alaskan coastlines, across the oceans, and through the Panama Canal. You can even take a cruise to the Arctic Circle or Antarctica.

Your cruise experience depends in part on where you go and also on the cruise line you choose. When you look to find the right cruise for your interests, consider where it's going and what kind of atmosphere you prefer. Carnival, for example, has a party atmosphere, while Holland-America is more elegant.

Ships also vary—some are floating cities with four thousand or more people, others are luxury sailboats with fewer than one hundred passengers. Antarctic cruises may use modified research vessels. Traveling by freighter is also a possibility, though these ships travel so slowly that Spontaneous Tourists may find it difficult to make the time.

Prices vary based on the cruise itinerary and on the size of stateroom that you want. If you book a stateroom by yourself, you'll be charged a fee called a "single supplement," which the cruise line uses to offset the money lost by leaving the other bed empty. Larger rooms, rooms on higher decks, and rooms on the outside of the ship generally cost more. Ironically, these are less appealing in rough seas, because the lower decks move less. Remember that modern cruises are one-class, which means you'll get the same access to the ship's amenities regardless of which stateroom you book.

Boarding involves a security screening similar to what you'd expect at the airport. There will be a mandatory lifeboat drill before the ship departs, and then you'll get underway. Life on a cruise ship is extremely pampering and includes far too much food. Fortunately, there's usually a fitness center onboard.

Whenever the ship stops in a port of call, you'll have some time to go ashore and see the area. You might join a formal tour, called a shore excursion, or simply go on your own. Do go, though, because the point of Spontaneous Tourism is to travel, not to stay in a floating hotel. Whatever you do, be sure that you're back aboard the ship by the announced time.

When you finish your cruise, there'll be instructions on what to do with your luggage (which is usually offloaded for you). Tipping is included as a daily service charge on your bill for most cruise lines, but you can change it if you want. If you've been outside of the United States, you'll go through Customs when you disembark, then you collect your luggage and you're done. It's a great experience. Try it!

Looking Ahead at the Cruise Industry

American workers are more productive than ever, but we also face overwhelming stress in a world of networked communications and global competition. Cruises provide a break from the hectic pace of everyday life and a chance to experience levels of luxury that most of us otherwise find only in dreams. Prices have been stable in the cruise market for several years, with excess capacity and competition helping first-timers and veterans alike enjoy a pampered life at sea that fits their schedules and budgets.

Spontaneous Tourists can expect these trends to continue. Cruising is big business—we're even seeing ocean liners designed to carry wealthy retirees around the world to live out their golden years in perpetual luxury. Profit margins help the cruise lines keep their ships well maintained and staffed, and there are so many itineraries that you're unlikely to exhaust the possibilities before you run out of cash.

There are also signs of a new industry in space tourism. Prices will remain out of this world for at least a decade, but by around 2020, it may be possible to take a trip to orbit for the price of a first-class airline ticket. Private sector companies have jumped on board with plans for everything from a space elevator to an orbital hotel. For the adventurous, the sky need not be the limit.

125

CRUISE TIPS

- As soon as time allows, set out to explore the ship. You'll feel more comfortable knowing your way around.
- If you're able, take the stairs rather than an elevator whenever possible. More than just being good exercise, it helps you to get a feel for what is located on which deck.
- Being on a floating hotel doesn't mean you should stay in your stateroom! Get involved in organized activities, such as games, sports, and classes.
- Don't sit alone at meals, even in the cafeteria. Find an empty chair at a table with other people and introduce yourself. Cruise passengers are friendly and like to meet people.
- Sign up for shore excursions as early as possible. You don't want to miss out on a great opportunity because you waited too long.
- When you go ashore, leave valuables onboard and use the same good travel judgment as if you'd arrived by air or some other way.
- Remember that American citizens are not allowed to go to Cuba or bring Cuban cigars or other property into the United States.

PART 3

Before You Leave

Planning your trip, figuring out passports and visas, deciding what to pack (and how to pack light), and dealing with foreign currency.

Chapter 6 Planning and Packing
Page 129

Chapter 7 Paperwork
Page 151

*"Always plan ahead. It wasn't raining
when Noah built the ark."*
—Richard C. Cushing

CHAPTER **6**

Planning and Packing

Before you leave and start exploring the world, you'll need to plan your trip. You have some big decisions to make (like where you're going), and then you'll want a basic idea of what to expect when you get there. Next, you can start packing. Spontaneous Tourists travel light, so we'll cover tips on how to take what you need, make it fit, and leave the rest at home.

Let's start by picking a destination.

WHERE TO?

Maybe some of you already have a place in mind that you'd like to visit. If you do, great! For the others, however, you don't need to choose a destination before you start planning a trip.

Many people who are just starting out as travelers look for cheap fares and plan their trips around the places they can afford to go. This approach works for domestic and international travel. In fact, it works especially well for travel abroad, because getting there is usually the biggest cost.

One big factor that affects the cost of any overseas trip is the currency exchange rate, the amount of local currency that you'll receive for each U.S. dollar. Local prices don't vary based on exchange rates, so if you can get more local currency for fewer U.S. dollars, that means you can buy more while spending less. The opposite also applies.

We'll talk more about exchange rates in Chapter 7, but the bottom line is that it's cheaper to travel to places where the U.S. dollar is strong against the local currency. Throughout 2006, the strength of the euro and British pound made trips to Europe extremely expensive, while Americans traveling to Asia, South America, and Australia enjoyed extremely favorable exchange rates.

Choose a destination where you'll get more for your money and where the cost of your trip is lower. That's the easiest way to save money on international travel.

Time to Study!

Once you've decided where you'd like to go, it's time to learn about it. Spontaneous Tourism is having the flexibility and sense of adventure to grab onto travel opportunities when they come up. That doesn't mean you have to leave without doing any planning at all, just that you don't have to take weeks doing it.

Fortunately, it's easy to plan trips these days, thanks to two great resources—guidebooks and the Internet.

Guidebooks

Worldwide interest in travel has sparked an explosion of well-written guidebooks that can tell you everything you need to know when you're planning to visit a new place. A few that are popular among American travelers—

- Lonely Planet *(www.lonelyplanet.com)*
- Frommer's *(www.frommers.com)*
- Rough Guides *(www.roughguides.com)*

- Fodor's *(www.fodors.com)*
- BakPak *(www.bakpakguide.com)*
- Rick Steves' Europe *(www.ricksteves.com)*
- Footprint *(www.footprintbooks.com)*

Guidebooks give you detailed information on the geography, climate, and culture. They cover what to see, where to eat, which clubs and bars are the best, and how you can spend less money while having a great time.

Pick a guidebook based on the style as well as the content. Go to a local bookstore, flip through one from each publisher, and go with the style that you like the best.

Guidebooks aren't only for foreign countries. You can get guidebooks for cities, regions, or even entire continents. A lot of American cities and states are covered, and you'll find a book to research virtually every nation in the world.

> Not everyone likes guidebooks. Some people feel that they can get much of the same information from the Internet for free. To me, having all of that information edited and bound in an easy to carry book is well worth the price.

Internet Research

The Internet is the greatest source of information that humanity has ever seen, more comprehensive than the best library or bookstore, and—aside from the cost of connecting—it's free. Just about everything is addressed somewhere on the Internet.

The problem with the Internet is the time that it takes to find what you want. We have powerful search engines that catalog Web sites and match our searches based on keywords, and they work quite well. Unfortunately, a lot of people make it their top priority to trick us by making their sites claim to be what we want.

Fortunately, travel is a particularly popular Internet topic. Spontaneous Tourists like you post their adventures in online journals (blogs), and they usually include pictures. You can find ratings of different places to stay and eat, tips for dealing with local officials, discussions of cultural events, and much more. These tend to be honest personal reactions rather than marketing hype. Many guidebook publishers also provide free mini-guides online. You'll find links to some of them at *www.spontaneoustourism.com*.

TRAVEL COSTS

Once you know where you're going, the next thing to consider is how much it's going to cost to get there. Travel costs depend on when, as well as how, you're traveling. For example, planes cost more than buses, but flying to London in the winter is much cheaper than going in the summer. Florida is the opposite, being more popular in the winter.

Wherever you're trying to go, discounted tickets can get you there at the best prices. An empty seat is lost money, and the higher the usual price, the bigger the cut can get. That means bus and even rail fares are relatively static, while plane and cruise ticket prices can vary widely.

Always be on the lookout for discounts. Be careful, though, that you don't miss the best opportunities to find them. Cruises get cheaper as their sail dates approach. Conversely, airfare to a specific destination usually costs more at the last minute.

Saving Money

No matter how you get there, travel tends to be the biggest cost of a trip. The farther that you're going, the more you're going to pay for a ticket to get you there. If you have to buy meals on the way, longer trips mean larger costs beyond the ticket price as well.

Combine Trips

By far, the biggest ticket prices are for international flights that cross the ocean. Depending on how much time you have, you can take advantage of the high cost of getting overseas by doing more while you're there. For example, fly to London and visit France on the same trip.

> If you'll be traveling around Europe, trains are a very popular way to go, but you'll also be surprised how cheap you can get flights on European low-cost carriers like easyJet, RyanAir, and German Wings. Some flights can cost as little as €9—less than $20!

Be Flexible, Save Money

If you're not picky about when you leave, you'll have an easier time finding discounted rates. Some Web sites allow you to specify that you'll consider dates "on or close" to the date chosen for your trip. Look at different times as well, because you can save money by traveling during off-peak hours. (Ideally, though, try to arrive in a strange city during daylight hours.)

Organized Trips

Tired of traveling alone? Want to visit an exotic place but don't know quite how to go about getting a visa and doing all of the paperwork? Interested in helping others?

These days, it's popular to avoid the travel agent and make your own reservations. The Internet certainly gives you the tools for that, but organized programs have a lot to offer. Merely sign up, pay the fees, and the organizers take care of the rest.

Tours and programs are available to fit nearly every budget and interest. There are plenty of day and weekend bus trips put together by interest groups, but most commercial and academic programs last at least a week. Humanitarian programs require considerably more investment, at least several weeks and often months or even years. While these programs are not for everyone, we'll cover them so you can decide what works best for you.

> ***Spontaneous Tourism*** **focuses on short trips for busy people. Readers interested in exploring the workings of longer trips should refer to Rob Sangster's *Traveler's Tool Kit*, a comprehensive reference for those planning to spend months exploring distant lands.**

Commercial Tours

Travel agents, tour companies, and community groups organize trips all of the time. You can sign up for anything from a bus trip to shop in New York City to a wilderness exploration of Incan ruins in South America. Travelers may find it difficult to narrow down the choices.

If you have friends or family who've traveled with a particular tour company before, that's usually the best place to start. Look for reviews in travel magazines and on the Internet. If people have had bad experiences, you'll probably find out.

School-Sponsored Visits

Universities and community colleges organize trips every year, usually during the winter and over the summer. They're made available to students first, but if there are spots left open, they usually accept other travelers.

DO YOU SPEAK ENGLISH?

If you're looking for a way to actually *live* abroad rather than just travel, English teachers are in demand in Japan, China, South Korea, and other Asian countries. If you're hired, you'll be paid a salary or living stipend, and the program will cover your roundtrip airfare and help you find housing.

You can get more information on the Teach English as a Foreign Language (TEFL) certificate at *www.tefl.com*. The only trade-off is that you have to commit to an entire year overseas.

Humanitarian Programs

Around the world, impoverished people live without adequate food, clothing, and shelter. International aid organizations do what they can to address these needs, but they depend on volunteers to help them.

As a volunteer, you might help build decent housing in central Africa with Habitat for Humanity or distribute supplies along a storm-ravaged coastline. You'll be responsible for a lot of your own costs, but helping others can be a very rewarding experience. Your efforts will also give you a chance to see places where you might not otherwise go.

Many volunteer opportunities require a commitment of at least a few weeks, sometimes a few months. There are some longer-term programs, as well. The Peace Corps places volunteers with local populations around the world to help them learn new techniques for things like farming and sanitation. AmeriCorps has a similar role within the United States. Both programs require a two-year commitment.

Eco-Tourism

Resorts are fun, but they generate a lot of trash. As it turns out, other countries don't have any better answer to waste than we do here in the United States. They burn, bury, or dump it in a river. Not good.

The relatively recent concept of eco-tourism is an attempt to address the impact that travelers have on the environment when they visit places. When you take an eco-friendly trip, you might (for example) stay in simple wooden cabins rather than a luxury hotel. You'll be comfortable, but you won't generate as much trash.

Eco-friendly trips aren't cheap. If they were, the amount of money that they contributed to the local economy would be less than traditional tourism, so no one would want to sell them.

Instead, what you'll find is that you're able to enjoy the country from a whole different perspective. Give it a try when you start visiting exotic destinations.

> Listing a trip as eco-friendly is easy, but no common standard certifies these claims, so be sure to ask questions up front.

Time to Buy

Once you've decided on your travel plans, it's time to buy your tickets. But when should you buy them? Do you grab today's price while it's available, or wait for tomorrow? It depends.

Bus tickets aren't sold on capacity, so it doesn't matter. With Amtrak, you have to buy your tickets at least three days in advance to qualify for most of the discounts. When you're flying, waiting until later to make up your mind can mean paying a lot more. Airlines assume that if you want last-minute reservations, you *really* need to get to your destination and will pay more to do it, (so the fare that was $99 a week ago can go for $400 or more on the day of the flight.)

At the same time, airlines that don't have enough bookings going into a weekend may offer roundtrip discounts between certain cities. These last-minute fares are generally published online and may have restrictive conditions attached, but they're a great way to save money.

Saving with Standby Fares

If you have a lot of flexibility, you might be able to save money by flying standby. Basically, you are put on a waiting list and sit by the gate. If there's an empty seat within half an hour or so of the scheduled departure time, you get it.

Standby tickets are very cheap, usually just a fraction of the cost you'd pay for a confirmed ticket. Not every airline offers this option, however, and some make it available only to students. Also, remember that you might *not* get a seat on the plane, and you'll need to have a viable alternative.

Don't Plan for Refunds

Airlines have a few different types of tickets, classified by a cryptic system of fare codes like Y, B, Z, V, S, and M. What precisely these codes mean isn't known to most mere mortals, but they define the restrictions placed on tickets—how they can be used, whether they can be upgraded, if exchanges are possible, etc.

Unrestricted full-fare tickets let you get back your entire cost if you have to cancel your plans. You can also make changes with no fees or penalties. The downside is that they can cost as much as five times more than the cheapest available fare. When you travel for business, the flexibility can offset the cost, but they're out of the price range for most Spontaneous Tourists.

137

Fare code Y indicates a full-fare economy ticket, and most airlines use C for a full-fare First Class ticket. Airlines may have other unrestricted tickets that aren't full-fare with different codes, but these vary by carrier.

You'll save a huge amount of money by purchasing non-refundable fares, which some airlines simply refer to as the "lowest available price." You can't get your money back for these kinds of tickets, but if you have to reschedule, you can apply their value to future flights to the same destination (minus a penalty fee, which may be as much as $100).

With non-refundable tickets, you'll still earn frequent flyer credit. Most also allow domestic upgrades (see the exception below). International upgrades are more restricted. If you want to request one, search for upgradeable fares.

DISCOUNTS VS. UPGRADES

Most non-refundable domestic tickets with legacy carriers can be upgraded. The exception is tickets purchased from discount sites like *www.site69.com*, *www.travelocity.com*, and *www.expedia.com*, which use special codes that don't allow upgrades. They do still accrue miles, however.

Outside of the airlines, refund policies vary. Amtrak will let you cancel your travel plans as long as the train hasn't left, but they will charge you a penalty fee in some cases if you have to rebook after the train has departed. (That's pretty fair, because the train left with an unfilled seat that they thought was sold.)

Greyhound refund policies vary based on the type of fare. For example, the heavily discounted E-Fares aren't refundable. As for cruises, policies vary by cruise as well as by company. Check with your booking agent to find out how a cancellation would affect you.

Beyond Travel Costs

Now that you know where you're going, and you've decided how and when you'll get there, you need to figure out how much it will cost you during your stay.

In the destination profiles included in Part Five, you'll find references to the U.S. Government's Per Diem (daily) rates for lodging as well as meals and incidental expenses, which are published each year. You can use these rates to get an idea of your costs, but remember that they're for business travelers staying in mid-level hotels and eating at mid-tier restaurants for three meals each day. These conditions may not apply to you.

We'll be taking a look at how you can save on lodging and food in Part Four. For now, you'll be happy to know that you can spend far less than the Per Diem rate on lodging and food.

TIME TRAVEL

Whenever you travel, time plays a significant role in planning. In addition to being in short supply, time has the added downside of being unreliable for travel purposes. Time changes as you travel, and that causes problems.

Let's look at how time works around the world, and then we'll consider how it affects you.

Time Zones

People like to know that 5:00 a.m. is the early morning and 11:00 p.m. is the late night. Since the Earth rotates, it's dark in London while it's afternoon in Los Angeles. To counteract that, governments divide time into zones and structure them relative to one another. (You can find an interactive time zone map at *www.timezonecheck.com.*)

The "core" time zone—the one that serves as the starting point against which all others are measured—is set on the prime meridian, the north-south counterpart of the equator. It goes through Greenwich, England and is commonly called Greenwich Mean Time, or GMT. (The military refers to GMT as Zulu time.)

Every other time zone is defined in terms of GMT. U.S. Eastern time is GMT-5, while Hawaii is on GMT-10. Head to Berlin, and your time zone becomes GMT+1. Notice that time zones move back an hour heading west from Greenwich and move ahead an hour going east.

But that's just the beginning!

Daylight Saving Time

For reasons relating to the orbit of the Earth around the sun, more hours of the day are spent in daylight during the summer than during the winter. Days get longer beginning with the winter solstice (December 21–22) and continue to do so until the summer solstice (June 21–22). At that point it changes, and days start to get shorter.

Since our society revolves around daylight, longer days mean more time to "get things done." The problem is that the days grow longer in both directions, eventually moving the sunrise too early for anyone to realistically wake up. No solution exists unless you move time itself.

To take advantage of the daylight, governments did just that when they established Daylight Saving Time (DST). When DST takes effect, time shifts forward by one hour, and daylight lasts into the late evening. As the days get noticeably shorter during the fall, countries return to "Standard Time" by removing that shift.

Most countries in the world, and all states in the United States except for Arizona, use Daylight Saving Time, but there are a few complications. Not all countries change their clocks to DST on the same days as America, although it's usually pretty close for practical reasons. To further confuse things, not all countries use that name for the time change. For example, the British call it "British Summer Time" (BST). Whatever term you prefer, though, if you're traveling in the fall or spring, plan with the summer time change in mind.

The International Date Line

As we've discussed, time moves back as you go west from Greenwich and moves ahead as you move east. Because the Earth is round, the zones must eventually intersect. The intersection comes on the opposite side of the planet from Greenwich, between Hawaii and Asia, and it's called the International Date Line.

To adjust for the opposing time changes that occur in each direction from Greenwich, crossing the Date Line results in a drastic shift. Moving west, you move back a day in time. Moving east, you move forward. In other words, it's instantly *tomorrow* when you cross the Date Line en route to Asia, but on the way back, it becomes *yesterday*.

Jet Lag

You've probably heard of jet lag, the condition of being unexpectedly tired after a long flight. Part of jet lag is the flight itself. When you fly, your body's moving at the same speed as the airplane (over 500 miles an hour in most cases). You're coping with a lot of acceleration, pressure changes, and muscle cramping—especially if you're flying in Coach and don't get up to stretch.

The fact is, though, that jet lag is more than physical stress. It's also the psychological effect of moving between time zones, suddenly finding yourself looking at the mid-afternoon sun when your body is thinking that it's midnight and time for bed.

Jet lag is not exclusive to flying. Travelers on trains or cruise ships, or people traveling by bus or car, also cross time zones. The reason that flyers are most affected is because airplanes move so much faster than other modes of travel that the time zones can change rapidly, maybe shifting by half a day or more on a single flight.

Dealing with Jet Lag

You can't really avoid jet lag, especially over long trips. The biggest cause of jet lag is the effect that time changes have on your sleep schedule. The best way to get past it is to be ready to follow the local time when you arrive.

If you have a flight that will arrive in early morning, sleep on the plane so you'll be waking up ready to start your day when you land. On the other hand, if you arrive at night, stay awake for at least the last portion of the flight so that you'll be able to fall asleep when you get to your bed.

Remember that your body clock is very affected by light. If you need to sleep when it's light outside, make the room as dark as possible and use a sleep mask. If you're trying to stay awake, avoid dark areas and don't wear sunglasses. They can trick your brain into thinking it's sundown.

> To help you sleep on a plane, you might try taking melatonin, a natural substance used by your body to regulate sleep. It makes you drowsy, and there aren't any side effects. Since it takes time to work, take it shortly before you board or about ten hours before the scheduled arrival.
>
> You may also want to obtain the Transmeridian Traveler booklet for more information on coping with travel stress *(www.transmeridiantraveler.com)*.

Delays

Labor action is much more common abroad than it is in the United States. There's a chance that you might arrive at an airport to find that flights have been delayed or canceled because of strikes at the airline, airport, or both. Terrorist threats can also result in sudden airport closures. Labor action is particularly prevalent in Europe, while terrorist threats may occur anywhere.

If you find yourself stuck at an airport, the first and foremost rule is to stay in good humor. People will be more helpful if you're friendly to them. For lengthy shutdowns, consider taking the train or even driving to an airport that isn't affected. Be sure to check for flight availability first, or it could all be for nothing.

THE ART OF PACKING

The challenge of packing is making sure that you don't forget anything. Americans tend to tackle this challenge with a brute force approach, bringing everything that they could possibly need and putting it all into several pieces of rolling luggage plus at least one duffle bag.

That works fine when you're going to a resort hotel where you'll be staying for a week. If you're taking a quick trip that involves a plane ride and two days at your destination, it can be overwhelming. Remember, you'll have to carry all of that stuff around with you, at least until you get to wherever you're staying. In an unfamiliar city, that may take a while.

Entire books have been written on packing, but Spontaneous Tourists bring what they need, put it into a bag that they can carry around without much difficulty, and leave the rest. Pack and then try carrying your luggage down to the nearest shopping center. If it's too heavy or too much hassle, redo it. You can bet that it won't be any more convenient to drag it up and down subway stairs or along a cobblestone street!

> Anne McAlpin is a packing expert, and her book
> *Pack It Up* is probably the definitive work on the
> art of packing. Spontaneous Tourists may want to
> visit Anne's Web site, *www.packitup.com*, for free
> checklists and other helpful packing ideas.
>
> You'll also find a basic packing list in Appendix F.

143

What to Bring

At a minimum, you're going to want to bring clothes and a personal hygiene kit with mouthwash, shampoo, toothpaste, and deodorant in travel sizes. Add a razor, shaving cream, and a set of blades. Ladies can usually pack their makeup and perfume in full or travel sizes. Bring a small bar of soap or a travel-size bottle of body wash, maybe some hair spray or gel, and toss in a travel toothbrush. You can fit all of this all into a very small zipper bag. (Pack the gels and liquids in a one-quart zip-top plastic bag for screening.)

> What is and isn't allowed in carry-on luggage varies by
> country. For domestic trips, visit *www.tsatraveltips.us*.

What you bring to wear depends on the climate and your personal preference. For a weekend, you may be able to wear the same pants twice, but take at least one clean shirt, underwear, and socks. If nothing else, it will give you something to wear if it rains.

Even on a long trip, don't pack more than a week's worth of clothes—they take up space. Remember, you can always wash your clothes during the trip if necessary. Also, bringing a second pair of shoes is optional, but it's not recommended. Shoes take up a lot of space in a bag, and it's difficult to pack around them. The only exception might be sandals if you're going to the beach.

Extras

Remember to pack any prescription or over-the-counter medication that you need, including things like eye drops. Your big exciting trip isn't the time to learn that one brand of allergy medication doesn't work as well as another. Anti-malaria pills may be needed in some countries, and travelers never know when water purification tablets may come in handy. Any contraceptives should also be brought from home.

Avoid bringing alcohol, which is subject to import taxes in many countries. It's easier to buy it there if you're inclined to have it. Don't bring illegal weapons or drugs, either, especially when you're traveling overseas. (A surprising number of travelers bring things that get them in a lot of trouble.)

You might not think of it, but bring a towel. Hotels usually provide towels, but travel hostels often don't. Having your own covers you if you stay somewhere that doesn't provide them. Depending on where you're going, you might need a beach towel anyway.

Plan on mailing postcards? If you're going on a domestic trip, bring stamps with you to save time. Overseas, try to get an idea of how and where you can buy stamps before you go. Post offices may be closed on the weekend.

For travel abroad, pack a copy of your passport identification page in your bag and some extra cash in case something happens to the money you'll have on you. My preference is to pack U.S. currency, which makes it harder for me to spend this "emergency cash" by accident.

If your trip is long enough that you may want to sleep, bringing a sleep mask and a set of earplugs can work wonders. Don't forget to take an umbrella or poncho in case it rains. Bring a cover or plastic bag to put over your backpack, especially if it has electronics inside.

Climate-Specific Items

Some of your packing will be dictated by the climate of your destination. For places that have beaches or swimming, you may want to bring a bathing suit, although you can swim in spare clothes if it comes down to it. Suntan lotion is best brought from home, because it's not always available overseas, and it can be expensive at the beach.

For treks through the woods or jungle, bring bug repellant that includes DEET. Treating your clothes with the synthetic insecticide permethrin may be helpful too. (DEET and permethrin compliment one another and are safe to use together. Take a look at *www.travmed.com/trip_prep/insect_permethrin.htm* for more information.)

For cold climates, dress in layers. Bring a hat, preferably a knit cap, and gloves. Mittens are better at keeping your hands warm in particularly cold environments. Personal heater packets may also be helpful.

High-Tech Gear

Flashpackers—backpackers who carry a lot of electronics—are increasingly common these days. A decade ago, supporting this kind of travel was tough. Today, though, hostels cater to the trend by offering extras like high-speed Internet access. Be sure to bring chargers for laptops, rechargeable digital cameras, and anything that needs to be plugged in. Bring extra batteries for everything else.

Adapters and Converters

Four different standard types of power plug are used in the world. You can buy a set of adapters that cover all four anywhere that sells luggage. Besides fitting the plug into the wall, though, you also need to plan for voltage differences. The standard electrical voltage in the United States is 110 volts, while most other countries use 220 volts. There are inexpensive power converters that turn 220v current into 110v current. First, however, you need to understand an important difference.

If you use an adapter to plug a 110v device directly into a 220v outlet, it will draw power too quickly and burn itself out within a few minutes or less. For these devices, which include basic electronics like curling irons and most electric razors, you need to plug the device into a converter first and then plug the converter into the wall using an adapter.

Most high-tech devices, on the other hand—things like laptop computers—have auto-sensing power supplies, which means they detect whether the current coming in is 110v or 220v and adjust their draw accordingly. Basic travel converters change voltage from 220v to 110v by cutting their strength in half, so if you plug an auto-sensing device into a converter, it will try twice as hard to pull power and will burn out of the converter within a few hours. If a device has an auto-sensing power supply, use an adapter to plug it directly into an outlet.

What Goes Where?

Spontaneous Tourists aim to have one bag, small enough to go in an overhead compartment. Even if you're not flying or if you plan to check your bag, planning for the size of carry-on luggage is helpful. You want it light enough to be carried around for a while. Now that you know what you're bringing, how can you get it all to fit?

First, think strategically when you pack. Start by putting the biggest things in at the bottom. If you're bringing a laptop, you may want to use a bag that has a special padded compartment for a computer or put your towel on the bottom and surround the laptop with clothes on all sides. Clothes can be stuffed in just about anywhere. They're soft, so use them as cushions to protect other items or hold them snugly in place.

Keep your poncho or other raingear near the top or in a separate pocket. It can start raining at any time, and you don't want to have to dig through your bag when it does. It's also a good idea to have a rainproof cover for your pack, even if it's listed as waterproof. Covers are especially important if you plan to be walking outside or if you're taking the bus in developing countries, where luggage usually rides tied to the roof.

> Do your clothes usually end up wrinkled when you pack? One way to avoid that is to roll them instead of folding them. It saves a lot of time, especially overseas where an iron might not be available.

Pack for Souvenirs

If your bag looks like it's going to be pretty full, pack a lightweight second bag in the bottom of your travel bag to hold souvenirs. You can probably buy another bag where you're going, but you don't know how much it will cost. You also don't know what you might buy (though we'll talk about souvenirs in Chapter 8).

The one thing you do know is that you're taking a trip, and you'll want to bring *something* back!

RECAP

Before you can travel, you need to pick a destination and learn about it. When you're just starting out and haven't been many places, it can be easiest to find places that are cheap. Once you have a location in mind, start researching by picking up a guidebook or using the Internet.

The biggest cost involved in most trips is the cost of travel itself, especially when going to another continent. You can save money by visiting several places on the same trip. Cheaper fares can also be found if your travel dates and times are flexible. Consider organized trips with tour companies, schools, and humanitarian groups for something a little different.

Time your purchases based on the industry. The price of bus tickets rarely varies, but train tickets are cheaper (and more discounts apply) within a few days of departure. Cruises have amazing last-minute pricing. Plane tickets, on the other hand, may be much more expensive if you don't book in advance. Keep refund policies in mind when you book fares as well. Refunds for train tickets are pretty liberal, but refundable airline tickets can cost as much as four times the lowest price. Use non-refundable fares instead, and pay the fee if your plans change.

If you travel enough, you're eventually going to encounter a flight that is delayed or canceled due to a weather delay or a labor strike. When the latter happens, try to get an idea of the scope of the strike and how long it's likely to last. You might be able to take a train or even drive to an airport not affected by the strike for less than it would cost to wait it out.

When you pack, try to figure out exactly what you need and leave everything else behind. The goal is to have one bag which you can carry on and easily carry around. A backpack is ideal. Pick up travel-size items for your hygiene kit, and keep the clothes that you pack down to a minimum. Always bring at least one change of socks, shirt, and underwear—even for a weekend—but don't pack extra shoes if you can avoid it. You can do laundry during longer trips.

The number of high-tech travelers is increasing, and even budget accommodations like travel hostels are taking them into account with services like free Internet access. Bring chargers and extra batteries. Most high-end electronics have auto-sensing power supplies that don't need voltage converters, but you'll need plug adapters to fit the wall outlets overseas.

Medication and contraceptives should be brought from home. A towel is good to have, and if you'll be sending postcards, get your stamps in advance for domestic trips. Pack extra cash in your bag, and pack for the climate. For example, bring a bathing suit for the beach or bug repellent for the woods. If you expect a lot of insects, consider treating clothes with permethrin.

Roll your clothes to keep them from wrinkling, and use them to pad and protect other items. Consider packing a flexible bag inside your main bag to carry souvenirs. Make sure that your raingear is readily accessible, and bring a cover for your bag as well.

PLANNING AND PACKING TIPS

- Before you start planning, know how much time you have for your trip from start to finish.
- For travel between countries on the same continent, the train or a bus might be just as workable as flying to get from place to place—and cheaper.
- If you're thinking of renting a car overseas, learn to drive a manual transmission. Automatic transmissions are not as easy to find abroad as they are in America.
- When you pick out a travel backpack, think about what it will be carrying. For example, many hiking packs don't hold laptops very well.
- In many cases, you can attach things to the outside of a bag using straps.
- You can use a plastic bag to protect your bag from rain instead of buying a special pack cover.
- Smaller planes have less space for carry-on luggage. You may want to check your bag if you don't need it for the flight.
- Be aware that some of the low-cost carriers in Europe and elsewhere around the world charge a fee for checked luggage based on weight.
- When packing for a flight, use the Internet to look up what items may not be allowed in carry-on luggage.
- Bring written prescriptions for all medication, especially if your name isn't on the bottle.

CHAPTER 7

Paperwork

Okay, so no one likes filling out forms, but if you're going to travel, a certain amount of paperwork will be necessary. Depending on where you're going, it may be a lot or just a little.

We'll start with the centerpiece of international travel, the passport—what it is, why you need it, how to get one, and how to renew it. From there, we'll go on to cover visas, crossing borders, and exchanging your dollars for foreign currency. We'll also talk about discounts and what you might need to get them. Finally, we'll take a look at vaccinations and medical insurance.

DO I HAVE TO READ THIS NOW?

Some of what we'll be covering here doesn't really apply until you go overseas—but that's something you'd like to do, or you wouldn't have picked up this book, right?

If your first few trips will be stateside, you might be tempted to skip some of this for now. If you at least browse through the topics, however, you'll know where to look when you're ready for travel abroad.

THE ALL-IMPORTANT PASSPORT

If you're going to be traveling abroad, you need to have a passport, which is a small booklet that proves your citizenship and records your movement over national borders. You don't need a passport to travel anywhere in the United States, including territories like Puerto Rico and Guam. If you're traveling outside America, though, you'll need to have one to leave—and more importantly, to come back.

U.S. passports are issued by the Department of State, cost $97 in total processing fees, and take about six weeks to obtain. If you're in a hurry, the process can be expedited to approximately two weekdays for an additional $60.

> Even if you don't have an overseas trip planned, if you're going eventually, get your passport now. That way, if you see a special fare suddenly become available for somewhere you'd like to go, you're all set.

The process for getting your first passport, as well as all of the possible situations that can apply if it gets lost, stolen, damaged, or taken away, is fairly complicated. To make sure you've got the most current information, visit the Department of State's passport Web site at *http://travel.state.gov/passport*.

Protecting your Passport

Physically, passports are fairly rugged and can take the abuse of travel. The identification pages, which prove your citizenship, are laminated to protect against water damage, and the cover is tough to tear. If yours is damaged, you'll need to get a replacement, which means time and money.

Anyone who sees your passport will know that you're an American. Depending on where you are, you may not want to attract that attention. You can have some control over both of these situations by purchasing a passport case or travel wallet in which to hold your passport.

Ownership of a Passport

Most people don't realize it, but your passport doesn't really belong to you—it's the property of the United States Government. (It even says so inside.)

What this means is that your passport must be surrendered to the United States upon demand by a duly appointed official or judge. It *also* means that it's illegal for someone else to confiscate your passport—a foreign government, for example. Your passport is your means of leaving a country. Without one, you simply can't leave. Safeguard your passport at all times.

> If your passport is lost, stolen, or taken from you, contact the U.S. embassy or consulate in your host nation *immediately.*

Renewing your Passport

Every ten years, you'll need to renew your passport. Your passport includes your photo, and we can probably agree that after ten years, that photo may not look much like you anymore!

Renewing a passport costs $67 and can be done by mail in most cases. Some exceptions exists, such as a name change or if your passport has been physically damaged. In these situations, you'd have to apply in person for the renewal.

VISAS

We hear "visa" these days, and our first thought is a credit card. Marketing people wanted to tell customers that their credit card was essential for crossing borders in life the same way that a visa was needed to cross borders around the world, so they called it Visa. Ironically, we use credit so much more than we travel that we don't even recognize the original meaning of the word.

A visa is a form of *endorsement* that categorizes your travel to another country. It's issued by the host nation, so it's a formal acknowledgement of your intention to travel to their country and proof that you've been approved to enter. In some situations, exit visas are also required to leave.

There are many different kinds of visas, and these vary from country to country. If you're going to a country for pleasure, or even on business if it doesn't involve taking a job within the host nation's borders, you'll probably need a *tourist visa*. Requirements for these are minimal, because in most cases, a tourist visa doesn't allow you to work or have access to social services.

Some countries include tourist visas as part of their entrance stamp instead of issuing them separately. Others don't issue them for American citizens or require them only for stays lasting more than a certain number of days. Some countries require visas in all cases. Getting a visa may or may not cost money, and it's handled through the embassy or consulate of the host nation.

154

> Some countries issue visas electronically, but most are processed by mail. If you have to obtain a physical visa, be prepared for problems. If the wrong visa is sent, you may not realize it until you arrive—especially if it's in a foreign language.

If you arrive at the border of a country that requires a visa for you to enter and don't have one, one of two things will happen. In some cases, you may be able to obtain the visa at your point of arrival. This can take some time, and you may be charged a fee.

Other countries are less accommodating and will simply turn you away. This second possibility is a particular dilemma if you're traveling from one country to another by going through a third nation. In these situations, you may not be able to continue your trip at all.

Exit Visas

Relatively few countries require an exit visa to leave their borders, especially for visitors. There are some that do, though—including Russia—and these visas are issued and valid only within a particular timeframe. If your exit visa expires and you haven't left, you'll be stuck waiting until a new one is issued, which may cost you time and money. Be careful.

WILL I NEED A VISA?

You might be inclined to think that whether or not you'll need a visa to visit a particular country depends on its relationship with the United States, but that's not always true. Australia, for example, requires visas for visitors coming from anywhere other than New Zealand. On the other hand, you don't need a visa to visit Brunei Darussalam unless you stay over 90 days.

The U.S. Department of State maintains a database of visa requirements for all countries online at *www.state.gov/travelandbusiness*.

155

CROSSING BORDERS

Now that you have what you need to cross borders, let's talk about the borders themselves. Borders are overseen by Passport Control personnel, who want to make sure that you should be there, and Customs officials, whose purpose is to ensure that whatever you're carrying is properly declared.

In some cases, you may not be permitted to bring something over the border. For example, many countries have bans on transporting certain kinds of weapons. In other cases, you can bring things in but have to pay duties (taxes) on certain kinds of items.

Each time that you cross a border, you'll go through Passport Control and Customs. The process varies from country to country, but it's similar in each case.

Passport Control

The official process of entering a country is handled by Passport Control agents. In the United States, these are part of the Department of Homeland Security. Other countries have their own approach, but in general, border control is a security check.

Present your passport and any Customs forms that you have to the Passport Control officer. (The U.S. Customs form for citizens and permanent residents is Form I-9.) He or she may ask you questions, which you should answer honestly. You might be asked where you'll be staying, how much money you have with you, and whether you can get more if needed, or to show a return ticket. Printed copies of itineraries are helpful if your airline uses electronic ticketing.

YOU'RE NOT IN KANSAS ANYMORE

You should be aware that the border officer is fully empowered to detain you for as long as needed if he or she feels that you are lying or pose some potential threat.

Short stays, in particular, might arouse attention. For example, a border officer might wonder why someone would visit London for twelve hours (not on business). It's not illegal to do something crazy like that. Maybe you got a cheap fare, had a free weekend, and jumped at the chance. Just show your printed itinerary.

Some countries put more emphasis on the border security process than others. The United States and Britain are on the tough end of the spectrum. They want to know where you're going and why. On the European continent and in Australia, the attitude is much more relaxed.

It's entirely up to each nation to decide on its own how it wants to approach control of its borders, so be flexible. (Actually, that's the best advice for travel in general.)

The Customs Process

After Passport Control, you'll go through Customs, which also varies from country to country. The purpose of Customs is to determine what you're bringing in, verify that it's legal, and decide whether or not it is subject to a duty (tax). Give your Customs form to the Customs officer, and answer any questions asked.

Odds are that you'll have little to declare when you arrive at your overseas destination unless you're doing business there. When you return to the United States, you'll go through Customs again. At that point you may have various souvenirs, perhaps items from the Duty Free shops, original artwork, and other things to declare.

> Most people think of Duty Free merchandise as being tax-free. That's not true. It's *sold* tax-free, but you may owe import taxes on it back home.

Import-export law is way beyond the scope of this book and can get complicated. If you'll be bringing back expensive items, check out the "Know Before You Go" section on the Customs Web site at *www.customs.ustreas.gov/xp/cgov/travel/vacation/kbyg*.

In most cases, you're allowed to bring up to $800 worth of items into the United States for personal use on a tax-free basis, and anything more is subject to various taxes and tariffs unless it meets certain exemptions. For example, any amount of original art may be imported tax-free, and items intended as gifts are often exempt.

> Be sure to save your receipts for overseas purchases. If you can prove what you paid, the value of your imported merchandise is based on that. If not, Customs will assess you duties based on appraised value.

157

Depending on what you declare, whether the Customs officer trusts you, and a bit of random luck, you might be required to go through physical Customs screening. If that happens, it's a little like being selected for security screening—it takes time and patience, but it's not actually difficult.

Whatever you do, don't lie to Customs! They're very good at spotting people who are smuggling undeclared goods into the country. Anything you purchased that's found in your possession but wasn't declared can—and will—be confiscated by the U.S. Government, and you will get *nothing* for it.

Ecological Declarations

If you're entering a closed ecosystem such as an island (including Hawaii or Puerto Rico as well as places like Australia), you may be asked to declare any foods, animals, or plants that you are bringing with you. Some things can't be brought in. For example, a burger purchased in the airport in Hawaii must be consumed in the airport, because tomatoes may not be imported from the mainland.

Good reasons exist for this level of concern. Ecosystems are delicate balances based on food chains of natural predators. Some plant, animal, or even fungus that is harmless enough in its native environment can devastate an ecosystem where it has no check on its expansion. The snakehead fish, introduced to North America from Asia, is one example of this sort of contamination. Relatively harmless in its natural habitat, it has devastated fish and wildlife populations in the United States and proven extremely difficult to exterminate through artificial means. Rabbits have proven equally problematic in Australia.

Beyond it being illegal to lie about these things, consider the potentially catastrophic effect that you could have on a foreign environment. Do the right thing—declare everything that you have, and let them make the determination.

CURRENCY EXCHANGE

One of the roles of a national government is to print (or coin) money. Most countries have their own currencies, and to pay for things in those places, you'll need to use their money. (You'll find a table listing the world's major currencies in Appendix E.)

That's where the money market fits in. Currency is traded similarly to stocks. Traders buy and sell based on expected performance, which in turn is caused partly by national events and partly by the trading itself. Unlike the stock market, money is traded 24 hours a day, seven days a week. The *exchange rate* between two currencies is the amount of one currency that can be obtained for a fixed amount of the other.

Exchange rates are expressed in ratios, where the money being offered (sold) is shown as a single-unit (i.e. one dollar) and the money being given in exchange (bought) is shown as a moving value—for example, 1 USD:0.6 GBP would mean that one U.S. dollar would purchase 0.6 British pounds. You can get the current exchange rates online at *www.forex.com*.

> Currency exchange rates are always changing. It's a little difficult to accept, but when you're overseas, you can't quite be sure what you're "really" paying for something in terms of the U.S. dollar.

Ways to Exchange Money

You don't need to track the currency markets to travel. Several different ways to trade your U.S. dollars for other kinds of money exist. They're all easy, but in each case, you'll pay a fee.

Exchange Desks

At the airport and throughout major cities in the world, you can request a particular type of currency and buy it based on the current rate. Hand the exchange agent $100 and tell her that you want Swiss francs, for example, and you'll be given the closest equivalent amount (and change if needed).

Most banks also have currency exchange desks. Depending on the size and location of the bank, the currency that you want may have to be ordered, which can take a few days, but they can get it for you, and it may be cheaper.

ATM Withdraws

Another way to get money exchanged is to withdraw it from an ATM in the host nation. The ATM performs the conversion based on the exchange rate at that instant and gives you local currency. Check with your bank, however, because you may be charged an extra fee for this convenience.

Using Credit Overseas

Buying with a credit card works similarly to using an ATM. The exchange is made given the rate at the instant of approval. Credit cards always charge a fee for currency exchange, but it varies from card to card. Call the customer service number and ask what rate applies. It may be less than what you'll pay at an exchange desk or ATM.

Credit cards were once not very popular in Europe, but they've really taken off over the last decade. The same is true in Asia and Australia, with varying degrees of acceptance in major cities throughout South America and Africa.

Of the American credit cards, Visa and MasterCard have large networks, and American Express has built an impressive following overseas. Discover is rarely accepted internationally. Diners Club is relatively unpopular in the United States but widely accepted in Europe.

Travelers' Checks

Once upon a time, everyone swore by travelers' checks. They were the wave of the future—a foolproof means of ensuring your money wouldn't be stolen. Here's how they work.

You buy the checks at the bank, signing on one of the two lines, but leaving the other blank until you're ready to buy something. If they're stolen, the thief can't use them without the second signature. American Express made these very popular with business travelers in particular, especially when credit cards were less useful overseas.

Travelers' checks are billed as being "as good as cash." They're backed by the financial strength of their issuing authority (always a major commercial bank, like American Express), and they're certified funds like money orders, so they should be widely accepted.

The problem is, a lot of places have a policy not to accept checks, and they don't really understand what a travelers' check is. As a result, they'll reject it. This happens even in the United States, and it's hard to argue the point overseas, especially in another language.

My recommendation? Credit cards have built-in theft protection, and they're widely accepted. Keep some cash on hand for small purchases, use a card for the rest, and don't risk having to find a bank to cash a travelers' check. There are also prepaid traveler's debit cards that avoid this pitfall.

The Price Trap

The biggest danger to the money of a Spontaneous Tourist traveling abroad is overspending. When we hear a price in dollars, our brains calculate whether this is a reasonable price based on what we expect it to cost, and we compare that cost to what we can afford. It works because we see all of our prices in dollars every day.

Go overseas and the game changes. You have no idea whether something is reasonably priced or not. It might be overpriced, or maybe it just costs more overseas than it does in the United States. On top of that, you're not really sure how many dollars you're spending when you see the price.

What happens? You compare not to what you'd like to spend, but what you have in your pocket. You open your wallet and find 50 notes, and the item is 10 notes, so you buy it. Later, it occurs to you that one note was $3, so you spent $30. Oops.

It's easy enough to get caught in this trap when you're using cash, but it expands when you're using a credit card. It can be tough to guess how much a purchase has set back your line of available dollars when you buy something in euros, especially since you pay a fee on top of the actual cost. You might not realize how much you've spent until the bill comes due!

LAND OF EXPENSIVE OPPORTUNITY

My first exposure to the price trap was in London. London is a prohibitively expensive city. On top of that, the exchange rate at the time that I went was about $2 for every British pound (£1).

All of the numbers were deceptively familiar—£4.50 for fast food, £9.00 for a movie theatre ticket, £14.50 for a steak dinner. These were prices that my American mind was used to seeing in dollars, so I happily paid them out of my stash of £100. Only later did I realize I'd spent $9.00 for a burger and fries, $18.00 on a movie ticket, and $30.00 for mediocre steak.

Trading Back

At the end of your trip, if you're fortunate enough to have any foreign cash left, you can trade it back for U.S. dollars at the airport exchange desk or you can take it back to your bank.

The exchange won't accept small change (too difficult to calculate the American equivalent), but that's okay. Foreign coins make great souvenirs, or even gifts for friends and family. In fact, depending on how much you have, you may choose to hang onto small bills as well, since you'll pay another fee to convert these back to dollars.

DISCOUNTS

A lot of companies offer discounts (called *concessions* in some countries) on their products and services. You can save money on lodging, travel, tickets for attractions, and even food by asking for a discount, if you qualify.

The trick is that each company decides on its own what groups of people deserve discounts. If you're part of an eligible group, you'll need to prove it, and then you'll be given the special rate.

Let's look at four broad groups of people who might be eligible and how they can prove their status.

Seniors

Discounts for the elderly are extremely popular in the United States and tend to be available abroad as well. In some cases, no proof is needed at all. In others, if they do ask, it's enough to show some form of photo identification that shows your birthday.

Sometimes, the senior rate is tied to membership in the American Association of Retired People (AARP). By far the largest advocacy group for the elderly, AARP has considerable clout within the United States and negotiates discounts on behalf of its members. In particular, you can expect to see a special AARP rate for lodging. If you aren't a member, you can't get the rate regardless of age.

Military

You'll find military rates available for lodging, travel, and some attractions—usually expensive ones. Military personnel can also get a monthly discount on recurring cell phone charges from all major providers. Discounts for movie tickets and food are increasingly rare, but they do still exist.

Requirements

When you look into military discounts, you need to understand both the scope and the limitations. Usually, military discounts apply to current personnel but *not* to veterans. You may also need to be on official orders or approved leave to qualify for the military rate (though this isn't always the case), and these special discounted rates might not earn miles.

SUPPORTING (SOME OF) OUR TROOPS

Many discounts are specifically for Active Duty military and exclude National Guard or Reserve troops. In a lot of cases, these restrictions were set up during the Vietnam era to protest that reservists were not called up to fight.

Today, these restrictions are outdated. The fact is that tens of thousands of National Guard and Reserve troops are serving all over the world in combat zones. When our heroes are home on leave, they deserve to be recognized.

Assuming that a discount doesn't require you to be on official orders, there's no reason you shouldn't get the discounted rate. Show your military I.D., and if you get a hard time, make them explain to you why your service doesn't qualify. You'll probably get the discount.

Even if you don't need to be on orders, bring your military I.D. with you for verification whenever you're using a military rate. Since the military rate is usually a deeper discount than other special rates, you're more likely to be asked to prove that you're really in the military. (Yes, there *are* people who lie about military status to try and get discounts.)

> Military discounts are almost always for the troops of their host country and don't apply internationally, so don't request one overseas unless you know that it applies to American troops. Besides, unless you're on official business, you don't want to show your military I.D. while you're overseas.

Veterans Advantage

Military discounts generally don't apply to veterans. If you're a veteran, you might want to consider joining Veterans Advantage, a discount program designed to get you special discounts on travel and other things.

There's an annual fee, so whether or not it makes sense depends on what benefits you'll be using. Visit *www.veteransadvantage.com* to read more about this program. If you decide that you'd like to join, you can sign up online.

Students

Students are usually offered deep discounts and concession rates. One reason for the offers is that students tend to be broke or close to it, so they can't afford to do things for full price. That wouldn't matter, however, if it weren't for another reason—vendors expect that students won't always be broke, and they want them to stay customers after they finish school (and presumably earn more money).

In some cases, you can get a student concession rate by showing a school I.D. For movie tickets in America, that may be fine—

but it doesn't get you far with higher priced purchases like travel and most student concessions overseas.

If you're a student, you can get a lot of benefits by having one or both of the two commonly accepted student discount cards. Graduate as well as undergraduate students qualify. They're very different, so we'll go over both.

Student Advantage

With a Student Advantage card, you can save on Amtrak and Greyhound tickets, Dollar rental cars, and lodging with Choice Hotels. You'll also save on purchases at Target, Urban Outfitters, and other popular stores, and get discounts on software products from vendors like Adobe and Microsoft.

To sign up for Student Advantage, fill out the online application at *www.studentadvantage.com*. The annual fee is $20, but you can add years at a discounted rate ($10 each) when you sign up.

ISIC STA TRAVEL
THE STUDENT EXPERIENCE

The International Student Identification Card (ISIC) is issued by STA Travel *(www.statravel.com)*. Unlike the Student Advantage card, the ISIC is a photo I.D. that includes your school and date of birth, and it's accepted around the world to get student rates.

To get an ISIC, you have to prove your enrollment status by submitting a current semester bill or course schedule, then pay $22. You'll get a card in the mail to which you add your own picture (sounds odd, but it's easy), and it's good for a year.

The ISIC is extremely useful for getting discounts overseas. Traditionally, it's been less accepted in the United States, where Student Advantage has a stronger presence. Amtrak now honors either card for student rates.

WHICH CARD DO I WANT?

The ISIC is a travel discount card for students; Student Advantage is a student discount card that includes savings on travel. For everyday purchases and travel within the United States, you'll find the Student Advantage card to be helpful. Overseas, go with the ISIC.

STA Travel also offers two other cards, one for young people (under 25) who aren't students and one for teachers. These cards are similar to the ISIC and might be helpful to overseas travelers who qualify. Visit the STA Travel site for details.

Affiliate Members

Aside from seniors, military personnel, and students, companies reserve special discounts for members of affiliate organizations. By far, the largest of these is the American Automobile Association (AAA), whose members get discounts on bus and rail travel as well as with most hotel chains. Others focus on specific industries, like the National Association of Railroad Passengers (NARP).

PROTECTING YOUR HEALTH

When you travel, you enter an environment different from the one that's familiar to you—and with that change of scenery come health considerations. Some of these, like the scope of your insurance coverage, may apply even within the United States. When you go abroad, vaccinations also enter into the picture. Let's look at what you need to know to stay healthy when you travel.

Health Insurance

Virtually alone among developed nations, the United States doesn't have a universal healthcare system for its citizens. Instead, it relies on a system of private insurance companies—some of which operate to make a profit—to subsidize a variety of services, including major medical procedures in the event of serious illness or injury.

Lower-income individuals and families may be covered by a joint state-national program called Medicaid. Senior citizens are generally covered by provisions of Medicare, which is similar in nature but funded solely at the national level. Millions of Americans have no coverage at all. It isn't a perfect system.

When you travel, the scope of your coverage becomes a factor. Even if top-notch medical care is available, you're not covered by the host nation's universal healthcare plan. You'll be expected to provide either proof of coverage that will pay on your behalf, or pay cash for the services you receive—before they're provided.

> **Medicare does not provide any sort of coverage outside of the United States.**

So, let's say you have health insurance. Does it work overseas? Some plans do, but there's a good chance that yours doesn't, and even if it does provide coverage, you may need to pay cash up front and then submit paperwork to be reimbursed. You need to know the limitations of your coverage before you travel.

An alternative is to get travel insurance to cover you for the duration of your trip. A number of providers offer travel coverage. One that you might consider is the policy offered through STA Travel *(www.statravel.com)*, which starts at $48.00 for an eight-day trip and can cover trips lasting a year or more.

Quality of Medical Facilities

Throughout the industrialized world, you'll find first-rate medical care on par with or close to the level of treatment that you find in the United States. If you need care in a developed nation, you shouldn't have any problems other than making sure you can pay for the services given.

Developing nations are a different story entirely. In many places, care is unavailable or extremely risky. In countries where care is lacking, make sure that your insurance policy will provide for an air ambulance to evacuate you to the United States or another country with modern medical facilities if you require sudden care.

Vaccinations

Many diseases, including malaria and yellow fever, have been eradicated in the United States but are commonly found in developing countries. Visit *www.cdc.gov/travel/reference.htm* to read more about vaccinations and precautionary care.

Certain destinations may list no vaccines as required but have some listed as recommended. Don't take the risk. Talk to your doctor, and get whatever vaccines make sense for your trip.

RECAP

Traveling overseas requires you to do some paperwork. The most important item to have is a passport, an official document in the form of a small booklet that proves your U.S. citizenship. Your passport is the property of the U.S. Government and must be surrendered upon demand by a duly appointed U.S. official or court.

Passports are fairly sturdy, but it's a good idea to protect yours in a carrying case. Be aware that anyone who sees your passport will know that you're an American. You need to have a passport to cross a national border, so if yours is lost, stolen, or taken away, contact the U.S. embassy or consulate immediately.

A passport is good for ten years, so apply for one as soon as possible if you eventually plan to travel overseas. You have to apply in person, but in most cases you can renew your passport by mail.

Some countries require special endorsements called visas for entry. A visa is an acknowledgement that you're approved to enter a country for a certain purpose, such as tourism or work, and to stay for a defined period. You may also need a separate exit visa to leave the country.

Be sure that you have all of the necessary visas before you leave on a trip. In some situations, a trip from one country to another may go through a third country that requires a visa. If you don't have the correct visa, you may not be able to continue or you may be required to pay heavy fines.

Whenever you cross a national border, you'll go through Passport Control, where you'll be asked questions about your trip as part of security screening. You'll also go through Customs and be asked to declare for tax purposes everything you purchased overseas. Always be completely honest in all cases.

Other countries use different money than the United States, so you'll need to exchange U.S. dollars for the currency of the country you're visiting. You can do this at an exchange desk at the airport or in a bank, by withdrawing money from an ATM, or using credit cards. The exchange rate of dollars to other currencies fluctuates at all hours of the day and night. You'll get the rate that applies at the time of the conversion.

Travelers' checks are supposed to be more secure, but you may run into difficulty using them, whether domestically or abroad. They aren't recommended for Spontaneous Tourists. Be conscious of prices overseas, and don't spend more than you can afford.

At the end of your trip, you can exchange the foreign currency you have left back to U.S. dollars, but you may want to give it as a gift or keep it as a souvenir. You'll pay a fee each time you convert currency.

Whenever you travel, be sure to take advantage of any discounts to which you may be entitled. Special rates are usually available for seniors, military personnel, and students. Members of organizations like AAA may also qualify for discounts. Be sure to have a way to prove your status whenever you're planning to use a discount.

For students in particular, two main programs exist. Student Advantage provides discounts for a variety of travel and non-travel purchases within the United States. For overseas travel, you'll probably benefit from having an International Student Identification Card (ISIC). You might choose to carry both cards, because their benefits don't generally overlap.

Before you travel outside of the United States, find out whether you have a health insurance policy that covers you abroad. Most basic policies don't, and you don't want to risk being denied coverage because you can't pay cash. Pick up travel health insurance before you go, and be sure to check if you'll need any vaccinations. It's better to err on the side of caution.

TIPS ON PAPERWORK

- Passports became mandatory for all air travel into and out of the United States on January 1, 2007. This requirement will be extended to land and sea travel on January 1, 2008.

- Make two copies of your passport's identification page for emergencies. Give one to someone in the United States and keep one separate from your passport.

- In some cases, if you arrive at the airport without a needed visa and it's available electronically, the airline can obtain it for you instantly for a fee. If not, you won't be able to board the plane. This is non-negotiable, because the airline absolutely doesn't want to have to bring you back!

- Leave electronic devices like cell phones off until you clear the Passport Control area.

- Be friendly to the Passport Control and Customs people, and always answer their questions honestly. If they ask you a lot of questions, you might get nervous. They understand that— it's usually the point of the questions. Don't worry about it.

- Use cash overseas to keep better control over how much you're spending.

- Exchange all of the money you plan to exchange at the same time to save on exchange fees.

- If you aren't sure whether a discount is offered, ask. Military discounts are common in the U.S., and student discounts are common overseas. You don't have anything to lose by asking.

- Carry your health insurance card or information with you at all times in case of an accident.

PART 4

While You're There

Where to stay, how to get around, ways to save money, taking good photos, meeting people, staying safe, and other tips to get the most out of your in-country time.

"The welcome ever smiles, and farewell goes out sighing."
—William Shakespeare

CHAPTER **8**

Lodging

If you plan right, you can arrive at your destination early in the morning, rested from having slept on the way, and spend all day going around soaking up culture and seeing new things. After dinner, you can even push yourself to stay out late and check out the nightlife. No matter how exciting your trip is, though, you'll eventually have to get some sleep.

After travel costs, lodging has the potential to be the biggest expense you'll have on your trip. Certainly, if you look up the Per Diem rates for most places, you'll see that the daily lodging cost is higher than the food allowance. These rates, however, are for business travelers, and since you're not there on business, you can easily spend less.

It all comes down to one question.

WHAT'S THE POINT?

Why lodging is needed at all seems like a silly question. People need to sleep, so they need a place to sleep, right? True—but if you look at the average American hotel, you'll see a different picture.

Fitness centers, pools, restaurants, and 200 channels of cable television have nothing to do with sleep. Neither does an over-sized garden tub, separate living room, or complimentary bath-robe. These features are about something else entirely. They're about giving you the illusion of a home away from home.

Nice idea—you show up in an unfamiliar place but have a lovely room with all the comforts you're used to. Go to that meeting, meet the customer for cocktails, then come back and relax in your room. It's ideal for the business traveler.

Wait! You're not there on business, are you?

As a Spontaneous Tourist, you don't need a home away from home. You need a place to sleep, because the point is to enjoy a new place, not a new hotel room. The more there is to do in the hotel, the less reason you have to leave it—and leaving the hotel is why you travel. That's the point.

THE RIGHT MINDSET

Americans have a more difficult time than most people in the world when we try to travel on a budget, because our standards are so absurdly high. As a culture, we expect to have our own space. The notion of a shared bathroom for the floor is absolutely alien to most Americans.

Ironically, a large and growing number of Americans should be able to relate to exactly this situation. If you lived in a college dorm—think back to those days—you had a twin bed, shared a bathroom, had a roommate... amazing, isn't it?

To be able to travel on a budget, you need to reacquaint yourself with this mindset. The closer you're able to get to it, the more you can save.

Defining Accommodations

Decide what you expect lodging to provide. With few exceptions, accommodations are a trade-off between luxury and price.

If you want a queen-size bed, you'll pay more than if you want a twin bed. Power outlets are pretty standard, but Internet access may not be. Is air conditioning crucial? If not, how much is it worth to you?

One thing to understand up front is that American standards for lodging are luxurious compared to anywhere else in the world. You can find American-style places to stay overseas, but they're expensive. With that in mind, let's take a look at some of the lodging options when you travel, at home and abroad. More information on the lodging covered in this chapter can also be found in Appendix C.

THE USUAL CHOICES

When Americans look for a place to stay while traveling, the first accommodations that come to mind for us are hotels and motels. They are the most visible sorts of lodging in the United States, so that makes sense.

You'll find hotels all over the world, and if you look within a given price range, they're pretty similar in terms of what they offer. Motels aren't as common overseas, in large part because they are associated with vacations that involve long drives. Driving, while done in most parts of the world, is not nearly as popular abroad as it is in the United States.

Since they're different, let's look at hotels and motels separately. Then, we'll cover one benefit that can apply to both.

Hotels

For our purposes, we'll define a hotel as a place that provides a large number of identical or nearly identical rooms, with private bathrooms, room entrances inside the building, a lobby for check-in, and a level of service that is at least equal to business travel standards. Luxury and business hotels differ somewhat, as discussed below.

Luxury Hotels

Every country in the world has luxury hotels and resort properties. In addition to major chains like Ritz-Carlton and Hilton, there are boutique hotels that blend luxury with local flavor. You may not experience life the same way that the locals do, but that's the point of these establishments—they spare no expense to provide a grand experience where everything is always perfect.

You can expect that everything in a luxury hotel costs more. Internet access isn't complimentary, the bottled water left in your room will be billed to you if you drink it, and room service has a mandatory 18% gratuity *plus* a service charge (on top of prices that are already higher than normal).

Staying in a luxury hotel will cost you upward of $200 per night in the United States. Overseas, add another $100 on average. These prices are *more* than the Per Diem rates for any locale. Government travelers don't usually stay in these places when they travel.

BEWARE THE MINI-BAR

Many hotels have mini-bars installed in their rooms. They claim that these are for your convenience, allowing you to get things like chips, soda, and alcoholic beverages at any time without having to leave the room.

They deliver on that promise, but you should be aware that the prices charged for items that you take from the mini-bar can be outrageously expensive—as much as $4.00 for a can of soda or $6.00 for a 4 oz. package of cashews. Most of the mini-bars are electronic, too, so if you pick something up, you've got a matter of seconds to put it back before it's automatically added to your bill—again, for your convenience.

Do yourself a favor and look over the prices for the mini-bar when you check in. If they're insane—and most are—then pick up snacks at a convenience store while you're out. Your wallet with thank you and your appetite won't notice the difference.

Business Hotels

The key difference between a luxury hotel and a business hotel is that business hotels tend to offer their amenities for free, while luxury hotels charge for them. Complimentary breakfast, Internet access, and use of an on-site fitness center are all traits of the typical business hotel.

The specifics vary by chain but are usually consistent for a particular hotel brand. For example, Embassy Suites always provides a full breakfast with custom-order omelet bar, while Hampton Inn offers a continental-style breakfast instead.

The Per Diem rates published each year by the U.S. Government are set with business hotels in mind, so you can expect prices at or near the published rate.

Motels

We've all seen motels in the course of our travels. Most are one or two stories tall with doors that lead from the outside air directly into the guest rooms. Popular brand names include Days Inn, Super 8, Motel 6, and Holiday Inn (not to be confused with Holiday Inn Express, which is a business hotel). There are also a lot of independently owned motels in America.

Motels are designed with vacationers in mind, especially families. The level of amenities in a motel is usually lower than a business hotel, and so is the cost. You can expect a clean, comfortable room without too many extra frills. It's easy to stay under the Per Diem rate at a motel.

Loyalty Programs

Most hotels and motels affiliated with a national or international chain offer a loyalty program, similar to the frequent flyer programs offered by the airline industry. By staying with the same chain, you can earn points toward free stays. Some programs also have tier status for preferred customers, giving these guests special gifts or upgraded rooms if available.

Ordinarily, the odds of staying with a particular brand of hotel enough times to get anything out of it would be pretty low for most Spontaneous Tourists. What you may not realize, though, is that a lot of different hotels are actually owned by the same parent company—and if you stay with any hotel in the family brand, you'll earn points toward a common loyalty program. You'll find a list of the six main loyalty programs and the brands that each includes in Appendix C.

One thing to keep in mind when looking at loyalty programs is whether or not the points expire. If they don't, you're bound to eventually get something out of your membership, even if you don't always stay with the same family of hotels.

> Travelers may prefer to earn airline miles or Amtrak Guest Rewards points instead of points in the hotel loyalty program. Most programs give you this option. In fact, one—the Hilton HHonors program—actually lets you earn both points and miles.

Another important consideration is that tier status with hotels is not as exciting as it is with an airline. A lot of stays are required to earn a tier level that will have much effect. So, while you might accept a slightly higher fare to fly with your airline of choice, don't pass up a nice-looking local motel in favor of staying at a more expensive motel that's part of a loyalty program.

THE HOSTEL EXPERIENCE

Hotels are nice, but they're quite a bit more expensive overseas than they are in the United States. One way to make your money go farther is to cut back on your lodging costs by staying in a hostel—budget accommodations for travelers. You'll find hostels all over the world, including here in the United States (though not in every city). They're very popular overseas, and it's not uncommon to be able to stay for $20 or less per night.

Most Americans have never stayed at a hostel and assume that it must be a miserable experience because it costs so little. Each hostel needs to be judged on its own merit, but most give you quite a bit for the very low rates they charge. The experience of staying in a hostel, however, is quite different from a hotel.

Hostels are designed with Spontaneous Tourists instead of business travelers in mind, and Americans in particular may take some time to adjust. Once you do, you'll probably agree that staying in a hostel can be a great choice.

Finding a Good Hostel

Not all hostels are the same. Some are better located, some offer more services, and some cost less than others. In general, hostels are clean and relatively comfortable, but even these traits can vary.

When you're looking for a hostel, it's helpful to find out what other people have thought about it. There are two main Web sites where you can search for hostels in a particular city— *www.hostels.com* and *www.hostelworld.com*—and they both provide ratings based on feedback. These ratings can help you find a place you'll enjoy.

> Pay attention to what the reviews say. If you're looking for a quiet place, and everyone gave a hostel five stars because it threw the best parties, look elsewhere.

Making Reservations

Both of the hostel sites mentioned above allow you to make reservations online for most of the hostels listed in their registries. Choose the type of bed you want (more on this later), provide a credit card for payment, print out a confirmation letter, and you're all set.

If you use this built-in registration service, you may be charged a modest fee (typically $2) which helps support the site. Your card will also be charged for some percentage of your first night's stay—10% is common—with the remainder due at check in.

Another option is to call the hostel directly. If it's a domestic call, or if you have questions, it might make sense to do this. On the other hand, for overseas hostels, you'll be paying international long-distance charges, and you may find that the person who answers the phone doesn't speak very good English. Making your reservation online avoids this problem.

Pay attention to the cancellation policy. It's usual for a hostel to require you to pay for your first night's stay if you cancel less than 24 hours before your planned check-in time.

Bedding

Staying at a hostel is closer to being in a college dorm than a hotel room. Most offer a few different choices for bedding (though not every hostel offers every type), and you may find a choice that's usually offered is sold out. Let's look at some of the options you may have.

Dorms

The cheapest way to stay in a hostel is in a dorm, a large room with a number of beds (usually stacked bunks). Dorms may be male, female, or mixed. The number of beds ranges from as few as three to 20 or more. You'll know which choices are available before you make your reservation, and you can go with whichever type you prefer.

Your first stay in a dorm might feel a little strange, especially if you live alone and are used to having your own space. The bed in a dorm, however, is perfect for most Spontaneous Tourists. You have a place to sleep when you're ready to sleep, and when you're awake, there's absolutely no reason to stay in the room.

BE PRUDENT, NOT PARANOID

Since a dorm is a shared space, be careful with your valuables. Don't leave cash or expensive electronics in plain view—that tempts fate.

At the same time, remember that everyone in the dorm is a traveler like you. It's unlikely that someone will steal your laptop out of the wire drawer underneath *your* bed just to put it in the wire drawer underneath *his* bed.

Hostels usually have lockers available, either for free or for rent at very low prices, but in general, don't bring a lot of valuables when you travel.

Some hostels have interesting variations on the dorm concept. One hostel in Zürich offers dorms that are rooms divided into six three-sided cubes with curtains to close them off from the main area—essentially private spaces, except without locking doors. As of March 2006, these were priced at a little more than $30 per night with breakfast included, an amazing rate in a city where hotel rooms usually approach $200.

Private Rooms

Sometimes, you want your privacy. Maybe you're not traveling alone, or maybe you're just not comfortable with the idea of a dorm. Among other things, a private room is good for new travelers who don't know what to think of the whole hostel concept—you still get your own space, but you pay less for it.

Private rooms in hostels may be available as singles, doubles, or quads. Single beds are either twin or full-size mattresses (twin being more common). Double rooms are geared toward couples, while quads are perfect for groups of friends traveling together. The average room will have a closet or wardrobe to hang clothes, a small nightstand, and maybe a table or luggage holder. Plain and simple—it's just a bedroom.

Shared vs. Private Bathrooms

Hostels commonly have shared bathrooms on each floor rather than each room having its own private bathroom. When you think about the amount of time in a given day that you actually spend in the bathroom, and then add in that everyone staying at the hostel has a different schedule, you can imagine that it's not very hard for everyone to share.

Sharing a bathroom sounds a little odd, but Americans actually do it all the time—in college, during military training, at fitness centers, and at camp. Once we get our own places, which is a very American concept, we stop associating shared bathrooms with being at home, even though we're used to thinking of our lodging as a form of home.

If you definitely want your own bathroom facilities in your room, it might be an option. What you need to do is look for private rooms that are listed as "ensuite"—a French word that means bathroom facilities are included in the room. What precisely you get with an ensuite room depends on what's normal for the country.

You'll definitely have a toilet, but it's hard to say beyond that. In many countries, the toilet—or loo, water closet, or whatever you want to call it—is separate from the bathroom, which is only for bathing. Actually, it's hard to understand why we combine toilets and bathtubs in the United States.

When you check into a private room, you'll be given a key, which might even be a real metal key instead of the key card you'd find in most hotels. You can leave whatever you want in your room when you're not there. Someone could still get in if he or she were determined to do so, so refer to the gray box for a discussion on valuables, but it's not very common for someone to steal from you in a hostel. (As a general rule, don't bring valuables when you travel.)

Some places include showers but no bathtubs, while other places will give you a bathtub but no shower. It's not even always the case that the toilet is in a separate room. However it's set up, you'll know that it's the authentic experience.

Enjoying your Stay

Beyond basic lodging, hostels provide a variety of other services for you to enjoy while you're staying with them. They have common areas where you can relax and prepare food, and you might even be able to stay for free in exchange for doing some chores. Let's look at what you might find.

Common Rooms

Hostels aren't just places to sleep. Most are built with relaxation in mind. Travelers staying at a hostel, however, also want to interact with their fellow guests, not sit in their rooms alone. That means the design includes recreation areas and focuses on community rather than personal space.

At a minimum, virtually all hostels will have a living room or lounge where you can watch television, maybe play pool or ping-pong, and hang out. Some go beyond that. At the Banana Bungalow hostel on Maui, for example, there's an outdoor hot tub.

Everyone at a hostel is a traveler like you, so it's pretty easy to meet people. You might even form some lasting friendships. As a bonus, wouldn't it be great to get to know someone from a country you're planning to visit on an upcoming trip?

Kitchen Facilities

Many hostels have kitchen facilities available for their guests to store and prepare their own food. It's almost always cheaper to buy food at a grocery store than to eat in a restaurant (even fast food), and some people who stay at a hostel are on long trips that last weeks or even months.

Even if you're just there for a weekend, you might want to use the kitchen. Just be sure to clean whatever you use when you're done so it'll be ready for the next person. That is actually a rule at some hostels, and not following it can get you banned from the kitchen for the rest of your stay.

Breakfast

Some hostels offer complimentary or low-cost breakfast to their guests. You'll see whether or not a particular hostel has breakfast included when you look at its profile on one of the hostel sites.

Hostel breakfasts are incredibly simple. It's not uncommon for the breakfast to be hot water, instant coffee, and toast with jam. A high-end breakfast might give you fresh coffee and tea, and add cereal or granola. On the European continent, this isn't too different from their usual breakfast anyway, so enjoy this *free* meal for what it is and have a more elaborate lunch with the money you've saved.

Internet Access

The increasing popularity of *flashpacking*—backpacking with a lot of high-tech equipment—has sparked a need for lodging that can support tech-savvy travelers. Hostels, dedicated to the needs of the world's Spontaneous Tourists, have responded by upgrading their facilities with flashpackers in mind.

Most hostels now have some form of Internet access, which might be anything from a computer for shared use to a full wireless network to connect your own devices. Depending on the hostel, you may have to pay a fee to use a shared computer, but if you do, it's usually not too expensive.

Jobs

Hostels need to have people change sheets, run the front desk, clean, and do other chores, but they can't afford to pay high wages. Travelers, meanwhile, may spend just about everything they have on airline tickets, then need a place to stay once they arrive. There's a natural overlap in this situation that lets everybody win.

At most hostels, you can get a job if you'll be there for at least some minimum length of time, usually two or more weeks. There may or may not be any pay—overseas in particular, actually paying wages can be a problem if you hold a tourist visa—but you'll be able to stay at the hostel for free.

If you're interested, it's best to call if you have questions about job availability, but you can also ask about a job when you arrive. You won't need to have previous experience.

Day Trips and Social Events

Some hostels provide tours or parties only for their guests. These can be a great way to see the area from a local point of view, make new friends, and save a lot of money. Not every hostel has these offers, but if they're available, you should try to take advantage of them.

OTHER KINDS OF LODGING

When you travel, your choice is usually between a hotel (or motel) and a hostel. Depending on where you're going, though, you might have a few other lodging choices as well.

Bed & Breakfasts

The idea of a Bed & Breakfast (or "B&B") goes back a long time. In fact, in colonial times, most of these places would have been called inns. B&Bs are houses in which the rooms have been converted into private lodging.

Think of a B&B as a luxury hostel for wealthier travelers. You'll usually find upscale old-fashioned amenities like antique furniture. The owner lives on the property (and may live in the house), and you'll have breakfast with the other guests in the common dining room.

Staying in a B&B can be fun, romantic, and a great way to experience small towns in the United States or abroad, but they're more common stateside. Cost varies, but don't expect to save a lot over a typical motel. Given the level of luxury afforded guests, you might even pay *more* for the experience.

The B&B market is heavily geared toward people traveling by car, so it's unlikely you'll find many of these along mass transit lines. Also, keep in mind that these tend to be quiet countryside retreats. There will be electricity and phones, of course, but wireless Internet access probably isn't on the list.

Campgrounds

The absolute cheapest type of lodging is one where you provide your own bedding. Long-term sleeping in your car is unsafe as well as illegal in most states, but campgrounds are popular around the United States as a way for travelers to save money and enjoy the outdoors.

What you get when you stay at a campground can vary depending on who runs it. State parks might host "primitive camping" areas, which include little more than some flat ground, a fire ring, and a source of drinking water. Other facilities are surprisingly developed, with platforms on which to pitch tents, bathroom facilities with hot showers, and vending machines or even convenience stores on-site.

In addition to public facilities, there are a number of independent campground networks. One that's particularly popular is KOA (Kampgrounds of America), which has sites throughout the United States and also overseas. You can search and make reservations online at *www.koakampgrounds.com*.

If you decide that camping is a good way to save money on your trip, be sure that you're prepared. Experienced campers will already know what gear they need to bring, but newcomers may want to do some research first.

Some campgrounds can be reached by bus, but others can't. If you aren't driving, check on this before making your reservations.

RECAP

When you look for lodging, have an idea of what you expect. Do you want a home away from home or a place to sleep? Americans tend to think in terms of hotels and motels, which give you personal space where you can return to relax at the end of a long day. You'll pay for this luxury, especially overseas where motels are less common.

If you do decide to stay at a hotel, sign up for any loyalty program that the family brand has for its guests. Tier status, if offered, won't give you the kind of elaborate benefits that you'd get from an airline, but you'll still be able to earn free nights over time. Earning airline miles or Amtrak Guest Rewards points might also be an option.

The alternative to staying at a hotel is to go with a hostel— budget accommodations for travelers. You can stay *very* cheaply in hostels, sometimes for less than $20 a night, and they're extremely popular overseas, though you can find them in a lot of American cities, too.

Hostel lodging is different from having a hotel room. You can get a private room, but it's very simple, usually with nothing more than a bed, nightstand, and closet or wardrobe. You can save even more money by getting a bed in a dorm, which is a shared space that can have four or more bunk-style beds and may be male, female, or mixed.

189

Shared bathrooms are pretty common in hostels. If a room has its own bathroom, it will be listed as "ensuite," but precisely what this means will vary by country, because toilets and bathing facilities aren't always in the same place.

Hostels usually have common rooms for guests to hang out, watch television, and play games. There might be free breakfast or coffee, and you'll probably have access to a kitchen. Most hostels these days have Internet access to cater to high-tech travelers, and if you'll be staying for a while, you can even get a job at the hostel in exchange for free lodging.

When you travel, you'll usually be choosing between hotels and hostels, but you might have other options. Bed & Breakfasts are similar to hostels in that they're standalone establishments with unique character, but the amenities tend to be upscale and rooms are private. Where available, campgrounds can also be fun and affordable places to stay.

LODGING TIPS

- If you have to cancel a lodging reservation, call as soon as possible to avoid paying a fee.
- Get a complete set of plug adapters, so you'll be able to use your electronics in any country.
- If you make any international calls, bill them to a credit card instead of using the hotel rate (which is usually higher).
- Be sure to look over your bill when you check out and question any charges that you don't understand. Even in luxury hotels, people make mistakes.
- Ordering room service usually has a service fee of 15% or more in addition to prices that are higher than usual.
- If you have elite status with a particular hotel chain, it's always worth the effort to ask for an upgraded room when you stay at one of their luxury hotels.
- Not all local hotels accept credit cards. If you're not sure and plan to pay with one, ask when you check in.
- Bring your own lock if you have valuables that need to be locked up when staying in a hostel.
- Some hostels want deposits for sheets, keys, and other items loaned to you during your stay. You might have the choice to leave your passport instead of cash—but it's not recommended.

"Certainly, travel is more than the seeing of sights; it is a change that goes on, deep and permanent, in the ideas of living."
—Miriam Beard

CHAPTER **9**

Out and About

Everything that you've done up to this point has been prep work. What you do while you're actually at your destination—your in-country time—is what will make it a great time to remember.

You packed, did your paperwork, found a way to get there, and booked a place to sleep. Now that you've finally arrived, you're not going to spend your time sleeping, are you? Of course not!

Wake Up!

Everyone needs to sleep, but you're in-country for only a few days. Set an alarm and try to wake up early—7:00, maybe 8:00 at the latest. Make the most of it, and sleep in when you get back if you're tired.

SEEING THE SIGHTS

What you see while you're in-country is up to you and your preferences. You can, and should, ask people who've been there for suggestions of what they liked, but don't think that you have to see it just because it was recommended. If you're not an art person, maybe you don't want to see an art gallery—and that's okay. Just because there's a famous statue doesn't mean that it's a requirement. Don't like the water? You're not obligated to go snorkeling on the coral reef just because it's there. This is *your* trip.

Of course, you decided to come, so there must be *something* that you'd like to see. Maybe you made a list on paper, or maybe it's more of a mental list—either way's fine. Consult a map, and put your list in an order that makes sense to you. Then get moving. More than anything else, the most limited resource you have is time.

Getting Around

Most cities have some form of mass transit. For the destinations featured in Part Five of this book, you'll find a short section on getting around each of them. If you're going somewhere not covered in the book, you'll be able to get an idea from your guidebook or research on the Internet.

Do you need a car?

Having a car means parking a car, which isn't only a matter of finding a place to park but also means *paying* for the parking—potentially $10 or more per day to let your car sit there. Overseas, in particular, rental cars tend to be incredibly expensive, and depending on the country, you may not want to be driving anyway.

> In a lot of places, including some American cities and most developed nations in the world, you can get a daily pass that allows unlimited use of the mass transit system. If you're going to be using the system to get around, you'll save a lot with one of these.

Basically, if there's an effective bus, subway, trolley, tram, or whatever else you can think of, plan to take it. Only get a rental car when it's actually necessary. When you do need a car, go with an established company that you can trust. Most of these companies have loyalty programs that let you earn credits toward free rentals. You'll find a list of the major rental car companies in Appendix D.

Do I need insurance?

Within the United States, buying the optional Loss Damage Waiver (LDW)/Collision Damage Waiver (CDW) is often unnecessary. Your personal automotive insurance may cover you, and many credit cards also include coverage for domestic rentals. Check into this, but if it applies to you, there's no need to spend extra money.

Outside of North America, it's a whole different issue. People in many parts of the world drive very aggressively by American standards, and damage to parked cars is also common. Since most of the coverage provided by credit cards and other programs doesn't apply outside of North America, you may want to protect yourself with an LDW/CDW policy.

Walking

In most cities, the easiest and most flexible way to cover short distances is on foot. Look around and see if everyone else is walking. If they are, then as long as there's no physical reason that you can't, you might as well walk too.

The shoes that you bring for a trip should always be chosen with walking in mind. Trendy shoes that look fabulous but leave you with blisters are a bad choice! If you want them for the nightlife, bring them along but leave them with your bag during the day.

Targets of Opportunity

As you go from place to place, there's a good chance that you'll pass by something that catches your eye. Time is of the essence, but if you've got your camera in a backpack, you're probably going to miss it. Keep your camera within easy reach, and you'll be ready to get pictures even while you're moving. (We'll cover *how* to take good pictures in Chapter 9.)

Getting In

Some things that you want to see will be free, like parks, monuments, and beaches. In other cases, you'll have to get tickets (i.e. aquariums, zoos). You might even be asked to make a donation and given a suggested value, which is very common for museums in the United States for tax reasons.

> **Americans are often surprised to find that museums in other countries charge a set ticket price for admission. These institutions generally receive little or no public funding, so it's very normal to sell tickets.**

Depending on the attraction and how popular it is, you may have to wait in line to get in. In some cases, you may be able to save a lot of time by buying a ticket online and then picking it up. If you know that you want to go somewhere in particular, check to see if this is an option.

Discounts

Many places that charge admission give special discounts for seniors, military personnel, students, and other categories of people. Review the section on discounts in Chapter 7 to get an idea of what you might need to take advantage of these special rates.

Pace Yourself

How long you spend seeing any particular attraction depends on three things—how much there is to see, how important it is to you, and what else is on your list.

You can fit just about anything into a few hours if that is your stated goal. For a museum in particular, this might mean spending just a few minutes at each exhibit and skipping around, but you'd get the highlights, and that might be more than enough for you. Aquariums can be seen top to bottom in an hour in almost all cases. Zoos, because of the ground you have to cover, depend on their size and layout.

Spontaneous Tourism isn't about running around trying to check off boxes. If you want to do that, fine, but the goal is really to take in the culture. In most cases, you get more out of spending a longer time seeing a few things than catching just a glimpse of everything. Don't feel as if you need to shortchange something important to see something else.

YOU REALLY *CAN* COME BACK

Many people want to see as much as they can when they travel because it doesn't occur to them that they'll ever have the time or money to come back.

The fact is, though, that travel is getting cheaper, becoming more important, and—once you get used to it—can be fit into just about any schedule. If you want to come back, you'll be able to do it. There's no need to rush.

FOOD AND DRINK

Sampling the local cuisine is one of the great joys of travel. Unfortunately, people are too often tempted by convenient, familiar foods from chain restaurants.

Don't give in! There's always local fare to be found, and it's worth the effort looking for it. The worst case is that you have something you don't like. That's a small price to pay, though, for knowing that you got to try something new that you might have really loved.

Meals

For travelers on a tight budget, it might be tempting to skip meals, but that's a bad idea. Travel puts a lot of stress on your body, and you need calories for energy. It's better to eat cheaply and intelligently than not at all. Here are some ideas.

Breakfast

Breakfast is truly the most important meal of the day. Eating breakfast revs up your metabolism, helps you wake up, and lets you pace yourself until lunch. There's even evidence that it helps with weight loss.

On the other hand, there's nothing that says breakfast needs to involve huge platters of eggs, bacon, pancakes, and fried potatoes. On the European continent, for example, breakfast is generally a light meal like a croissant or bagel.

Ideally, try to find lodging that includes some form of breakfast, and make due with what's included (even if it's only toast and jam). If you go out, keep your breakfast simple to save time and money.

Lunch

Some countries place more emphasis on lunch than others. Generally speaking, the later that dinner is eaten, the more substantial the lunch. For example, in Spain and France lunch is a leisurely experience that may take several hours, even during the work week. Don't think that you're wasting time having lunch, especially in countries where it's part of the culture. Then again, don't feel obligated to stop for a long meal if it doesn't appeal to you.

What you do for lunch is just another question of how to spend your limited resources—time and money. Whether or not you're traveling alone plays a role as well, because it's more appealing to have a long lunch if someone else is with you. If you'd prefer to keep moving, get a quick lunch instead.

A NOTE ABOUT FAST FOOD

You'll find fast food chains in most countries. There's nothing wrong with stopping by one of these if it helps you stretch your limited budget farther—but work it into the cultural experience!

Look for a foreign fast food chain, and eat there if one's available. If you do go to a McDonalds, there's usually at least one sandwich that isn't available in the United States (and sometimes the whole menu's different).

Dinner

If you can only afford one big meal each day, make it dinner. In some places, including France and Spain, dining involves many different courses. Other cultures tend more toward single-plate meals. The point, though, is to take some time to relax after a busy day and before going out for the evening.

Find a place where you can have good food brought to you—not necessarily expensive, mind you, but well-prepared—and make sure that it's somewhere local. Chain restaurants give you get the same thing wherever you go. Food is a huge part of culture, and when you travel, you want to have something that you can't get just anywhere.

Whether it's fried alligator in New Orleans, conch chowder in Key West, or horse meat in Geneva, there are bound to be things that you wouldn't get at home. If you're not sure what you'd like, ask the server to recommend something!

Other Considerations

Aside from the meals themselves, there are some other things to think about when it comes to eating and drinking on trips. Many of these considerations come up more often when you're traveling overseas.

Tipping

In the United States, it's normal to leave a gratuity (tip) to cover the service provided by a waiter or waitress for a meal. The usual amount is between 10% and 20% of the bill depending on the quality of service received. Not to leave a tip is an insult.

This custom isn't universal, though. In some countries, a service charge is automatically included in the bill, and an additional tip isn't required. It might even be seen as condescending.

Find out before you leave whether giving a gratuity is expected, acceptable, or not desirable. If you forget to look it up, ask someone at your hotel or hostel.

Alcoholic Beverages

Assuming you're of legal age, there's nothing wrong with drinking alcohol with a meal or while you're out on the town. In many countries, it's a part of the culture. Wine, for example, is very popular in France, and Germany is known for its beer halls. There are also countries where drinking is frowned upon or even illegal, but in those cases, you won't be offered alcoholic beverages with dinner.

Always drink responsibly, and tailor your behavior to your surroundings. What you definitely *don't* want to be is the drunk American who's drawing attention to yourself. Aside from annoying people, you mark yourself as a target for crime if you're intoxicated—especially if you're alone or everyone in your group has also been drinking.

Water

The United States is the only country in the world where virtually all water is potable (safe to drink). If you're washing your car and get thirsty, you can drink from the hose and you'll be fine.

Elsewhere, including Western Europe, it's common to have separate plumbing for the clean water used for bathing or drinking and the work water used to wash cars or water plants. Drink from a hose in such a place, and you could end up in the hospital. It's not safe.

Standards for water vary enormously, even within the industrialized world. Taiwan, for example, is a First World nation, but you don't want to trust the tap water. Mexico, China, India, and a lot of other places are certainly out of the question. Contrary to what you might expect given its status as an American territory, the tap water in Puerto Rico isn't recommended for drinking either.

The best idea when it comes to water is to research whether or not it's safe. You can get this information from the Internet or most guidebooks.

If you read that the water in a given place isn't safe, accept it as fact and don't take the risk. Locals may be immune to bacteria that might harm you.

SO WHAT IF THE WATER'S NOT SAFE?

Drinking plenty of water is important in every climate, so if the tap water isn't safe, you'll need a backup plan. Basically, you have three options:

- Buy bottled water, ideally a brand that you recognize. Most bottled water is filtered for bacteria.

- Boil water for fifteen minutes, and you can trust that it's safe to drink. There are also ultraviolet purifiers that work in just a few minutes.
- Use water purification tablets, which clean the water of harmful bacteria using iodine. You can drink water purified in this manner for several weeks without any problems.

Keep in mind that ice is almost always made from tap water. If you're in a country where the tap water isn't safe, order drinks without ice. You'll find that having drinks served over ice is uncommon in most countries anyway, so this won't present much of a problem.

Coffee

Coffee is served in many places around the world, but it isn't always the same as what you might be used to drinking. In Hawaii, for example, coffee beans are grown on the Big Island (the blend is called Kona, after one of the cities), and it has a different flavor than the Columbian-grown beans that many mainland Americans are used to having. Most people are familiar with Espresso, an Italian form of strong coffee. French coffee is similar, served in small cups with froth. Arabian and Turkish coffees are also very different. Then, in some places, you'll find that they don't drink coffee at all. Former British colonies, in particular, tend to prefer tea, which also comes in dozens of varieties.

All of these are worth trying, of course, but if you want coffee the way that you'd get it in the United States, try asking for "American" coffee. They'll probably know what you mean.

NIGHTLIFE

At the end of the day, most of the museums and monuments will be closed, but that doesn't mean you should go to bed. You'll find a lot of culture by getting out and mixing with the locals.

Things to Do

Guidebooks can really help when it comes to finding ideas for nightlife. Whoever works at the front desk can probably make good recommendations. If you're staying in a hostel, ask other travelers. What exactly you're looking for in terms of nightlife depends on what you like. In most places, you'll find enough options to make sure you don't get bored.

Let's look at some of them.

Clubbing

You'll find dance clubs in most cities around the world, even places where the level of development isn't very high. One reason for this is that clubs draw tourists, who bring money. Another is that clubs give young people somewhere to go to burn off extra energy, meet each other, and have fun.

If you're the clubbing type, you probably already know to be careful of pickpockets and such while you're dancing. That's especially true overseas if you bring your passport for identification. Be extra careful that you don't lose it.

Bar Crawls

People who like to mingle and drink when they go out but aren't big on dancing might prefer to hit some local bars. In cities, bars are generally pretty busy on weekends. Bars are also more likely to host local live bands than clubs, which tend to play recorded dance music. Get in on a game of pool or darts, and see if there are local specialty drinks that you can try.

The biggest challenge with a bar crawl away from home is that if you're alone, you need to be sure that you don't drink too much to get back to where you're staying—or so much that you become a tempting target for criminals. In developing nations, travel in groups where at least one person is completely sober.

Shows

Places like New York City and Sydney are clear candidates for musicals and operas, but even small towns might have theatres performing plays on weekends. It's usually possible to get discounted tickets at the last minute, especially if you're entitled to some sort of discount, like a student or military rate.

Don't limit your scope to traditional theatre, either. Maybe you can find a comedy club or a coffee shop that hosts local personalities. Dinner theatres can also be great fun. You'll find commercial dinner theatres like Medieval Times and Arabian Nights throughout Orlando. Ask around to see what local places are recommended.

> Sometimes, the problem is that there's so much available that it gets confusing and hard to make a decision. You'll find this to be the case in Las Vegas, for instance, where the casinos compete to offer guests the most elaborate entertainment.
>
> If you run into this situation, go with your first choice and plan to come back for another visit.

Beach Parties

If you're on the coast, there might be beach parties going on. In a lot of cases, you don't need to know anyone at a beach party to join in—just walk up and say hello. Bonfires make beach parties more fun and easier to spot. Unfortunately, it's illegal to have bonfires on most beaches on the East Coast of the United States, but these are allowed and very popular on the West Coast, most of the Hawaiian islands, and internationally.

Stargazing

In busy cities, there's no way to see the stars—the light from the buildings blocks all but the brightest of them. Not every trip is to a city, though, and if you find yourself in a small town, it might be fun to just sit outside and observe the cosmos.

Movies

You might think at first glance that it's a waste of time to go to the movies while you're traveling, but that's not necessarily true. Granted, within the U.S. mainstream movie theatres work pretty much the same way. Maybe there's an independent theatre, however, that's showing something you wouldn't be able to see back home.

Overseas, odds are that most of the movies playing aren't films you'd find in America. Stopping by to catch a foreign film can be a fun way to spend a few hours, especially just before going home. Be warned in advance that foreign movie theatres tend to be more expensive than their American counterparts.

Catching Up

When you travel, you leave behind the hassles of everyday life, which presents a great opportunity to reconnect. If you're traveling with someone, you might just want to sit somewhere and talk. Of course, this isn't much of an option when you're traveling alone.

Speaking of being alone, most people would agree that it isn't much fun—so let's spend some time talking about meeting people.

Meeting People

Whether you're traveling alone, with someone else, or in a group, it can be fun to meet new people when you travel. If you're a natural social butterfly, you'll find that it works about the same way in other cities as it does at home, even overseas (though it can get a bit tricky if you don't speak the same language). But what if you're not terribly outgoing?

Well, that depends. If you're not willing to talk to people at all, you just can't meet anyone. Antisocial behavior is pretty much a barrier to socializing.

On the other hand, maybe you have a hard time starting conversations? Or what if the opposite is true—you can get anyone to talk to you but don't have anything to say? Let's go over some pointers.

> This chapter isn't about "hooking up" on
> trips. If that's your interest, you'll still have to
> say hello first—then you figure it out.

Starting Conversations

People meet all of the time. If they didn't, we'd all be very lonely and wouldn't know one another. A lot of people, though, don't feel comfortable talking to someone they don't know. So, they wait for someone else to start talking to them.

Saying Hello

The passive approach isn't the best way to go about meeting new people. Take an active role!

Now, the most common question is *how* to start talking to someone. What are you supposed to do—just walk up and say, "Hey, how's it going?"

Yes, that works in almost all situations. As an opening line, it's perfect. Someone who doesn't react well to that didn't want to be approached at all, so you would've had the same response. Other simple ideas, like asking someone's opinion on the music or to recommend a drink, also work as starting points.

Confidence

People are social by nature, and it's now been proven that the human brain responds very empathically to what's going on around it. How you feel about yourself manifests in your body language—tone of voice, posture, etc. If you act like you're not worth talking to, don't be surprised when others agree!

What you need to do is project confidence. Say hello believing that you're worth talking to, and you'll see a marked difference in how you're treated. Don't confuse this with arrogance, however. Coming across as if people are beneath you will generally annoy them, especially if you're an American overseas.

Dealing with Rejection

Not everyone wants to talk—or might just not be inclined to talk to *you*. It's not that there's anything wrong with you. People have a split-second to decide whether they want to move beyond a simple hello. They base their decisions on a lot of things, and it's not your fault.

What *is* your fault is if you use their disinterest as an excuse to stop talking to anyone else. You need to become comfortable with rejection and not take it personally. Big deal—someone who didn't know you before still doesn't know you! Does it matter? Not in the least.

Don't let it bother you, and don't be rude, either. Just say something like, "Well, have a good night," or even nothing at all, and walk away. There are plenty of other people to meet. Who knows? Your casual acceptance might even spark the interest of the person who had just thought you weren't worthwhile. (It happens more often than you might think.)

What to Talk About

Of course, some people *will* want to talk to you. So now you've said hello and exchanged names. Where do you go from there?

Keeping a conversation going is the real challenge when it comes to meeting people. Some people just don't click when it comes to personality. Others can't find anything to talk about. It's a problem.

As you try to find something you have in common with your new conversation partner, some topics are safer than others. Sports are popular. What kind of music do you like? Maybe you can talk about what you've seen so far or are planning to see before you leave. Stories about places you've been work really well with others who also travel.

On the other hand, politics and religion are generally bad choices for new acquaintances. People tend to feel strongly about these issues, and they're also very personal—maybe too personal for a first meeting.

TOO MUCH INFORMATION

Be especially careful about discussing politics or related subjects overseas. People in many parts of the world might have views very different from yours and may become agitated or hostile. Disclosing things like military affiliation could even make you a target for terrorism.

Moving On

Having met someone, you don't want to just wander off, do you? It would be better to set up a way to stay in touch. You can exchange phone numbers, but it's a little less intrusive to exchange email addresses. It's more useful, too. You're probably far more likely to email someone you've just met than you are to call.

Understand that when you part company, you have absolutely no way to ensure that you'll ever hear from the other person again. Odds are actually strongly against it. But does it really matter? Of course not. The worst case is that you don't stay in touch, and that's where you'd be anyway.

Above All, Stay Safe

Make sure that you have your identification with you when you go out—something that shows your age, especially if you plan to drink. Safeguard your valuables, and keep track of where you are, so you can get back to your bed when you're ready.

As we covered already, getting drunk can make you a target. Don't set your drink down or let anyone else touch it. There's safety in numbers, so don't go out and drink too much if you're alone.

SAFE SEX FOR TRAVELERS

Who you might get involved with on your trips is your business, but keep in mind that sexually transmitted diseases—including but not limited to HIV—are found all over the world. Impoverished countries have much higher infection rates than their developed counterparts, but HIV affects plenty of Americans, so it shouldn't be a surprise that it affects Europeans, Australians, and people from other developed nations as well.

If you do engage in sexual activity with someone, be sure to protect yourself with latex condoms or other protection—and bring it from home, so you can be sure it was manufactured to a high quality standard. We know *way* too much about how STDs spread for there to be any excuse not to be prepared.

RECAP

All of the prep work for a trip is focused on getting you to your destination—but whether or not the trip is a success depends on what you do once you get there.

Wake up early. You've only got a few days, and you can sleep on the way back. Have an idea of what you want to see, and try to put your plans in order. In some places, it's absolutely necessary to have a car. Maybe there isn't mass transit at all, or it works but is extremely slow to get around. When you need to have a car, get one—but avoid it if possible, because cars add a lot of cost and tend to spend most of their time parked anyway. (Cars are especially pricey overseas.)

However you get from place to place, try to walk between places that are close together. Carry your camera with you to get photos of things that catch your interest. Some of the best photos are targets of opportunity that you wouldn't find on a map.

If you're going to need tickets for something, see if you can buy them in advance and save time. Keep in mind that American museums typically have a suggested donation for admission, but most museums overseas charge fixed ticket prices.

Don't rush to see everything you can. It's better to spend more time doing a few things that interest you rather than to focus on checking off boxes on your list. Remember that you can always come back for a second visit when you have time if you know that there are other things you'd like to see.

Try not to skip meals, but it's certainly possible to save money by eating light. See if you can get an included breakfast as part of your lodging, or stop by a bakery for a croissant or bagel. You might want to stop for a sit-down lunch, but there's nothing wrong with getting fast food to keep your budget intact. Just make it cultural, maybe choosing a foreign fast food chain or getting a sandwich not sold in America.

If you can only afford one sit-down meal each day, make it dinner. Avoid chain restaurants, and order something you wouldn't be likely to find back home. You can always ask the server to recommend something if you're not sure what to order.

Consume alcohol in moderation. Be aware that not all countries have water that's safe for drinking. If you're not sure, don't order ice with beverages, because ice is almost always made from tap water. Coffee is fine, because it's boiled, but you may find that the flavor or style isn't what you expect.

Get out and experience the nightlife wherever you go. Choose from clubs and bars, theatres, opera performances, stargazing, or even relaxing and talking with a traveling companion. Ask local people what they recommend or talk to your fellow travelers.

It's also a lot of fun to meet new people. Be friendly, say hello, come across as confident, and if someone doesn't want to talk to you, don't worry about it—there are lots of other people around. If you do meet someone and want to keep in touch, exchanging email addresses makes more sense than phone numbers in most cases.

Make safety a priority when you go out on the town. Remember how to get back to where you're staying, and be careful not to drink too much—especially if you're alone. When traveling in groups, it's a good idea to have at least one person stay sober. Be responsible when it comes to sexual activity, too, because STDs are found worldwide.

Whatever you do, make sure that you have fun. The more that you see and experience, the broader your perspective of the world becomes. That's what Spontaneous Tourism is all about.

TIPS WHILE OUT AND ABOUT

- Don't be afraid to try foods that sound strange! (Escargot tastes like mushrooms, horse meat tastes like beef, and alligator tastes like chicken.)
- If you decide to bring your passport when you go out, keep it in an inside pocket where it can't be lost or stolen. A better idea is to carry a copy of the identification page and store the original in a safe place.
- Use cash to pay for drinks, even if credit cards are accepted. You'll probably spend (and drink) less, and you can also leave whenever you're ready.
- Put the cash that you plan to spend in your pocket, and either leave your wallet in a safe place or keep it separate from the cash.
- Don't leave your drink unattended. Drugging is typically linked to sexual assaults in the United States, but overseas, it's more often used to rob unsuspecting tourists.
- Terrorism is a real threat these days. If you're confronted by someone, you may have just a moment to discern whether someone is a robber or intends to harm you.

  Should you be threatened by a robber, hand over your cash immediately. There's no reason to risk losing your life needlessly, and whatever is taken can be replaced.

  If, however, you genuinely believe someone intends to kill you, do something while you can. There *is* a time for action, and Americans have already learned that lesson the hard way.

CHAPTER 10

Making Memories

Travel can be a life-changing experience. No matter how many stories you have to tell when you get back, however, people who didn't go with you won't really be able to share in your adventures just by hearing about them. Over time, even you'll forget a lot of what you did—unless you link the trip to physical objects, which make memories clearer and stronger.

Fortunately, that's easy to do. When you travel, write postcards and mail them back to family and friends. Take lots of photos, and put them on a Web site or in a scrapbook that you can show to everyone who wants to hear about your trip. Buy souvenirs from each place you visit. You don't need to spend a lot, and it'll make your trip that much more exciting.

Let's look at these ideas a little more closely. In this chapter, we'll cover some practical information on writing postcards, taking good photos, and picking good souvenirs.

POSTCARDS

You've probably gotten at least one postcard from someone you knew who was traveling. Postcards are really great—they're cheap, personal, and specific to the place that you're visiting. People who get your postcards get an idea of what it's like where you are.

Of course, you might say that you could just as easily take a digital photo and attach it to an email. Part of what makes postcards so special, though, is that they're handwritten—not very common these days. They'll also arrive with a postmark from the place where you mailed them, and it's fun to get postmarks from distant or exotic places.

> Don't bring postcards back and mail them from home. The postmark is important—it says that you were *really there.*

Buying Postcards

You should buy your postcards as soon as possible after you arrive. That's because postcards take time to write, and you don't want to wait until the last minute to write them. If you already have the cards, you can pull them out when you have nothing better to do—say, while you're waiting at a bus stop.

The average price of postcards varies from place to place, but they're not expensive. In the United States, it's not uncommon to get five or more for $1. They may cost a little more overseas, but if you find a shop that wants you to pay more than 75¢ per card, you're paying too much.

Postage

In the United States, standard-size postcards have a special reduced rate. If you have an oversized postcard, you might want to take it to a post office to make sure it's eligible for the postcard rate, or you might put regular first-class letter postage on it instead. (It's the same price to send mail anywhere in the United States, which includes territories like Puerto Rico and even U.S. military bases overseas.)

When you go abroad, it's more complicated. Every country is responsible for deciding how its own postal services will work. It's not even necessarily the case that mail is a public service! Australia, for example, has an official post office but it competes with private companies in a deregulated market. It can be tricky.

There's another hurdle, as well. The hours of operation for postal employees vary by country, and they can be downright inconvenient for tourists. In France, for example, post offices aren't open on weekends at all. Some countries have postage machines where you can buy stamps, and others don't.

What can you do?

Well, start by looking around at the airport to see if there's a post office or an automated postage machine. If you can't find one, ask if you can buy stamps wherever you buy postcards. (This is really hit or miss, even in the United States.) If they don't sell stamps, ask if they can tell you how to get to a place where you can buy them.

Failing that, ask when you get back to where you're staying. Hotels generally go to great lengths to make sure their customers' needs are met, and if they don't actually sell stamps, they can probably help you. Hostels, meanwhile, are run for travelers, so they'll at least have an answer for you.

Writing Postcards

The fronts of postcards are different wherever you buy them, but the back portion is almost identical around the world. Put the stamp at the upper right corner, just as you would for an envelope. There may be lines or a box on the right side of the card—that's where you write the address (with "USA" at the bottom when you're traveling abroad).

There might be a section at the bottom that's blocked off from the rest of the card. Leave that for the post office to use. You've got the left side of the card to write your message (and you can use whatever other space is left on the card, too).

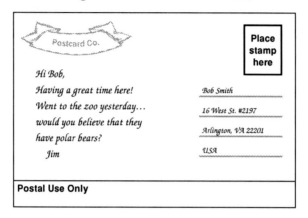

WE DELIVER, EVENTUALLY

When you send postcards from overseas, don't be surprised if they take a week or more to arrive. Postcards are bulk-mail shipments, and in a lot of cases, they're packed onto cargo ships. Your friends and family will have to be patient.

In developing nations, take your postcards to the post office and ask the clerk to hand-cancel the stamps while you watch. The value of international postage may be more than you realize compared to local wages, and if the stamps are stolen, your postcards will never arrive.

THE BEGINNER'S GUIDE TO PHOTOGRAPHY

Once upon a time, all cameras used film, which came in small rolls labeled with numbers. Most people were loosely aware of how to load a camera with film. They didn't really understand the numbers—something called "film speed"—but they'd been told that higher numbers were more versatile, so they cheerfully bought the fastest (and most expensive) film that they could find.

A click, maybe a flash, some winding, and that picture was done and gone. After 24 exposures, the roll was rewound, removed, and placed into a plastic canister, its contents unknown. Only when the film was developed using a chemical process would people get back prints that they could look through in the hopes that at least a few were worth keeping.

Choosing a Camera

You can still pick up a 30mm auto-focus film camera for less than $30, but film costs several dollars per 24-exposure roll even for the lowest quality and slowest speed. Getting that film developed costs money, too, and you'll be paying for photos that might not be worth keeping.

> Film developers usually won't charge you for any prints that are blurry or otherwise defective, but that doesn't include the photos that just aren't interesting.

What do you want to do with your photos, anyway? If you're making a scrapbook, you'll want physical prints, but you'll need digital pictures if you plan to post them online. Developers can provide you with a CD of your pictures as digital images, but that can cost you another $10 or more per roll of film.

There's a better way.

Go Digital!

Digital cameras use computer technology to interpret reflected light and render what they see as image files. When you take a digital picture, you get to see it on a built-in display—while there's still time to take another if it didn't come out.

As a Spontaneous Tourist on the move, you'll love the flexibility that a digital camera provides. Special settings let you take pictures of moving objects and landscapes as well as take photos at night—and when you get back, you can post your photos right to the Web.

Once clearly inferior to film photography, digital photography has made enormous progress over the past five years. Prices have also come way down, so much so that entry-level digital cameras can be bought for less than $200 and produce results at least as good as a 30mm film camera.

Things to Consider

Choosing a digital camera is a tradeoff between cost, size, weight, quality, and features. Most people focus on resolution, which is the sharpness of the camera's images measured in mega-pixels (MP). Realistically, anything 5MP or higher is going to produce results better than most photo printers can render, so look at this, but don't obsess about getting the highest possible resolution.

Instead, consider other factors. Optical zoom is measured in times-magnification (i.e. 3x, which is three-times) and helps you get pictures from farther away. You can safely ignore digital zoom, which is a software function that won't help you get better pictures, but a higher optical zoom is extremely useful.

Check what kind of batteries a camera takes before you buy it. If you have a camera that uses AA batteries, you can always buy some in a pinch. Some cameras use specialty batteries, however, and they may not be readily available on the road or in other countries. In these situations, it's a good idea to have a charger *and* a spare battery.

> Regular alkaline batteries run down quickly when used in digital cameras, especially if you're using the real-time LCD viewer. Rechargeable batteries tend to work better.

Also pay attention to the expansion card a camera uses. There are several different formats—CompactFlash (CF), SD, and xD among them—as well as a number of proprietary cards that only work with a particular brand and model.

Performance doesn't vary much between the different formats, but if you go with a camera that uses a proprietary card, keep in mind that you'll probably pay more for cards and they'll be harder to find. Of the standard formats, xD cards also tend to cost more than the others for the same storage size. Get a card that's one gigabyte (1GB) or larger, and storage won't be much of a concern.

Whatever camera you buy, you don't want it to get damaged when you travel. Choose a high-quality carrying case, one that's padded and has storage space for things like extra batteries. Sometimes, a good carrying case comes with the camera, but if not, you can buy one separately.

Research

Don't buy a digital camera on a whim. It's an expensive purchase, and while just about every camera sold in stores today can at least be rated good, you might pay more than you need to and get less than you could've gotten if you'd checked into it.

There are lots of resources to help you figure out which digital camera is right for you. Consumer Reports *(www.consumerreports. com)* reviews digital cameras several times a year and breaks down its results into entry-level, mid-tier, and advanced (categories). You have to pay to access the Consumer Reports site, so you might also want to check out Imaging Resource *(www.imaging-resource.com)*, which has freely accessible reviews.

The Photographic Process

Now that you've got a good camera, you need to learn to take good pictures. There are five key steps that make a good photo— holding the camera, lining up the shot, using light, getting the right focus, and actually taking the picture. Let's look at each of these one at a time.

Holding the Camera

Digital cameras have digital displays that let you see what they're seeing in real-time. It's great when you take home movies, but people typically use this feature to take their photos as well. What's wrong with that?

Well, nothing—as long as you don't mind risking blurry photos from the movement in your hands. If you want good pictures, you need a steady camera—and you have a lot better chance of getting that if you turn off the LCD screen, hold the camera up to your eye, and look through the viewfinder.

> Using the LCD screen on your camera for live capture also uses a lot of power. You'll drain your batteries in half their usual lifespan if you make a habit of it.

The Rule of Thirds

Most people who are new to photography place the subjects of their photos in the very center. If you do the same, you'll end up with pictures that are dull—it's just the way that the brain processes pictures.

A photo technique called the *rule of thirds* can help. When you get ready to take a picture, mentally overlay what you see with a tic-tac-toe pattern—two horizontal lines and two vertical lines. Line up the shot so that the horizon follows one of the horizontal lines instead of the center, and put the intended target of your shot on one of the intersecting lines. Because of the way that the human brain reacts to images, your photos will appear less flat and more interesting when printed.

Centered   Rule of Thirds

Lighting

Photography is all about light. A camera processes reflected light and uses it to create an image. The quality of that image is closely tied to the quality of the lighting used to create it.

It's usually better to have a lot of light. When there's good lighting, you don't need to worry about things like changing the aperture. Sun glare can be a factor outdoors, but you can compensate for that by standing with the sun behind you or lining up a photo so that the sun is blocked. (Ideally, block the sun with something other than the main target of your photo, or else it may come out too dark.)

Cameras come equipped with flash features to create light whenever ample lighting isn't available. In general, you'll want to use a flash whenever you're inside, but there are exceptions. For example, you can't use a flash when you're taking a photo of something behind glass, because the glass will reflect the flash back. Also, a flash only works on things that are close enough to be illuminated, so you can't use flash photography to capture pictures of things that are far away (like the stars, or a cityscape at night).

In situations like these where a flash isn't useful, you can compensate for the lack of light by adjusting the *aperture* to allow more light in. You can also slow the *shutter speed* to give light more time to enter. Usually, the best results come from some combination of the two.

> A slower shutter speed makes a camera particularly vulnerable to movement, because the picture is literally being taken for the entire time the shutter is open. Hold the camera very steady, or rest it on a still object. You might also use a tripod.

Focus

A lens is only capable of holding one distance in focus. If you're taking a picture of something right in front of you, the background will be blurry. When you're taking a landscape photo, whatever appears in the foreground will be less sharp.

There's no way to avoid this. Truth be told, you don't *want* to avoid it. Focus is part of what makes the intended subject of your photo "pop" off the page. It helps someone looking at the picture to direct his or her attention. The worst possible scenario is that *nothing* is in focus, in which case you just have a blurry picture.

Digital cameras have settings that can help you with the right focus. If you're taking a picture of someone from a fairly close distance—say, eight feet or less—you'd want to use a portrait mode, which will place the focus closer to the camera. If you're standing on a cliff trying to get a photo of the lighthouse in the distance, though, you want a landscape or panorama mode that will sharpen the far-away view.

Taking the Photo

Everything's lined up, you've got the camera steady, lighting is good, and now it's time to take the picture. All that you need to do is press the button—but if you do it too quickly, there's a good chance you'll ruin the picture.

You might think that pressing the button on a camera simply releases the shutter and takes the picture, but it's actually a two-part step. When the button reaches the halfway mark, it activates the focusing feature. Depressing the button all the way is what releases the shutter. If you simply press the button all at once, the camera may not have time to focus, in which case you'll get a picture that isn't as good as it might have been.

To focus the camera first, press the button halfway and wait a moment. Once it focuses, be sure to keep the camera steady before you take the picture. Since your body moves when you breathe, that means you want to stop breathing—in a way that won't interrupt the photo.

There are two natural pauses in your breathing cycle, one when you finish inhaling and one when you finish exhaling. The ideal pause is when you finish inhaling. Press the button halfway down to start the focus, inhale, stop breathing, press the button to take the picture, and then exhale. You'll minimize your movement and get better pictures—especially if you've slowed down the shutter speed.

PHOTO ETIQUETTE

Not everyone likes cameras. If you'd like to take a photo of a person, ask his or her permission first. In some countries, it's customary to give some small payment to a person being photographed.

There are also places where you may not be allowed to use your camera for cultural, religious, or security reasons. If you violate these rules, your camera may be confiscated. In certain cases, taking photos of places considered strategic by the local government may get you thrown in jail!

Taking photos is part of the fun of travel, but be smart. In the developing world, it's usually easier to ask for permission than forgiveness.

Editing

It's always been possible to touch up photos, but until recently, only a professional could do it—and you had to pay a lot for the service. One of the most exciting things about digital photos is that you can download them to a computer and work with them just like any other image files. Using a photo editing package, it's easy to remove red eye and balance colors. With some instruction, you can remove blemishes and scratches, too. All that you need is the right software.

Most people are familiar with Adobe Photoshop®, a powerful professional-caliber editing suite. It costs hundreds of dollars, and while it's widely regarded as a bargain for those who need its capabilities, it's overkill for most home users. Instead, check to see what software came with your digital camera. A lot of cameras today come bundled with basic editing software that can do most of the things that you would want to do. These tools are free with your camera, and they also tend to be very easy to use.

Printing

You don't need to print digital pictures at all if you only want to post them to the Web or share them electronically. There are lots of cases, however, where you *want* physical prints—maybe for a scrapbook, or to put in picture frames.

Look through the photos that you have and decide which ones you'd like to have as prints. Do any editing that's needed and copy the images over to a CD, then take the CD to any photo lab that does digital printing (which most do). They'll import the images that you provide and print your photos on the same high-speed printers that produce photos from developed film.

Another option is to upload photos directly from your computer to an online service, crop them, and have prints mailed to an address of your choice. Shutterfly *(www.shutterfly.com)* is one of the most popular services that do this, allowing you to select sizes from wallet through 20 x 30 as well as use your images for custom calendars, postcards, and other gifts.

If you'd prefer to print your photos at home, you can do it on a photo printer using special inks and glossy photo paper. The difficulty with this approach is that virtually all color inkjet printers these days claim to be photo printers and back up the claim with lots of confusing numbers and proof images that were specifically chosen because they look good. Actual results vary, and many of these home photo printers are exceptionally slow and expensive to operate in terms of ink.

It's a matter of personal preference as to whether you'd like to print from home. At less than 25¢ for a 4 x 6 print with turnaround times of just a few days, it's easy to do without the photo printer and outsource your printing to the professionals.

SOUVENIRS

People like to keep track of where they've been. Sure, you could just write it down on a list—but wouldn't it be more fun to bring something back with you? Most people think so, which is why you'll find so many shops selling shirts, hats, and other "swag."

Collectibles

A lot of people collect things when they travel. In most cases, they pick things that have the name of where they went, and just about anywhere that has a tourist industry will cater to that by selling hats, mugs, shot glasses, and other items. Get the same thing everywhere, or mix and match. It's up to you.

Unique Items

If you don't want "touristy" stuff, another idea is to buy unique items from each place that you go. You might buy a bone carving in Alaska, a bottle of champagne in Paris, and a woven rug in India—whatever catches your interest. Purchasing original art is particularly easy because there's no import duty when you bring it back to the United States (but be sure that it's really original, because the exemption doesn't apply to copies).

Passport Stamps

One of the best souvenirs that you have is your passport. Whenever you leave one country and enter another, your passport gets stamped to record your arrival. Some countries also stamp your passport when you leave their borders.

Each country has its own unique passport stamp. Some are more elaborate than others, but they always include an indication of the place and the date of the stamp, which gives you a handy record of your travels abroad. In most cases, collecting passport stamps is also free.

The Quest for Stamps

Collecting passport stamps has changed a lot over the last decade. The United States stamps all passports upon entry, but if you want to have more than a collection of American stamps on different dates, you'll want to plan ahead.

Here's a list of tips for you to consider:

- Any country that requires an entry visa will always stamp your passport when you arrive.
- Countries that require exit visas, and some others, stamp your passport when you leave.
- Crossing the U.S.-Canada border by land won't get you a stamp. (Traditionally, people doing this haven't even needed a passport. That's changing, but it's not clear whether the new rules will mean passport stamps.)
- Flying into Canada is processed as standard international travel—you need to have a passport, and you'll get a stamp.
- Your first entry point into the European Union will get you an E.U. stamp from the nation where you arrive. The Schengen Protocol makes travel local between most E.U. members as well as Norway and Iceland so movement between these countries won't get you stamps.
- Britain and Ireland are part of the E.U., but they didn't adopt the Schengen Protocol, so you'll get a stamp for any travel between British or Irish territory and another E.U. nation.
- All countries are allowed to stamp passports, but not all do it as a matter of border control. Liechtenstein, for example, charges a small fee for an official tourist stamp.

Gifts

Do you have a friend who loves Swiss chocolate? Pick some up when you visit Switzerland. Maybe your parents would like to try that bourbon marmalade that they have at the Tower of London. How about a bottle of Australian wine for your coworker's housewarming party?

Travel offers a lot of opportunities to pick up great gifts. If you have a general idea what your friends and family like, you can take advantage of a trip to do some shopping. You might even find some things for a lot less than what they cost back home.

PREMIUM NAME, BARGAIN BASEMENT PRICE

You'll be particularly surprised at how cheaply you can buy things in developing nations like China and Vietnam. Shoes and clothes that cost a small fortune in America are sold for pennies on the dollar!

That's because most of the cost of consumer goods covers the advertising that companies do to make you want to buy them in the first place. When you buy them at the source, you avoid those markups.

RECAP

Travel's more exciting and memorable when you associate your trips with physical objects. On each trip, write and mail postcards to your family and friends.

Decide before you leave who's going to get what, and make sure that you have everyone's correct address. Buy the cards early and write them whenever you have free time (like while you're waiting for a train or bus).

Postage can be tough to find when you're traveling. You can mail a postcard to anywhere in the United States (including

American territories like Puerto Rico and even U.S. military bases overseas) for the same rate, so buy your stamps in advance and bring them with you. Use a standard postcard stamp for normal-size postcards and go with letter-rate postage for oversized cards.

When you're traveling abroad, it may be difficult to find postage, especially on weekends. Look for an automated post-age machine at the airport. If you don't see one, ask where you can get stamps when you check into your lodging. Either way, buy your stamps as soon as possible and get your postcards in the mail so you don't have to worry about it when you're getting ready to leave.

Plan to get a digital camera instead of using film to take pho-tos when you travel. Digital cameras can hold a lot more pictures, and you'll know if they came out reasonably well as soon as you take them. Digital cameras also have lots of features like high-speed and nighttime settings. When you choose a camera, don't focus on resolution (mega-pixels). That's important, but so are things like optical zoom battery type and weight.

Taking photos involves five fundamentals. Hold the camera steady, and for best results, use the viewfinder instead of the LCD screen to line up your shot. When you aim, use the "rule of thirds" to create more interesting pictures, and remember that you can only put one distance in focus. Light is important to pho-tography. Natural light is the best, but a proper flash can work well. Don't use a flash when photographing through glass or the light will reflect back. Compensate for low light by adjusting the aperture or slowing the shutter speed.

Use a three-step photo-taking process. First, press the button halfway down to activate the focusing feature. Wait for the natural pause, then stop breathing and press the button to take the photo.

Most digital cameras come with photo editing software that can do things like remove red eye and correct color balance. You can print photos yourself, upload them to an online printing ser-vice, or take them to a photo lab.

Pick up souvenirs when you travel. Start a collection, either of one specific kind of item or just by picking up something interesting from each place that you visit. Original art can be imported duty-free. Passport stamps help you keep track of international travel, and collecting these can be fun. You might also find that a trip is a good opportunity to pick up unique gifts.

229

TIPS FOR MAKING MEMORIES

- Decide in advance who's going to get postcards, and make sure that you have all of their addresses before you leave.
- Send postcards early in your trip if possible so that they'll arrive before you get back.
- If you're planning to post your photos to a Web site, either take them in lower resolution or convert them so they won't take as long to load.
- Any photos that you might want to print should be taken at the highest resolution to give you flexibility when it comes to cropping and scaling.
- Always take a lot of pictures. Some of them won't turn out nearly as well as you thought they would (even if they looked good on the display).
- If you're using a film-based camera, remember that each speed of film has a specific use—but in a pinch, the highest speed is the most versatile.
- Consider taking black-and-white pictures, or converting images to grayscale with a photo editor. Some pictures that are merely "okay" in color can be very dramatic in black and white.
- Between inks and paper, using your own photo printer can cost a lot more than having your photos professionally printed.
- Pack breakable items like glasses between layers of clothing for added protection.
- If a passport control officer looks at your passport and tells you that you can go without giving you a stamp, ask for one. Lots of people want stamps, so they're usually happy to oblige.
- Gibraltar is British territory, so you need a passport to enter and leave. One benefit of this process is that a visit to Gibraltar gives you a chance to pick up a Spanish passport stamp even if you came to Spain from another E.U. country.

PART **5**

Where You Might Go

A selection of domestic and international destinations ideal for new travelers, chosen to give you the skill and confidence to go anywhere in the world.

"The whole object of travel is not to set foot on foreign land; it is at last to set foot on one's own country as a foreign land."

—G.K. Chesterton

CHAPTER **11**

Travel at Home

Domestic Destinations for Spontaneous Tourists

The United States is an enormous country with an incredibly diverse array of cultures and climates. Americans exploring their homeland will find not only some of the biggest cities in the world, but also beaches, mountains, waterfalls, islands, and glaciers. We have amber waves of grain, spacious skies, and wonders to be found from sea to shining sea.

For new Spontaneous Tourists, the United States provides the perfect opportunity to practice travel skills comfortably, knowing that they're still at home. You'll be amazed how much variety you'll find throughout the country.

DOMESTIC DESTINATION PROFILES

With so much to see, exploring the United States is pretty intimidating. To get you started, I've selected sixteen destinations I would recommend to Spontaneous Tourists. They certainly aren't the only places worth seeing, and I don't even claim that they're the best in the country. What I've tried to do is to give you a list with places that are each unique in what they offer travelers.

Visit as many or as few as you like, and add other destinations to your domestic travels. The more diversity that you experience at home, the better prepared you'll be when you travel abroad.

What's in a Domestic Profile?

These profiles aren't guidebooks. There's a lot more to see and do in each place than I have space to write. Besides, plenty of great guidebooks exist already.

Each profile gives you a snapshot of a destination. You'll find the nearby airports and local train station, along with the three-letter codes that you can use to make reservations with your favorite airline or with Amtrak and the address of the central bus station. Check the ship icon to see if it's a cruise destination. I've also included a short list of things to see and do while you're there.

Cost Estimates

Each year, the U.S. government publishes Per Diem (daily) rates for destinations throughout the United States. These rates are a good way to compare average costs for business travel, including mid-range hotels and restaurants.

> You can easily spend less than the Per Diem rate (especially on food). Depending on your preferences, you can exceed it as well. Use it as a guideline to help you plan.

The Per Diem rates shown are current as of 2007 and are separated into lodging (L) and what the Government calls "meals and incidental expenses" (M&IE). The incidental expense rate is three dollars for the forty-eight lower states covered by General Services Administration (GSA) Per Diem tables, while a special committee sets the rates for Alaska, Hawaii, and U.S. territories like Puerto Rico.

You can get the current Per Diem rates online from several sources, but the most convenient source is *https://secureapp2.hqda. pentagon.mil/perdiem/perdiemrates.html*. The Pentagon site references current data for both domestic and international destinations.

PER DIEM AND TAX RECORDS

For those of you who are self-employed, the Per Diem rate plays a big role in recording business travel expenses for tax purposes. When you're on business travel, you may be able to claim the Per Diem M&IE rate instead of keeping individual receipts for all meals and incidental expenses.

Of course, this isn't a business tax guide, so consult your tax preparer for detailed information.

Budgeting Time

People are busy, and fitting travel into the schedules of hectic lives takes some finesse. Don't get drawn into the trap of thinking you need to stay somewhere for a week in order for it to be worthwhile. If you do, you may end up not going anywhere at all.

You can see a lot more than you realize with only two days of in-country time. You can see most of the places listed here if you leave on Friday evening and come back on Sunday. Puerto Rico and Alaska are three-day weekends from most places. Set aside a four-day weekend for Hawaii to cover the long flights.

Remember that Spontaneous Tourism is about experiencing new places, not merely rushing around to check off every box on your list. See the things that you want to see—even if that means stopping by a coffee shop and skipping a museum. Above all, have fun!

New York City
New York, USA

Four-star hotels or hostels, pizza or fancy restaurants—you can find it all here. Art flourishes, business thrives, and nothing stops at sundown. New York City is the largest city in the United States, and you'll find nowhere else like it. From the moment you arrive, you'll feel the difference.

2006 Per Diem Rates: (L) 201-282 ♦ (M&IE) 64	
	• John F. Kennedy International Airport (JFK) – AirTrain to subway • LaGuardia Airport (LGA) – Bus service to downtown • Newark-Liberty International Airport (EWR) – AirTrain to New York-Penn Station
	• New York-Penn Station (NYP) – Acela, regional Amtrak, NJ Transit, and LIRR service; direct subway access • Grand Central Station – Metro North service
	• Port Authority, 625 8th Ave. – Greyhound and regional bus lines; East Coast Chinatown buses; direct subway access
	• New York Cruise Terminal –Canadian coastal itineraries; Transatlantic service on the Cunard line

Getting Around

Other cities in America have light rail, but New York's subway is by far the most extensive mass transit rail system in the country. It operates 24 hours a day and any trip is a $2 flat fare regardless of the distance traveled, including transfers.

New York City has five boroughs, but when people say "New York," they're usually thinking of Manhattan. The Bronx, Brooklyn, Queens, and Staten Island are more often referred to by name.

If you arrive by train at Penn Station or bus at the Port Authority, you'll have direct access to the subway. None of the three airports have that luxury. LaGuardia offers bus service, and Kennedy and Newark-Liberty offer AirTrain service to subway locations. Another option is to take a taxi, which is a flat $50 fare from the airports to anywhere in Manhattan.

THE MARVELOUS SUBWAY

The subway is one of the defining characteristics of New York that makes it so different from the rest of the country. Because it has extensive service throughout the city, and virtually everyone uses it, it's a social equalizer like nothing else.

In general, subway stations are noisy, hot, and crowded, but they're almost always safe. The sheer size of the system can make it tricky, so ask for directions if you aren't sure. Once you get the hang of it, you'll enjoy the convenience it offers.

Buses go nearly everywhere if you can figure out which one you have to take, and transfers from the subway to the buses are free and automatically tracked on farecards. Also, New York City has more taxis than anywhere else in America.

It's common to take the subway to a general area and then walk, especially when the weather is nice. The streets of New York are amazingly crowded, so if you're traveling with other people, have a plan in case you get separated.

Driving here is not a good idea—there's a huge amount of traffic, and parking is difficult to find and very expensive.

237

Sightseeing

Seeing everything that New York has to offer would be difficult in a lifetime. In fact, there's so much that to offer more than a few highlights would take away from the enormity of the trip. Fortunately, it's easy to see enough in a weekend to make a big impression.

The **Empire State Building** was at one time the tallest in the world. It was surpassed by Chicago's Sears Tower in 1973, but you'll still want to check it out both for its charming Art Deco design and the views it affords of Upper and Lower Manhattan. Some visitors may also want to visit **Ground Zero**, the site of the World Trade Center buildings destroyed on September 11, 2001. (The memorial is now under construction and scheduled for opening on September 11, 2009.)

You'll find the **South Street Seaport** in the city's financial district, just a short walk from the famous bull statue of **Wall Street**. This revitalized area is now home to upscale boutiques and restaurants and also affords an opportunity to walk across the **Brooklyn Bridge**.

To experience Manhattan culture, turn your attention to the artistic side of New York. The **Metropolitan Museum of Art** (the "Met") attracts thousands of American and foreign visitors each day. The recently renovated **Museum of Modern Art** (MoMA) appeals to more abstract tastes. Are you a fan of the stage? Most of your favorite shows are playing every day on **Broadway**, and you'll find hundreds of smaller theatres around the city. Stroll through **Central Park**, or take a carriage ride for about $50.

The **Statue of Liberty** and **Ellis Island** are both tempting destinations for travelers and reachable by ferry. If you'd prefer to avoid the congestion of going in person, you might enjoy the view from one of the **Circle Line**'s harbor tours. Visit *www. circleline42.com* for schedules.

Take the time to wander the packed streets beneath the dazzling lights of **Times Square**, but be careful to keep any companions in arm's reach in case you get lost among the crowds. **Rockefeller Center** is home to an ice skating rink as well as the City's Christmas Tree in the winter, and its observation deck offers another chance to see the city from high in the sky.

Wander through the lobby of the legendary **Plaza Hotel** en route to the reincarnated **FAO Schwartz** toy store. Did you know that New York has the largest **Chinatown** in the country? See as much or as little as you like. You'll always find more waiting when you return.

Washington, D.C.
USA

Monday through Friday, Washington is the seat of the U.S. Federal Government. On weekends, however, the Congressmen and lobbyists leave, and the tourists arrive. Monuments and museums, embassies and concerts, the nation's capital is a mixture of business and pleasure.

2006 Per Diem Rates: (L) 150-192 ♦ (M&IE) 64

- Washington-Dulles (IAD) – Bus service to Metro
- Reagan National (DCA) – direct Metro access
- Baltimore-Washington International (BWI) – MARC or Amtrak to Union Station

- Union Station (WAS) – Acela, regional Amtrak, MARC, and VRE service; direct Metro access

- Washington Greyhound Station, 1005 1st St. NE – Greyhound and regional bus lines; East Coast Chinatown buses

- No cruise ship terminal

Getting Around

The D.C. metropolitan area subway system is technically called MetroRail, but it is universally referred to as "the Metro." There are also several different bus lines, including the free Downtown Circulator, the Arlington ART bus, and the MetroBus network (simply called "the bus" to avoid confusion with MetroRail).

Union Station and Reagan National both have direct Metro access. If you fly into BWI on a weekday, you can take a MARC regional train to Union Station, but on weekends, the only choice is Amtrak (or a taxi—but the trip is very far). From Washington-Dulles, you can pay around $15 for the Washington Flyer express bus to the West Falls Church Metro station or take the commuter 5A route to the Rosslyn Metro for less than $3.

METRO VS. SUBWAY

You'll see many differences between the Metro and the New York City subway. The comfortable and attractive stations are readily noticeable, but there are four big differences that might catch visitors off guard.

First, while the Metro is America's second-largest subway system, it's much smaller than its cousin. Metro service includes over 100 stops in the District, Maryland, and Virginia, but you can't get everywhere on it. For example, it doesn't go to Georgetown, a popular section in Northwest D.C.

Second, whereas New York's subway runs at all times, the Metro closes each night. The last trains leave downtown around midnight during the week and 2:00 a.m. on weekends and holidays. (New York actually has the only 24-hour subway in the world.)

Third, Metro fares aren't flat rate. They depend on where you start and stop a ride—which means you can't share fare cards, because once a trip starts, a new one can't start until the first one ends. It's also more expensive during peak weekday hours than other times.

Lastly, you can't eat or drink on the Metro or in Metro stations. It's illegal, and you can be fined and even arrested.

Taking the Metro is by far the easiest way to get around. The stations are spacious, clean, well-lit, and extremely safe. Walking is also popular, and in some areas (especially around the National Mall and throughout the downtown area) you may find "Golden

Triangle" hospitality guides who can help direct you if you get lost.

Sightseeing

The District of Columbia is small compared to other major cities, even when you add in neighboring Arlington County. There's a lot to see and do, though, so you'll have a busy weekend.

Everything starts on the **National Mall**, the promenade that runs between the U.S. Capitol and the Lincoln Memorial. You can spend hours visiting all of **the monuments**, including the new World War II Memorial. (A monument to Dr. Martin Luther King, Jr. is scheduled for completion in 2008.)

As you walk, you'll pass some of the 17 museums that make up the **Smithsonian Institution**, the largest museum complex in the world. Admission is free to all Smithsonian facilities, including the **National Zoo** (a short trip from Downtown on the Metro) where you'll find Tai Shan, one of America's famous panda cubs on loan from China.

Within walking distance of D.C.'s small Chinatown, you'll find the **International Spy Museum**, which opened in 2002. You have to buy a ticket, but you won't want to miss it—or the **Holocaust Museum**, which is also unique though considerably more somber.

For several decades, it's been the Northwest section of the District that's drawn the most attention—tourists and locals alike flock to the upscale boutiques and nightlife of **Georgetown**, or the independent bookstores and clubs in the gay and lesbian community around **Dupont Circle**. Rising property values have led to large-scale renovations, and the impacts are very visible. The **U Street corridor** has remerged as a thriving center of African American culture, nightlife, and local music, and new construction is underway in the Northeast.

Many visitors to D.C. include a visit to **Arlington National Cemetery** as part of their trip. The hourly changing of the guard ceremony at the **Tomb of the Unknowns** and the **Eternal Flame** at the grave of President Kennedy are both popular, but it's really the visit itself that matters—Arlington is a memorial to all American soldiers who have given their lives since our country was founded.

If you haven't already seen the magnificent Great Hall, stop into **Union Station** before you leave. Enjoy the food court or one of several restaurants, and take the opportunity to do some shopping. Its central location makes it a convenient endpoint whether you're taking a plane, bus, or train.

243

San Francisco
California, USA

San Francisco is a vibrant coastal city with a culture as unique as its climate. You'll find a thriving art scene and a place of social and environmental activism. The San Francisco Bay area is also home to some of the world's leading high-tech companies. What's so interesting is the synergy between the two.

In most cities, the activists find themselves at odds with the business owners at every turn. Here, it's more likely that the owners *are* the activists, creating socially responsible products for a healthy and thoughtful customer base. Not only has the sky not fallen, but the city is doing better than many of its more polarized counterparts. It's a model that the rest of the country should study.

2006 Per Diem Rates: (L) 130 ♦ (M&IE) 64

	• San Francisco International (SFO) – direct BART access • Oakland International Airport (OAK) – direct BART access
	• Free shuttle bus from MacArthur BART station to Emeryville Station (EMY) – regional Amtrak service
	• Transbay Terminal, 425 Mission St. – Greyhound and regional bus lines; West Coast Chinatown buses
	• Fisherman's Wharf Piers – Pacific, Alaskan, and Transcanal itineraries

Getting Around

The Bay Area Regional Transit (BART) rail system provides long-haul service within the San Francisco Bay area, including to and from both major airports. Within San Francisco, a light rail system called the Mini is supported by an extensive mass transit network, which includes cable cars, electric buses, and trolleys.

If you're up for it, you can get to most places on foot. San Francisco is known for its hills, but if you do get tired, it's easy to find a taxi.

> It's usually 20 to 40 degrees cooler in San Francisco than in the rest of the Bay area. Bring a jacket or a sweater, even in July, because it gets chilly when the sun sets.

Sightseeing

The Embarcadero BART station is adjacent to the historic **Ferry Building**. Recently renovated and now home to wine bars and boutiques, its noticeable clock tower is a landmark. To the left are dozens of numbered piers, some still in commercial use while others are tourist attractions. **Fisherman's Wharf** is at the far end.

As you walk, you'll pass the **Aquarium of the Bay** and the **Pier 39** shopping complex. Stop for some delicious clam chowder or other fresh seafood. You can also take the ferry to visit infamous **Alcatraz Island**. Plan ahead, because lines may be long, even during the summer when several tours run each day. Nearby **Angel Island**, the gateway for immigration from the Far East, is also reachable for tours.

When you get to the Wharf, you can climb aboard an old-fashioned tall ship or explore a submarine at the **Hyde Street Dock**. The most crooked street in the country, **Lombard Street**, is at the top of the Hyde Street hill. You can walk, but why not take the **Powell-Hyde cable car** to the top?

San Francisco has a famous **Chinatown**, which is best entered through the ornamental gate at Grant Avenue and Bush Street. It's the perfect place to buy postcards, since they can be found here as cheaply as eight for $1 along with bargains on silk robes, artwork, and other Chinese items. There's a **Japantown** in the city as well.

Along **Mission Street**, you'll find an impressive collection of museums, including the unique Museum of the African Diaspora as well as museums of contemporary art and Mexican culture. Downtown, **Yerba Buena Gardens** offers a unique blend of landscaping and modern architecture, while the Asian Museum is located near the **Civic Center Plaza** on Market Street.

The most famous landmark in San Francisco is probably the **Golden Gate Bridge**. You'll be able to see it from high points in the city, including on your way up the hill to Lombard Street. A particularly striking up-close view can be had during a visit to Civil War-era **Fort Point** on the shore.

The Castro, the center of San Francisco's thriving gay and lesbian community, is a popular tourist destination and is home to some great nightlife, but it's too far away from the center of town to reach on foot. Pick up the Mini and you can get there pretty quickly.

If you have time, stop by **Golden Gate Park**, the largest manmade park in the country. The **Japanese Tea Garden** is located on the grounds and offers a serene opportunity to relax and enjoy tea in the mid-afternoon.

Chicago
Illinois, USA

Famous for its cuisine and archi- tecture, infamous for a history that includes Al Capone, the "Windy City" was largely destroyed by the Great Fire of 1871 but was rebuilt to become one of the jewels of America's industrial age. Hit hard by the rise of glo- balization and the decline of domestic manufacturing, twenty- first century Chicago has reinvented itself again as a corporate center in the global marketplace.

2006 Per Diem Rates: (L) 136–169 ♦ (M&IE) 49–64

	• O'Hare International Airport (ORD) – direct CTA access (but at least 45 minutes from downtown) • Chicago-Midway Airport (MDW) – direct CTA access
	• Union Station (CHI) – Regional Amtrak service (transcontinental hub)
	• 630 W Harrison St. – Greyhound and regional bus lines
	• No cruise ship terminal

Arriving by Train

Chicago's Union Station serves as a main junction between Amtrak's Northeast and Westbound train routes. With the excep- tion of only a few routes that go across the southern United States into Florida, all cross-country rail travel involves a stop in

Chicago, which means it's easy to visit Chicago on most domestic rail itineraries. Even if you have only a few hours' layover, you can duck out to see the Sears Tower—it's just a few blocks away from Union Station.

Getting Around

The Chicago Transit Authority (CTA) operates a light rail system that includes several different color-coded lines. One of these, the Green Line, is famously known as the "El" because it runs on elevated tracks overlooking the city.

Tourists can pick up single- or multi-day passes that provide unlimited access to the CTA trains as well as the interconnecting buses that provide access to most every part of the city. The downtown area is also serviced by a system of free trolleys.

Unless you plan to visit the outlying areas away from the city, you won't need a rental car to see Chicago. If you do get one, you may find that it's easiest to park in central locations and walk to everything in the area. Alternatively, taxis are plentiful in this bustling metropolis.

Sightseeing

A great way to start is with the **Sears Tower,** presently the tallest building in the United States and the third-tallest in the world, measuring 1729 feet to the tips of its twin antennae. For $12, you can take a trip up to the **SkyDeck** and learn about Chicago's rich history while enjoying a panoramic view of the city.

Chicago is on the shores of Lake Michigan, and many of the most famous attractions in the city can be found on or near the waterline. One of the most striking is **Navy Pier,** a family entertainment and shopping center with everything from an enormous Ferris wheel to an indoor arboretum and fountain garden. The **Children's Museum** is at the front and you'll find the amazing **Stained Glass Museum** off the underground mall.

At the southern end of Lakeshore Drive is the world-renowned **Field Museum**. At the entrance, you're greeted by a dinosaur skeleton. Walk through a life-size simulated ant colony or learn about the man-eating lions that were the basis for the film, "The Ghost and the Darkness." With a huge amount to see and do, you may have to save some of it for your next trip.

Conveniently located next to the Field Museum is the **Shedd Aquarium**, where you'll find sharks, dolphins, and Komodo dragons. Spend an hour or two enjoying its wonders, then walk a few hundred yards to the **Adler Planetarium** for a cosmic show.

Feeling hungry? A **Chicago-style hot dog** is served on a poppy seed bun and topped with mustard, onions, tomatoes, peppers, and a dill pickle spear. You can order one from a street-side vendor or seek out one of several hot dog cafés throughout the city. There's also an assortment of German food to be found in the area around **Lincoln Square**.

One more museum beckons. The **Museum of Science and Industry,** offers a dazzling array of technological and scientific wonders that include coal mines, trains, and a chance to climb aboard the German submarine U-505 captured during the Second World War.

New Orleans
Louisiana, USA

The most famous city in the only state whose laws are based on the French Napoleonic Code instead of English Common Law, New Orleans (pronounced by locals more like "N'awlins") is known for its nightlife, music, and riverboats. More recently, it's been in the news for the devastation it suffered through the hurricanes of 2005.

Fortunately for Spontaneous Tourists, American resolve (or stubbornness, if you prefer) has kicked in, and the rebuilding is underway. Travelers will find the French Quarter open for business, and while there are some buildings with evident damage, most of what you'll see on a weekend trip is back to pre-disaster standards.

2006 Per Diem Rates: (L) 103–133 ♦ (M&IE) 59

- Louis Armstrong Airport (MSY) – bus service

- Union Passenger Terminal (NOL) – Regional Amtrak service

- 1001 Loyola Ave. – Greyhound and regional bus lines

- Julia Street Cruise Terminal – Caribbean itineraries

Getting Around

The French Quarter is the place to do most of your exploring, and it's easy enough to walk (though a map can be quite handy). A streetcar system can get you around the Quarter and out to the historic houses of the Garden District. There's a ferry to the Zoo, and buses will take you just about anywhere else.

Sightseeing

Certainly, New Orleans' most famous attraction is **Bourbon Street**, half a dozen blocks of drunken debauchery that masquerades as having some connection to music. Go, by all means, but don't miss out on the many **jazz clubs** throughout the city.

One of the best ways to get your bearings is to take a mule-drawn **carriage ride**. Look for the mules near **Jackson Square**, site of an historic brewery that's now an upscale shopping mall. The rides are cheaper if a few people come along.

The **Napoleon House** was built to serve as a refuge for France's self-proclaimed emperor. He never had the chance to see it, but today it serves some of the finest seafood gumbo to be had in New Orleans.

Head to Decatur Street and stop at **Café Du Monde** to enjoy coffee and fresh doughnut-like beignets drowning in powdered sugar 24 hours a day. A few blocks down from Jackson Square, you'll find the **Farmers Market**, busy most of the time with people selling Cajun spices and fresh foods.

Ever seen a white alligator? They have one at the **Aquarium of the Americas**. Of course, if you're not picky about color, you can pick up some **fried alligator** at several places along Canal Street. (Tastes like chicken. Really.)

If you have time, you'll find **riverboats** that serve as cruising casinos. Gambling is illegal in Louisiana, but not on the Mississippi River.

251

Orlando
Florida, USA

The title is already taken, but Orlando is the real mall of America. In addition to being home to nearly a dozen theme parks, it offers endless shopping centers and strip malls featuring nearly every department store, restaurant, and boutique chain in the United States.

Spontaneous Tourists will want to visit the various amusement parks in depth, but keep in mind that many of these take at least a full day to enjoy. You can easily spend a week or two in Orlando, but if time is short, don't worry. We'll also look at some ways to get a taste of a few of the parks to fill your weekend trip.

2006 Per Diem Rates: (L) 83–101 ♦ (M&IE) 49

	• Orlando International Airport (MCO) – bus service
	• Orlando Station (ORL) – Regional Amtrak service • Auto Train service at Sanford, FL (SFA; 27 miles from Orlando)
	• 555 N John Young Pkwy. – Greyhound and regional bus lines
	• Cape Canaveral (approximately one hour away) – Caribbean itineraries

Getting There

Flying to Orlando is very popular, with most airlines offering daily flights to Orlando International Airport (MCO). Amtrak provides service with its Sunset Limited route (ORL), or there's the Auto Train, which can bring you and your car to Sanford, a short 27 miles from Orlando.

Getting Around

Orlando has an extensive public bus system, but the area is so spread out that you'll spend hours getting from place to place. Get a rental car for this trip.

Sightseeing

When people think of Orlando, they think first and foremost of **Walt Disney World**. Encompassing the Magic Kingdom, Epcot Center, Animal Kingdom, MGM Studios, and more, Disney World is large enough to be a city unto itself. If you want to see it, make this your *entire* weekend. It has too much, and it's too expensive, not to give it at least two days.

On the other hand, you can get a taste by visiting **Downtown Disney**, an area of shops and theme restaurants that feature Disney characters—and it's free. Universal Studios' **CityWalk** is also free, though the other parts of the Universal Studios theme park do charge admission and parking.

See alligators, llamas, exotic birds, and a petting zoo at **Gatorland**. It only takes half a day to see everything, so spend the other half of the day at **Sea World** enjoying orcas (killer whales), dolphins, and seals as well as penguins and polar bears.

> No matter what politicians tell us to get our votes, we have ample scientific evidence that global warming will make polar bears extinct. See them while they last and advocate strongly for zoos that create habitats to house them.

When you get tired of theme parks, head north to **Winter Park** and enjoy dozens of small shops selling clothing, pastries, and artwork. **Wall Street Plaza** is a popular nightlife spot whose brick streets are lined with bars, clubs, and restaurants.

It's a bit outside of the downtown, but if you have time, consider a trip to the **Kennedy Space Center**. You can see one of the Saturn V rockets that took Americans to the moon and even touch a piece of Martian rock. **Space shuttle launches** are also public, but you'll need tickets in advance.

Niagara Falls
New York, USA
Ontario, Canada

Niagara Falls is the name of two cities, one on each side of the Niagara River that forms the border between the United States and Canada. Each has dazzling views of what is by far the most spectacular waterfall display in the country. You'll enjoy seeing this natural wonder, and the trip will provide you with an opportunity for some casual international travel. A trip to Niagara Falls is also a romantic experience to share with someone special.

2006 Per Diem Rates: (L) 60–83 ♦ (M&IE) 44

	• Buffalo Niagara International Airport (BUF) – Metro Bus access
	• Niagara Falls, NY (NFL) – Regional Amtrak and VIA Rail Canada northbound service • Niagara Falls, Ontario (NFS) – Amtrak and VIA Rail Canada southbound service
	• 303 Rainbow Blvd. – Greyhound and regional bus lines
	• No cruise ship terminal

255

Getting Around

Buffalo's Metro Bus system provides service to and from Niagara Falls. Also, a fairly inexpensive trolley operates within the city and stops at or near the various hotels. Traffic can be a problem during the warmer months, so you may prefer to avoid it by walking. You'll have less trouble finding parking outside of peak tourist season.

Buffalo has a light rail system called Metro Rail that provides service in and around the city. It doesn't extend out to Niagara Falls, but if you decide that you'd like to visit the nearby city, keep in mind that a paid fare is only needed for the underground portions of the line. Above ground, Metro Rail is free.

Sightseeing in Niagara Falls, New York

Niagara Falls actually includes three different waterfalls. **American Falls** pours 150,000 gallons of water over its edge for a 150-foot drop every second. **Horseshoe Falls**, on the Canadian side of the border, is a dual waterfall that flows around a central barrier to create two different parallel streams. **Bridal Veil Falls** is the smallest of the three.

The Falls themselves draw visitors 24 hours a day, 365 days a year. Most other attractions, including the **Aquarium of Niagara** and the famous **Seneca Casino**, are also available year-round. The winter months are popular with birdwatchers and tend to be less congested. You won't lose out on a great view—the Falls are **illuminated** every night from shortly after sundown until at least 10:00 p.m., an incredible sight to behold. Another unique view can be had from **Luna Island**, located between American and Bridal Veil Falls.

If you come during the summer months, you'll enjoy some special treats. **Fireworks** are set off over the falls at 10:00 p.m. every Friday and Sunday during the summer. A summer visit also means a chance to visit the **Cave of the Winds**, where wooden decks 175 feet down at the base of Bridal Veil Falls put you within feet of the surging water. The **Maid of the Mist** steamboat tour, also offered during the warmer months, costs about $12 per person and lets you view the Falls from the lake.

Sightseeing in Niagara Falls, Ontario

It's a quick walk or drive across the **Rainbow Bridge** into Canada. New border security requirements are being phased in over several years beginning in 2007, and you'll need to show a passport effective January 1, 2008. Until then, a government-issued photo I.D. is enough.

The highlight of the trip is probably the **Journey behind the Falls** tour, a self-guided walk through tunnels that extend for 150 feet behind the waterfall. Check it out, and then explore the gardens of nearby **Queen Victoria Park**. When you get hungry, have lunch or dinner overlooking Horseshoe Falls from restaurants at the tops of the nearby **Konica Minolta Tower** or **Skylon Tower**.

You may also want to do some shopping while you're in Ontario. Keep it to $300 or less if you want to avoid Customs duties at the border.

Miami
Florida, USA

You can feel the excitement from the moment you arrive. Sure, people live and work here, but there's a sense in the air that they only work as much as they *have* to in order to get back to the beach—and what a beach. The water is crystal clear, it's warm and sunny, and everyone is smiling. Life is good, and Miami is a place to party!

2006 Per Diem Rates: (L) 93–144 ♦ (M&IE) 59

	• Miami International Airport (MIA) – bus connections to Tri-Rail and MetroRail
	• Miami Amtrak Station (MIA) – regional Amtrak service (but not Tri-Rail)
	• 4111 NW 27th St. – Greyhound and regional bus lines
	• Miami Cruise Terminal – Caribbean and Transcanal itineraries

Getting Around

Miami-Dade County operates a light rail service called MetroRail that can take you from Palmetto to South Miami. Service is fairly linear, but MetroRail is supplemented by extensive MetroBus service. Also, the MetroMover, a free automated shuttle, provides service in the downtown area. Getting around isn't a problem.

The Bilingual City

The Cuban exiles that fled to Miami in the 1950s when Fidel Castro came to power were among the wealthiest and most highly educated people in Cuba. Their impact has created a unique culture and a bilingual city where Spanish is an equal counterpart to English, not the language of an impoverished underclass. That's what makes Miami so important as a destination.

For the last fifty years or more, Americans have benefited from overwhelming economic superiority that forced the world to learn English. Those days are fading, and we need to understand the value of speaking several languages. A trip to Miami is helpful, because it's a place where both languages have obvious value. (One might say that Miami is our version of the Canadian city of Montréal.)

Sightseeing

The road running along the waterfront is called **Ocean Drive**, home to an assortment of super-hip clubs, bars, hotels, and restaurants as well as the architecture of the historic **Art Deco District**. You'll probably spend a lot of your time on or around **South Beach**, 23 blocks of white sand and crystal-clear water.

This is the party center of Miami, full of beautiful people with bright-colored sports cars that cost far more than most people will ever have. Drink specials are common throughout the day and most places stay open into the very early hours of the morning.

> You may notice women sunbathing or swimming topless on South Beach. Yes, it's allowed. Remember, it's impolite to stare.

But Miami is more than beaches and nightclubs. The world-acclaimed **Miami City Ballet** and the **Bass Museum of Art** can both be found in the Art Deco District. Downtown, be sure to attend the **Miami Museum of Art** and the **Florida Grand Opera**. Galleries and exhibitions are scattered throughout the city, including the Latin America-themed **Diaspora Vibe Gallery** in the Design District.

Between 12th and 27th Avenues, the road otherwise known as Southwest 8th Street takes on a new identity as **Calle Ocho**, the main thoroughfare of **Little Havana**. See cigars rolled by hand in tabaquerías as you pass. Buy pastries from one of the many bakeries. Spanish is the language of business here, but if you don't speak it, just point.

On the last Friday of every month, the street is packed for **Viernes Culturales**, an exhibition of dancing, artwork, and other cultural symbols. Any other day, you can see a delightful array of artwork at the recently renovated **Tower Art Center**. Gift shops with imported items from Latin America abound with an endless array of food choices available when you get hungry.

For a completely different experience, head to **Everglades National Park**, the largest subtropical wilderness in the country. Join a ranger-led hike through the wetlands, or take an **airboat ride** across the "rivers of grass." Along the way, you may see alligators. If not, you can see thousands of them at the **Everglades Alligator Farm**.

TWO NATIONAL PARKS?

Biscayne National Park is also in Miami, but since it's a marine park, it's almost entirely underwater. There are kayaks and canoes for rent, as well as guided boat rides. During winter and spring, boats are also available to ferry visitors to and from the camping sites on Boca Chita and Elliott Keys.

Without a boat, you'll be limited to the Dante Fascell Visitor Center and the quarter-mile Jetty Trail.

San Antonio
Texas, USA

Texas, the third-largest and second-most populous state in the country, is already a blending of cultures. San Antonio, however, is a point of convergence even for Texas.

In this city, you'll find a mixture of historic and modern architecture and artwork as well as cuisine that blends American and Mexican palates ("Tex-Mex"). Some Spanish is spoken, but San Antonio doesn't feel like a modern bilingual city—the vibe is more of a place that embraces its Mexican influences.

2006 Per Diem Rates: (L) 89–96 ♦ (M&IE) 54

	• San Antonio International Airport (SAT) – Downtown Shuttle and VIA city bus service
	• San Antonio Station (SAS) – Regional Amtrak service
	• 500 N Saint Mary's St. – Greyhound and regional bus lines
	• No cruise ship terminal

Getting Around

Downtown San Antonio is a place to walk. Most of the things you'll want to see are in the same general area with bus service if you get tired. You can also take advantage of the traditionally styled VIA streetcars that operate in the downtown area.

You might want a rental car if you plan to head to the outlying areas of the city. On a trip that spans several days, you can save money by waiting until you're done with downtown before getting the car. Otherwise, you'll merely be paying to park it.

Sightseeing

Downtown San Antonio has a lot to offer within a very short distance. **The Alamo** is located in the heart of downtown, almost comically integrated with the surrounding bustle of shops and traffic.

Exhibits tell the story of how the defenders of this old Spanish mission held off the attacking forces of Mexican General Santa Anna for more than a week. The delay was long enough for General Sam Houston to rally a Texan force to defeat the Mexicans and pave the way for Texas to become a state in 1845—in turn leading to the Mexican-American War.

Walk through **Hemisfair Park**, the site of the 1968 World's Fair, and see the **Tower of the Americas** built for that occasion. If you like, take an elevator ride to the top and enjoy a panoramic view of the city.

The soul of San Antonio is the **Riverwalk**, a narrow canal along which you'll find shops, greenery, and a delightful collection of restaurants featuring American and Mexican cuisine. Enjoy a **canal cruise** through the Riverwalk area or wander on foot, then stop for shopping at the **Riverwalk Mall**.

A quick trip on a VIA streetcar takes you to the **San Antonio Zoo and Aquarium**, open every day of the year and home to a dazzling array of wildlife. Not far away is the **Japanese Tea Garden**, where you can wander among serene pools and lush gardens before stopping to enjoy some of the Garden's signature beverage. Admission is free.

The Hawaiian Islands
USA

Everyone wants to go to Hawaii. Mainlanders save for months or years with the goal of one day taking their dream vacation to the distant tropical state.

Amazingly, when they finally go, most squander their opportunity by staying at an all-inclusive resort. Fortunately, you won't make that mistake. As a Spontaneous Tourist, you want to get the *real* Hawaiian experience, right? Great, because you'll find a *lot* to see and do.

You'll need at least three days to make a trip worthwhile. With four or five—and a willingness to make the time count—you can fit in everything that we'll cover here (including trips to all three islands mentioned).

263

> "Aloha" means both "hello" and "goodbye" in Hawaiian. "Mahalo" means "thank you."

A Plethora of Adventure

There are eight islands that make up Hawaii. Spontaneous Tourists will find the broadest range of flights to Honolulu on the island of Oahu. From there, you can take inter-island flights to Maui or Hawaii (referred to as "the Big Island") for as little as $39 each way. It's usually a little more expensive to visit the other islands—Kauai, Lanai, Molokai, Niihau, and Kahoolawe.

2006 Per Diem Rates: (L) 72–188 ♦ (M&IE) 93–130

- On Oahu, Honolulu International Airport (HNL)
- On Maui, Kahului Airport (OGG)
- On Hawaii, Kona International Airport (KOA) or Hilo International Airport (ITO)

- No rail service to the Hawaiian Islands

- No roads connect to the Hawaiian Islands

- Departure points vary by island; Pacific itineraries
- Inter-island cruises by Norwegian, operated as American-flagged ships

Getting Around

Even on Oahu, bus service is limited outside of Honolulu. In most cases, you'll want a car to get around. Some hostels, like Banana Bungalow on Maui, have their own transportation and offer different trips each day of the week. If those sorts of arrangements are available where you're staying, they can be fun and help you save money, but find out as much as you can in advance.

On the Big Island, tour buses travel to the most popular spots, including Hawaii Volcanoes National Park and the Black Sand Beach. If you want to avoid driving, buying a ticket with one of these companies is your best alternative. Be aware, though, that some secluded spots—like Green Sand Beach—are only reachable with four-wheel drive.

Oahu

When tourists think Hawaii, they're probably thinking of Oahu. This is the most "touristy" of the islands, heavily developed and dominated by military presence. The state capital, Honolulu, is the island's largest city, and every stereotypical Hawaiian theme can be found here (to excess).

Start with **Waikiki** on the southeastern shoreline. The beach is home to resort hotels where luaus are held several times a week—staged, of course, for the benefit of visitors. Wages and housing prices in Hawaii are generally low, but you'll find luxury accommodations and high-end stores lining **Ala Moana Boulevard**.

Head to the north of the island and you'll find **North Shore**, a very different environment with rough seas and adventurous surfers who challenge its waves on a daily basis. When you're ready to eat, try a **plate lunch**—it's a Hawaiian concept that gets you an entrée and a few sides at a cheap price.

You'll have to drive out past the airport to get to the U.S. Naval base at **Pearl Harbor**, site of the Japanese attack that brought America into the Second World War. Come here to see the **U.S.S. Arizona**, the only battleship permanently sunk as a result of the bombing on December 7, 1941. Pearl Harbor is also home to the **U.S.S. Missouri**, the ship that hosted the Japanese surrender that ended World War II.

Oh, and if you need anything—snacks, toothpaste, liquor, souvenirs, postcards, clothing, magazines—stop at one of the 24-hour **ABC Stores** that you'll find on most corners. Prices are reasonable, and the selection is good.

> What mainlanders typically call a "Hawaiian shirt" is properly called an "Aloha shirt," and it's the standard business dress for Hawaii. No matter who you're meeting, an Aloha shirt and khakis will be fine.
>
> Buy at least one while you're here—but be sure to get one actually made in Hawaii!

Maui

A short hop away from Oahu and its money-making tourist attractions is Maui, a much less expensive place that has recently attracted the wealthy elite of the world on its western shores.

Shun **the resorts of Kapalua**, though, and look toward the center of the island near Kahului Airport.

The sleepy town of **Wailuku** has a handful of local restaurants (and one McDonalds), its own stage theatre, and scenery for some great photographs. You'll find Banana Bungalow, a popular travel hostel on Maui, in the town as well.

Makena Beach is not to be missed. It has two parts—the main beach and a secluded clothing-optional one that involves climbing over a rock wall (not nearly as difficult as it sounds). Every evening, there's a **sunset party** on Makena, with hundreds of people who come to dance, sing, and relax. Unlike the luaus of Waikiki, this is a *real* celebration—as popular with the locals as it is with visiting surfers and other tourists.

Three hours from Kahului on the southwest of Maui is **Haleakala National Park**. If you have the time and means to get there, it's a great place to hike and take spectacular photos. Wilderness cabins and camping are also offered.

The Big Island (Hawaii)

Hawaii is by far the largest of the islands in the chain, and it's actually getting bigger each year as new land is created by volcanic activity. Despite a recent tourist boom, most of the island is undeveloped, with the small population focused in two major cities—Hilo, in the northeast, and Kona, on the western shore.

The highlight of a trip to the Big Island is **Hawaii Volcanoes National Park**. Located in the southeast of the island, the Park is open 24 hours a day, features over 150 miles of trails to walk, and is one of the few places in the world where you can see live lava flows. Given its high altitude, weather can get chilly, so bring a jacket.

The Park is nearly 100 miles from Kona but there is ample lodging, including the on-site **Volcano House** and a number of

Bed & Breakfasts in nearby **Volcano Village**. (Travelers coming from Hilo are only 25 miles away.)

What you do at the Park depends on your interests, physical condition, and how much time you have. Tour buses go to all of the major attractions, but it's easiest to get around by car. Start at the Visitor's Center to get your bearings. Next door is the **Volcano Art Museum**. The **Steam Vents** are also nearby.

Probably the best first stop after getting oriented is the **Thurston Lava Tube**, which includes a brief but enjoyable walk through a section of the Hawaiian rain forest. **Crater Rim Drive** offers a half-dozen scenic overlooks from which you can take pictures of dormant volcanic craters as well as landscapes sculpted of hardened lava.

To see the lava flows, follow **Chain of Craters Road** for about 20 miles. When you reach the roadblock, it's a half-mile walk to the end of the road—not because they stopped building it, but because it was covered by lava years ago. At night, you'll be able to see a bright glow on the horizon showing you where the lava is still actively flowing. In daylight, you'll see a massive plume of steam.

The adventurous will decide to hike two miles across the **Lava Delta** to the **Viewing Area**, where you can often see the lava flowing into the ocean. This is the highlight of the Park, but it's not something to be done lightly. If you're planning to make the trip, be prepared for hard trekking.

PREPARING FOR THE LAVA DELTA

The hike from the end of Chain of Craters Road to the Viewing Area is dangerous and requires planning. The terrain is jagged, so you'll need good hiking boots. Hardened lava is similar to glass, so walk carefully and protect yourself against a fall with long pants, a jacket, and gloves. Have a first aid kit to treat any injuries if you do slip.

The lava flow gives off tremendous heat, even at a considerable distance, so as you approach the viewing area, you'll dehydrate rapidly. Bring two or three quarts of water for the trip to stay hydrated. There may also be volcanic gases in the air. The levels of these gases are monitored and the trek is off-limits when they reach high levels, but people with asthma or breathing problems should avoid making this trip.

Bring a good flashlight and extra batteries in case you have to walk back in the dark. There is no lighting beyond the roadblock, and when the sun goes down, you don't want to try to walk across the Delta in darkness.

Never cross a safety rope. New land formed by hardened lava is often unstable and may collapse without warning. The ropes make sure you know where the safe areas are.

Follow these planning tips, and you can have a safe and enjoyable trek.

Less than a mile outside of the park, you'll find tranquil **Volcano Village,** home to a variety of cafés, restaurants, stores, and lodging accommodations. It's a good place to stop if you've got a long drive back to one of the coastal cities.

Beaches on the Big Island are not as well known as those on the other islands, mostly because Hawaii's size means they're farther away. The northeast **Kohala coastline** is where you'll find the tourist beaches and the resorts that go with them, but the real jewels are to be found on the southern coast.

About 25 miles south of Hawaii Volcanoes National Park on Route 11, there's a sign posted for the **Black Sand** (Punalu'u) **Beach**. Famous for the nesting grounds of Hawaiian sea turtles as well as its volcanic sand, Black Sand Beach is frequented by most of the tour companies and surrounded by resort housing. (It actually isn't the only beach with black sand, but it's the most conveniently located.)

If you head farther west along Route 11, you'll see a sign for **South Point,** which is both the southernmost location on Hawaii and by extension the southernmost reach of the United States. Many people see that sign and visit the Point. Far fewer turn left at the end of that road and follow an incredibly rugged dirt track for two or more miles to reach secluded **Green Sand** (Papakolea) **Beach**. You need four-wheel drive and a degree of audacity to reach this beautiful spot.

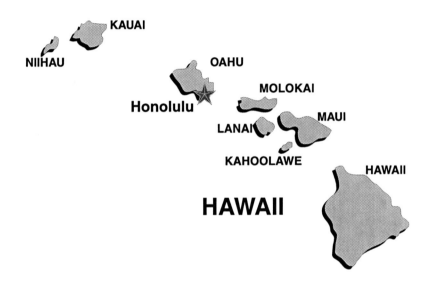

The Hawaiian Islands

Philadelphia
Pennsylvania, USA

Philadelphia, the seat of our nation's power before it was a nation, served as the capital of the United States from 1790–1800. In 1776, the Continental Congress met there to declare independence from Great Britain.

As you wander the streets of "Philly," you'll see beautiful architecture and meet friendly people. This city loves to eat, and you'll find endless opportunities for good food and drink as you indulge in education and entertainment wrapped into one.

2006 Per Diem Rates: (L) 125 ♦ (M&IE) 64

- Philadelphia International Airport (PHL) – direct SEPTA access

- 30th St Station (PHL) – Acela, regional Amtrak service, and SEPTA regional rail; direct subway access

- 1001 Filbert St. – Greyhound and regional bus lines; East Coast Chinatown buses

- Cruise Terminal at Pier 1 – Caribbean and Canadian coastal itineraries

Getting Around

The subway in Philadelphia has two lines, the north-south Broad Street line and the east-west Market-Frankfort line. A trolley covers some of the same area as the subway, and SEPTA regional rail provides access to outlying areas as far as Delaware and New Jersey. High-speed PATCO trains connect Philadelphia to the casinos of Atlantic City.

Numbered streets in Philadelphia run north-south, divided by Market Street. The Schuylkill River flows north-south as well, dividing the city in half at what would otherwise be 28th Street. West of the river, which includes the Amtrak-SEPTA hub, is University City. East of the river is Center City.

Since you can't go to all places using the rail-based transit systems in this city, lots of people rely on the bus system. As a Spontaneous Tourist, you'll find that most places you want to go are reachable by rail or the free PHLASH downtown bus system. This is also a great city to walk around, so you won't need a car.

Sightseeing

The most famous relic in Philadelphia is certainly the **Liberty Bell**, forged in the days before America's existence and now known throughout the world as a symbol for freedom. You can see the historic bell on display in **Independence Hall** after passing through a security screening process.

City Hall sits in the center of Penn Square and is a useful landmark for navigating the city. **Suburban Station**, part of the now-defunct Pennsylvania Railroad, is on one side of the Square. To the West is **Love Park** (also called John F. Kennedy Plaza), home to the city's trademark "Love" sculpture. Take a beautiful walk down the flag-lined Benjamin Franklin Parkway to the **Philadelphia Museum of Art**, made famous by the movie *Rocky* for the 72 steps that lead to its entrance. (It's rather long, so you may prefer to take the PHLASH bus.)

Other museums line the Parkway as well. The **Franklin Institute** is science-focused with a lot of fun hands-on exhibits that deal with electricity and sound. Visit the Rodin Museum, devoted to the works of artist Auguste Rodin, and see his acclaimed **Gates of Hell** sculpture.

South of Penn Square, Broad Street becomes the **Avenue of the Arts**, where you'll encounter many of the city's theatres including the Kimmel Center. Along 9th Street in South Philadelphia, the **Italian Market** offers opportunities to buy fresh produce. There's also **Antique Row** for collectors and hobbyists.

At the intersection of 9th Street and Passyunk Avenue you'll find the two rivals that claim mastery of Philadelphia's most famous food, the cheesesteak. Both **Pat's King of Steaks** and **Geno's** are open 24 hours a day and have lines almost constantly. Specify American, Provolone, or Cheese Whiz, and order your cheesesteak "wit" (with onions) or "witout" (no onions). You'll pay around $7, but it's an experience no visitor should miss. (**Gianna's Grille,** two blocks off South Street at 6th Street, offers a cheesesteak for vegetarians.)

Shopping is as much a pastime in Philly as eating. East of Penn Square is **The Gallery at Market East**, the nation's largest downtown shopping complex. If that doesn't impress you, the vast **Plaza and Court of King of Prussia** is the country's largest shopping complex and is reachable by connecting bus. Unless you're an avid shopper, you can probably skip that on a short visit. Instead, browse the locally owned shops on **South Street**.

Across the Delaware River, Camden, New Jersey, has the **Adventure Aquarium** where you can pet stingrays and swim with sharks. It's also where you'll find the Navy's most decorated battleship, the **U.S.S. New Jersey**. If you've got time for a day trip to Camden, you can take the RiverLink ferry from Penn's Landing or get there via the PATCO train system from Center City.

The U.S.S. New Jersey is an Iowa-class battleship, the same class as the U.S.S. Missouri anchored in Hawaii at Pearl Harbor. See both if you can, but if Camden is more reachable than Honolulu, take advantage.

The **Philadelphia Zoo** is north of University City, not far from the Museum of Art but on the opposite side of the Schuylkill River. Enjoy breathtaking views from 400 feet in the air on the **Zooballoon®**, then check out the new big cat exhibit that opened in May 2006 with nearly twenty endangered felines, including snow leopard, puma, and black jaguar cubs. Unfortunately, there hasn't been trolley service to the Zoo since December 1995, but several bus routes can take you, so make it part of your trip.

Las Vegas
Nevada, USA

Glitz, glamour, neon lights, and spectacular shows, all set to the sound of slot machines—that's Las Vegas. While many have imitated it, the gambling capital of the United States has never been duplicated.

Coming to Las Vegas isn't just about gambling, though most people do gamble at least a little. You need to experience the place, because this is one of America's "fun towns," a place we can go to unwind. It wouldn't work if enacted on a large scale—but having *one* Las Vegas works quite well.

	2006 Per Diem Rates: (L) 99–112 ♦ (M&IE) 64
	• McCarran International Airport (LAS)—bus and taxi service
	• Las Vegas Station (LSV) – Regional Amtrak service
	• 200 South Main St. – Greyhound and regional bus lines; West Coast Chinatown buses
	• No cruise ship terminal

Getting Around

You don't need a car to get around Las Vegas. There are taxi, shuttle, and limousine services at the airports, and "The Strip"—where most of the main casinos are located—has a variety of light rail systems to maximize your support of the local economy.

GAMBLING IN LAS VEGAS

Whatever people think, casino games are rarely "rigged." There's no need—in all cases, the fair rules of the game give the House (the casino) an advantage.

If you're good, you can shave that advantage down to the point where your odds are worth the effort. If you're lucky, you can come out ahead. Make no mistake, though—if you keep playing long enough, you'll lose. Just because you've lost ten times in a row doesn't mean you can't lose next time as well. Probability doesn't work that way.

It's easy to lose control in Las Vegas. Don't gamble to make money. Don't keep playing to "get even." If you win big, congratulations—it does happen—but assume you'll lose everything you're willing to bet, and stick to that limit.

The Vegas Experience

The main tourist attractions in Las Vegas are the casinos. Much more than just places to gamble, they're lavish resorts that cost hundreds of millions of dollars to build. Each is unique in theme and style, from Egyptian designs at the Luxor to the Venetian's Italian canals. Some are newer than others, some flashier, some more refined.

Inside, you'll find fast food, four-star restaurants, and mid-level cafés. Most have buffets. (Confusingly, most buffets advertise that they've been voted the best in Vegas, but they're all pretty good.) Each casino also has its own signature shows, such as the Round Table fantasy dinner theater at the Excalibur, as well as seasonal and fixed-set performances by musicians, comedians, and other celebrities.

There was a time when food in Las Vegas was very cheap, but no longer. On the other hand, gamblers get free drinks at most casinos, regardless of what or how much they play. Just ask one of the waitresses wandering around the floor.

Traditionally, the big-time casinos have all been located on or very near **The Strip** in the heart of the city. Recently, there's been a move toward building casinos that are outside the main urban area. The advantages to casino owners of building "off the Strip" is that there's a lot more space, land prices are much cheaper, and—most importantly—patrons are less likely to leave. These casinos are fabulous resorts—but to get the Vegas Experience, you'll want to be on The Strip.

You'll be able to carry around your drinks from place to place, since there are none of the open container laws you find in most cities. Contrary to popular belief, however, prostitution—legal elsewhere in Nevada—is *not* legal in Las Vegas. It clashes with the family-friendly theme that casinos are trying to portray these days.

Key West
Florida, USA

In 1982, the Government decided to establish a checkpoint at the top of the Florida Keys to search for smuggled drugs. Key West residents, annoyed that they were required to cross a border within their own country, registered a protest by declaring their independence as the Conch Republic—then surrendering one minute later.

Despite their relatively short period of formal independence (though you can still find Conch Republic souvenirs everywhere), the people of Key West are noticeably different from other Florida residents. Most people imagine Key West to be a party spot like Miami, but, in fact, it's a sleepy little fishing town except for the few times each year when people come from out of town to cut loose.

2006 Per Diem Rates: (L) 132–200 ♦ (M&IE) 64

✈	• Key West International Airport (KEY) – rental car and limited taxi service
🚂	• No rail service to Key West
🚌	• 3535 S Roosevelt Blvd. – Greyhound and regional bus lines
⛴	• Truman Annex –Caribbean itineraries

There are no open container laws here, and the locals are more interested in fishing, snorkeling, and relaxing than anything else. Relax, enjoy fresh seafood, and listen to the music.

Getting Around

The main road in Key West goes around the perimeter of the island. The eastern side is where you'll find most of the chain stores for groceries and fast food, while everywhere else you'll find local shops and bars.

Even though the island is only three miles wide, you'll want to have some sort of vehicle. If not a car, maybe rent a bicycle or motor scooter. The Conch Train, an old-fashioned trolley system, is also effective for touring the island.

Sightseeing

Most of the Key West experience is *being* in Key West with its endless opportunities for **diving** and **fishing**. The tourist highlights include the **Southernmost Point**, which marks the limits of the continental United States 90 miles from Cuba. (It's poorly maintained, but people still have photos taken in front of the garishly-painted marker.)

Enjoy fresh seafood at a seaside restaurant, and be sure to sample the **conch chowder**, which is made with imported conch due to over-fishing of the domestic stock. See the spectacular **sunset** from Mallory Square dock, then head down to **Duval Street** to shop and check out the nightlife. Be sure to check out the **Hogsbreath Saloon**, a local landmark.

San Diego
California, USA

It's hard to say what's so great about San Diego. Ask just about anyone who's been there, though, and you'll get a wistful sigh and a comment about how much they loved it. Located at the bottom of California, just across the border from Mexico, San Diego has it all—a dreamlike climate, gorgeous beaches, and a friendly atmosphere.

2006 Per Diem Rates: (L) 120–127 ♦ (M&IE) 64

	• San Diego International Airport – Lindbergh Field (SAN) – direct bus service
	• Santa Fe Station (SAN) – Amtrak service (Pacific Surfrider); direct trolley access
	• 120 W Broadway – Greyhound and regional bus lines; West Coast Chinatown buses
	• Cruise Ship Terminal – Pacific, Mexican Riviera, and Transcanal itineraries

Getting Around

San Diego's Metropolitan Transit System (MTS) is made up of the typical commuter bus network and a system of high-speed trolleys. Since you can transfer between the two for free, they operate as a single system. MTS can get you just about anywhere you want to go, even to the Mexican border.

Of course, many places in the city are best explored on foot, including the Gaslamp Quarter and Old Town. The mild San

Diegan climate makes walking a pleasant experience even during the winter months. If you get tired, taxis are easy to find.

San Diego is one place where it's fairly easy to find parking, even downtown. If you plan to drive to Mexico, however, let the rental company know. Some companies don't allow it, and if yours doesn't and something happens to the car, you'll be held liable for its entire cost.

Sightseeing

The **San Diego Zoo** is widely regarded as the best in America, so you'll want to be sure that it's high on your list. The trip also gives you a chance to try out the MTS trolley and bus system.

You'll need between four and six hours to see everything in the main zoo, including the giant pandas and polar bears. From there, you can take MTS about 35 miles north to the 1800-acre **Wild Animal Park**, where you'll have a chance to see lions, elephants, and other safari wildlife in a natural habitat.

The **Gaslamp Quarter**, a short walk from downtown, is the home of San Diego's trendy nightlife. As the sun disappears, crowds arrive to enjoy the hundreds of restaurants, bars, and clubs. If you want to get a table for dinner, a reservation is a good idea. There's also **HillCrest**, San Diego's Gay and Lesbian neighborhood, which has an eclectic mix of restaurants, coffeehouses, shopping and nightlife.

On the Bay, you'll find the floating **Maritime Museum** and an opportunity to tour several old-fashioned tall ships as well as a Soviet-era diesel submarine. Take the trolley north to **Old Town** for authentic Mexican restaurants, and shop for high-quality crafts in the market.

Five minutes farther north is beautiful **Pacific Beach** with its historic **Crystal Pier** and a hotel that puts you directly over the ocean. Pacific Beach is where you'll find Mission Bay Park and the world-famous **Sea World** adventure park. It's also home to the hottest beach bars in southern California.

Unlike beaches on the East Coast, the beaches in southern California allow fires as long as they're built in fire rings. It can be tough to find one of the rings during the summer, but other than that, you just need to be sure to put it out before you leave.

Traveling to Baja

San Diego isn't far from the Mexican border, and lots of people who come to this city take the opportunity to cross into Baja and visit **Tijuana**. It's a great chance to take a quick international trip, and it's easy—the Blue Line trolley goes all the way to the border at the San Ysidro-Tijuana station.

CROSSING THE BORDER

Americans don't need visas to visit Mexico for 72 hours or less. Starting in 2007, though, we'll be phasing in requirements for passports at border crossings. You'll need a passport for all international travel effective January 1, 2008.

Tijuana is a great place to shop for Mexican cigars, leather goods, and other local merchandise as well as the usual souvenirs. Bring cash and avoid using the ATM, which charges conversion fees. You don't need pesos, because the vendors accept U.S. dollars. Oh, and haggling is encouraged. Above all, have fun!

Juneau
Alaska, USA

With a population of fewer than 40,000, this small town in Southeastern Alaska is known as the country's most scenic state capital. Nestled between the waters of Alaska's Inside Passage and coastal mountains, surrounded by the Tongass National Forest, Juneau is unreachable by any highway, instead welcoming its travelers by air and sea (plus the occasional dogsled).

Tourism is the backbone of the economy here, and you'll find all of the comforts of modern civilization. Just being here, you can't help but get a sense of the pioneer spirit that was—and still is—required to live in this spectacular place that we call Alaska.

2006 Per Diem Rates: (L) 69–189 ♦ (M&IE) 55–107

✈	• Juneau International Airport (JUN) – bus service
🚂	• No rail service to Juneau
🚌	• No roads connect to Juneau
⛴	• Franklin St Cruise Terminal – Alaskan Inside Passage and Northern Tier itineraries

When to Visit

Peak season for tourists in Juneau is during July, but you'll find it a bustling place from May through September, when cruise ships arrive in port on an almost-daily basis. During this time of year, it's warm enough to wear shorts, and everything that Juneau has to offer will be open, including shops, restaurants, and other attractions.

Beginning in October, the cruise ships stop coming, and Juneau settles in for its relatively long winter. You can still wander as you like, because even by the end of October, it's still in the low 30s on average, but most of the places that cater to tourists will be closed. That isn't necessarily a bad thing, but it's something you need to know before you plan your trip.

Getting Around

Juneau's bus system is called Capital Transit. Fares are $1.50 and there are local and express routes between the downtown area, Auke Bay, and the Mendenhall Valley. The bus doesn't go all of the way to the Glacier, but it's only a mile and a half from the closest stop.

Spontaneous Tourists will find the bus to be a cost-effective way to explore Juneau, but there are other options, including taxi-vans and rental cars. During the tourist season, guided tours are also available.

Sightseeing

From the moment you step off the plane or ship that brings you to Juneau, you'll be overwhelmed by natural beauty. Majestic mountains shrouded in soft mist accentuate the rustic look of local buildings, creating endless opportunities for memorable photos.

You'll take plenty of pictures while you're here, of course, but start with a trip to **Centennial Hall**, which houses the Tourism Center. The helpful staff will recommend things for you to see based on your interests and how much time you have. Then, head next door to the **State Museum** and learn about Alaska's rich history, or visit the **City Museum** next to the State Capitol on Main Street.

Wander along Main Street, up Front Street, and onto Franklin Street, stopping into any of the **downtown shops** that catch your interest. Besides the usual souvenirs, **original Alaskan art** is also available, including carvings made from whale bone and mammoth ivory. Stop into the **Red Dog Saloon** to see Wyatt Earp's pistol on display and enjoy local Alaskan ale, then continue down along the waterfront.

> The Red Dog is a historic landmark that also serves to mark the border of "tourist country." The shops past this point are either owned by folks from "Down South"—the Alaskan term for the lower 48 states—or meant only for tourists, so they won't be open outside of the tourist season.

Just beyond the cruise ship dock, you'll find the **Mount Roberts Tramway**. For around $25, you can take the tram to the top of the mountain. The 360-degree panoramic view afforded by the loop trail at the top makes this a particularly good deal on a clear day. There's also a restaurant on the mountain where you can have lunch.

BEAR ETIQUETTE

Black bears are native to the Juneau area, and from time to time, you may see one—usually out near the glacier, though it's not unknown for them to come into town on occasion.

The natural inclination when you see a wild animal may be to appear calm and unthreatening. If you feel threatened, you may even be inclined to run. Neither of these is the right choice when dealing with a bear. Bears are predators, and they chase prey. If you run, you're identifying yourself as prey.

What you need to do is make it clear to the bear that you are, in fact, a human—the top land predator in the world, a creature to be feared and avoided. Talk, wave your arms, and make noise. Back away from the bear slowly, and don't turn around. Once you're out of the bear's sight, it's a good plan to steer clear of that area.

Much of Juneau's history involves the mining industry, which was responsible for its original boom and remains part of the town's modern economy. The **Last Chance Mining Museum** and the **Thane Ore House** offer a look into the hard work that built so many American cities. (The Ore House has the added benefit of a nightly salmon and halibut bake.) You can also take the **Juneau Steamship** from Marine Park and experience a real steam engine in operation.

When you've finished with all of these manmade attractions, it's time to head to the one that was here before the town—the **Mendenhall Glacier**. The closest bus stop is Dredge Lake, from which it's less than two miles to the visitor center. The walk is beautiful, with the road surrounded on both sides by the **Tongass National Forest**, which you may be surprised to learn is a temperate rain forest.

Once you arrive, stop into the visitor's center, then enjoy the spectacular view of the Glacier. With its miles of hiking trails, you can walk for hours, but keep an eye on the time. Part of the road isn't lit, so if you came by bus, you want to be back down to the part that is before it gets dark.

Puerto Rico
USA

The United States laid claim to Puerto Rico at the end of the Spanish-American War and granted U.S. citizenship to its people in 1917. It was governed as a non-incorporated territory until 1951, when Puerto Ricans approved a referendum to draft their own constitution. The island became a self-governing commonwealth on July 24 of that year.

Contrary to what most mainlanders assume, there's little sentiment in Puerto Rico for independence, which was offered—and rejected—in 1951. Today, pro-independence parties in Puerto Rico poll less than 5% of the vote. The real debate is over whether the island should remain a commonwealth or become America's 51st state.

2006 Per Diem Rates: (L) 62–195 ♦ (M&IE) 57–75

	• San Juan Luis Munoz Marin International Airport (SJU)
	• No rail service to Puerto Rico
	• No roads connect to Puerto Rico
	• San Juan Cruise Ship Terminal – Caribbean itineraries

No Passport Required

American citizens traveling to Puerto Rico aren't leaving U.S. soil and don't need passports. Foreign travelers will need to complete the same paperwork and visa requirements as they would to visit the U.S. mainland.

> Puerto Rico is by far the most accessible of the Caribbean islands, making it a popular stop with short flights available to other destinations. Except for trips to the U.S. Virgin Islands, though, you'll need your passport to do that.

Getting Around

The Metropolitan Bus Authority (AMA) operates an extensive public bus network in San Juan. There's also the Tren Urbano, a light rail system that's intended to connect 16 stations throughout the area though its actual implementation has been plagued by cost overruns and delays. Save time by using the plentiful taxis called *publicos* to get around. Fares are shared among the passengers, so having more people makes it cheaper.

If you plan to explore outside of the city, you'll need a rental car, which will cost you more than you'd pay in most mainland cities. Think carefully before passing up the liability damage insurance, because Puerto Ricans are aggressive drivers by U.S. standards. Merging is extremely competitive, horns are blown constantly, and lane markers are more like recommendations than hard rules. You'll also encounter road signs in Spanish and distances measured in kilometers.

One thing that you'll notice immediately is that police almost always have their light bars on when they're driving. Do your best to ignore it. You only need to move out of the way if you hear their sirens.

CAR SAFETY IN PUERTO RICO

Theft is very common here. Don't leave valuables in your trunk, which an experienced thief can open in seconds. Many people leave their cars empty and unlocked to avoid damage.

In some outlying areas, there are also problems with car-jacking. If you approach a red light at night in a secluded area, it's legal (and recommended) to slow down, pause, and then continue without waiting for the light to change.

Sightseeing in San Juan

The capital of Puerto Rico is located on the island's northeastern shore. **Old San Juan**, founded in 1521, immerses you in restored 17th-century Spanish architecture. Streets are paved with gray stone, and everything has an artistic flair. The **Plaza de Armas**, the main square of the old city, is flanked by four statues representing the seasons, while a bronze statue of city founder Ponce de Leon can be found in the center of the **Plaza de San Jose**.

Built during a period of unrelenting warfare, much of the old city's architecture has a military purpose. The six-story tall coastal fort known as **El Morro** offers an exceptional view of San Juan Bay to accord its long-gone cannons the ability to fire on attacking ships in the 1700s. The **Castillo de San Cristóbal**, completed in 1771, is one of the largest fortifications built in the Western Hemisphere. Even the Governor's Mansion, **La Fortaleza**, was originally built to be a fortress.

San Juan offers more than historic sites with a dozen museums, including the **San Juan Museum of Art and History**. Concerts, plays, and operas are performed at the **Centro de Bellas Artes** (Fine Arts Center). There are several exceptional beaches and a number of casinos, including the flashy **Ritz-Carlton Casino** on the Avenue of Governors. Many of the nightclubs and hotel bars are open all night, especially in the tourism-focused areas of

Condado and neighboring Isla Verde, and you'll find an array of tempting restaurants and cafés to fit any budget.

Sightseeing outside of San Juan

Puerto Rico isn't a large island, and if you have a rental car, you can see a lot in a relatively short period of time. In general, Spontaneous Tourists will want to make San Juan and its vicinity the scope of one weekend trip and save trips around the island for a separate trip.

Rio Camuy Cave Park is in the northwest, near Arecibo. The park covers 300 acres above ground, but its highlight is the underground network of caves that includes one of the longest subterranean rivers in the world. On the west coast, you'll find the tiny town of **Rincón**, where surfers come to enjoy world-class waves. In the south is **Ponce**, Puerto Rico's second largest city.

Sightseeing on the Spanish Virgin Islands

Four islands and a number of smaller cays sit off the coast of Puerto Rico, collectively known as the Spanish Virgin Islands even though their status today is Puerto Rican and thus U.S. territory. **Culebra** is the most developed, with only a handful of restaurants and some seaside villas. Its **Playa Flamenco** is considered one of the most beautiful beaches in the world.

Vieques, once the site of a U.S. Navy proving ground, is now being rediscovered along with a number of unspoiled beaches, including popular **Sun Bay**. Wild horses are more commonly seen than cars on most parts of the island. **Mosquito Bay** is a magical place that glows with the organic light of single-celled creatures called dinoflagellates. Recently restored **Isabel Segunda**, the last fort built by the Spanish in the Western Hemisphere, houses the **Vieques Museum of Art and History**.

Daily flights and a fast ferry service run to both Culebra and Vieques from San Juan.

WHAT ABOUT THE OTHER ISLANDS?

Off the west coast, **Mona** is small and uninhabited except for people who bring their own boats over for day picnics.

Visitors aren't permitted on **Cayo Santiago,** home to scientists studying imported monkeys, but boats often cruise by to watch the monkeys play.

Puerto Rico and the U.S. Virgin Islands

PLENTY MORE TO SEE!

Beyond the 16 destinations profiled in this chapter, the United States has thousands of other places worth seeing. Don't limit yourself to the places we covered here.

Go to Los Angeles and see Hollywood, or take the train to Glacier National Park in Montana and enjoy the serenity of nature. Wander Boston, Seattle, or Houston, and then see a revitalized Columbus, Ohio. Gear up for the long flights to Asia by visiting the exotic U.S. territory of Guam, often overlooked even by frequent travelers—or stop by equally forgotten small towns in the Appalachian mountains of West Virginia.

Get out and travel. Grab a discounted weekend airfare or take advantage of special rates on Amtrak and Greyhound. With so much to do in America, the only real mistake is sitting at home. When you're ready, there's an even bigger world out there waiting for you.

"You can't cross the sea merely by standing and staring at the water."
—Rabindranath Tagore

CHAPTER **12**

Travel Abroad

Foreign Destinations for Spontaneous Tourists

For all of the wonders you can find in the United States, the real discovery comes when you cross national borders. Attitudes, customs, and laws vary widely around the world, and many things that you take for granted at home may be very different. One thing that's fairly consistent is that people tend to be friendly toward visitors. They appreciate that outsiders are interested in learning about their history and culture.

Travel is the ultimate educational experience. When we travel, we gain insight into the world and the lives of others while at the same time learning about ourselves. It's impossible to become fully immersed in a culture in a few days, but that's okay. Spontaneous Tourists don't claim to be experts—only that they have a better grasp of things than their less-traveled counterparts who stay at home and assume that everyone in the world thinks the way they do.

INTERNATIONAL DESTINATION PROFILES

You've traveled America, and now you're ready to venture out into the broader world. Passport in hand, you wonder where to start. Choosing your first international destination is thrilling, but it can be a little intimidating as well, because there's a lot riding on your choice.

A good time abroad means you'll want to go again. If you have a bad time, however, your first trip may be your only trip. With that in mind, I've picked eight destinations outside of the United States that I consider perfect for new Spontaneous Tourists. They represent a diverse array of cultures and are places you'll enjoy, have fun, and learn a lot without feeling too confused.

What's in an International Profile?

There's a lot to do in these places. You could easily spend a week or more visiting without seeing everything—if you had time. Spontaneous Tourism assumes that you don't, so each profile gives you a snapshot of a destination. We cover the airports that serve each destination and include the three-letter codes that you can use to make reservations with your favorite airline. Also look for information on the local languages, currency, and whether train, bus, and cruise ship service is available.

Each profile includes a cost estimate from the U.S. Government along with a short list of things to see and do during your visit. If you're particularly adventurous, this might be enough for you (especially in the English-speaking locales). As with the domestic profiles, however, these aren't meant to be or replace guidebooks. The goal is to give you a sense of why you should go and what to expect.

Cost Estimates

The U.S. Department of State publishes foreign Per Diem (daily) rates on an annual basis. These rates are a helpful way to compare average costs as long as you remember that they're intended for business travelers, who stay in mid-range hotels and eat three meals in restaurants each day.

The 2007 Per Diem rates are separated into lodging (L) and what the Government calls "meals and incidental expenses" (M&IE). The incidental expense rate varies by country and is usually substantial, because many products and services cost more overseas.

> It's a real challenge to exceed the foreign Per Diem rate on food, and it's not difficult to find lodging that costs less. Don't let what may look like high Per Diem rates keep you from traveling.

You can get the current Per Diem rates online from several sources, but the most convenient source is *https://secureapp2.hqda.pentagon.mil/perdiem*. The interactive menus at the Pentagon site give you one source to reference data for both domestic and international destinations.

PER DIEM AND TAX RECORDS

On overseas business travel, as with domestic trips, you may be able to claim the Per Diem M&IE rate for your host country instead of keeping individual receipts for all meals and incidental expenses. Be sure to consult your tax preparer for detailed information.

Budgeting Time

Finding time to travel is always difficult, but people are particularly resistant to traveling overseas for brief periods. The thinking is, why take a long trip to spend a short time in-country?

This point seems valid but can quickly become self-defeating. Can you afford to spend a week or two in Paris? If you're a student or recent graduate, you may not have the money. Working professionals, on the other hand, probably don't have the time. If every trip has to wait until you can spare ten days, you won't take many trips.

Spontaneous Tourism is about experiencing new places, not relocating to them. Forget for a moment how far you're traveling and imagine it's an American city. You'd go to New York for the weekend, so why not London? Travel time makes a trip to Asia a four-day minimum, but you don't need a month.

Look for cheap fares. Leave after work. Fly overnight and get back early on Monday morning. Be creative. Do whatever it takes. But find a way to go, or you'll only look back at a lifetime of regrets for what might have been.

London
United Kingdom (Europe)

Americans always enjoy going to London. There's a lot to see, it's easy to get around, and while you'll definitely know you're in another country, the similarities of language and culture keep it from getting uncomfortable. Of course, it's the similarities that make the differences stand out, and seeing London demonstrates that the way that we do things in America isn't the only way that they can be done.

2007 Per Diem Rates: (L) 307 ♦ (MI&E) 173	
Languages: English (official)	
Currency: Pound Sterling (£)	**Visa: No, up to 6 months**

- Heathrow International Airport (LHR) – direct Underground access, Heathrow Express train service to London
- Gatwick International Airport (LGW) – direct National Rail access, Gatwick Express train service to London
- Stansted Airport (STN; hub for European low-cost carriers) – direct bus access, Stansted Express train service to London

- Paddington Station – National Rail service; direct Underground access

- Victoria Coach Station, 164 Buckingham Palace Rd – National Express, Eurolines, and several dozen other lines with service to Britain, Ireland, and Europe

- London Cruise Terminal – Icelandic, Scandinavian, British Isles, and Baltic itineraries

Getting Around

You'll find the London Underground—a large-scale subway system commonly called the Tube—to be a fast and reliable way to get around. It doesn't go everywhere, but it can get you at least close to most places, and it's fairly affordable by London standards. Fares are based on origin and destination, or you can buy a daily pass (highly recommended) that makes things a lot less complicated.

When you leave a Tube station, follow the signs that say "Way Out." The term "Exit" is not nearly as popular in Britain as in the United States.

MIND THE GAP!

In the United States, it's commonly understood that there's a space between the edge of a train and the edge of the platform at which it stops. Apparently, even after decades, this is still news to Londoners, as the train operators give a helpful reminder to "mind the gap" whenever the train stops. It's become a cultural phenomenon, and you can even get merchandise with the slogan.

Buses of all shapes and sizes, many of them red two-level designs, carry people throughout London every day. People are much more willing to take the bus in London than in the United States, perhaps in part because gasoline is so expensive.

Taxis are available throughout the city as well, though you may not immediately recognize them. They're black, not yellow or other bright colors as they would be in most U.S. cities.

Planning to drive? You can rent a car with a U.S. driver's license, but if you're staying in London, it's not recommended. Rental cars are very expensive, petrol (gasoline) will cost you around $7 per gallon, parking is tricky, and it's no minor skill to adjust to drive on the *left* side of the road from the *right* side of the car. If you're driving into London, you may also have to pay a congestion tax of £8 (around $16).

It's a lot easier if you're heading out of the city, because most roads are divided and traffic circles are more common than intersections. Even then, be careful to stay to the left and pass on the right, and remember that different countries have different styles for their road signs.

Sightseeing

Walking around London can get confusing, so it's convenient that many of the famous sites are close to Tube stations. **London Bridge** is very photogenic, and you can walk across it on your way to or from the **Tower of London**, which houses the crown jewels of the British royal family. Take the guided tour led by one of the Beefeaters—it's very entertaining.

The **British Museum** offers visitors an astonishing array of artifacts, including the famed Rosetta Stone and a collection of Egyptian mummies. If time allows, it's also worth taking a tour of **Windsor Castle**, or just exploring the shops that surround the famous royal residence.

The English aren't known for their culinary skill, and much of the local fare is rather tasteless to an American palate, but there's some good food to be had. Stop in an **English pub** for a steak and kidney pie or a plate of fish and chips. Drinking is much more entertaining, with popular drink choices including light British ales like Stella Artois as well as some excellent bitters.

Wait until nighttime to visit **Piccadilly Circus**, an entertainment district in the downtown area. The only thing that I've seen similar in look and feel to its neon splendor is Times Square in New York City, and even so, it's quite different. Wander through nearby **Soho** to find the densest concentration of clubs, cafés, bars, and restaurants in London.

GATEWAY TO EUROPE

Flying to London from the United States is among the cheapest of international flights, with most domestic carriers offering special rates on a regular basis. More than just giving Americans ample opportunities to visit London, these flights also give Americans a cheap way to visit the rest of Europe.

Like the United States, Europe has an array of low-cost carriers, including EasyJet, German Wings, and the famed discount Irish airline RyanAir. These carriers take no-frills to a new level, but most fly out of London-Stansted Airport. With low-cost flights starting around $15, Europe is easier to reach than you think.

Montréal
Canada (North America)

Canada and the United States share a border and a great deal of history. In fact, Canada and the United States are so similar that at first glance, the differences are barely noticeable—unless, of course, you visit the province of Quebec, famous for its separatist attitude and use of French as its official language.

Located in Quebec, Montréal is the second-largest French-speaking city in the world. Americans who visit will discover a gracefully bilingual city with a unique blend of familiar and foreign culture and all the charm of Europe, without having to travel too far from home.

2007 Per Diem Rates: (L) 212 ♦ (M&IE) 128
Languages: French (official), English (common)

Currency: Canadian Dollar (CAN$)   **Visa: No**

- Montréal-Trudeau International Airport (YUL; commonly called Dorval Airport) – shuttles to station centrale d'autobus

- Montréal Gare centrale (MTR) – VIA Rail Canada and Amtrak service; adjacent Métro access

- Station centrale d'autobus, 505 boul. de Maisonneuve est – Greyhound and Orleans Express service; adjacent Métro access

- Montréal Cruise Terminal – Eastern Canadian and New England itineraries

---

BONJOUR! HOW MAY I HELP YOU?

Most people in Montréal speak both French and English. French is prevalent, so you're typically greeted with "Bonjour!" The conversation will continue seamlessly in English if you respond with "Hello!"

This friendly and accommodating attitude is one reason Montréal makes such a great destination for Spontaneous Tourists just getting started in their international travels.

Getting Around

Montréal has an established subway system called the Métro, which operates similarly to the subway of the same name in Washington, D.C. Announcements and instructions are made in French, but it's easy enough to tell what's happening. There's also an extensive bus network that goes anywhere the Métro doesn't provide service.

Between the Métro and the buses, you certainly don't need a car to get around Montréal. Travelers who decide to bring a car, though, will find it easy to navigate the streets and find parking.

Sightseeing

The oldest building in Montréal is **Séminaire de St-Sulpice**, which was built by arriving priests in 1657. Next door to it is the **Basilique Notre-Dame**, a cathedral that holds 4000 people. Montréal has nearly two dozen museums, including the **Musée McCord d'Histoire Canadienne** for those interested in the history of Quebec Province and the excellent **Musée des Beaux-Arts** for fine art. The **Musée d'Art Contemporain de Montréal** caters to more modern tastes. Visitors with just a day or two, however, may prefer to skip all of the museums on this trip.

McGill University is set in the middle of Vieux Montréal, and its campus provides a lovely place to walk. Climb the hill to **Parc du Mont Royal** and enjoy a panoramic view of the city as well as the campus below.

At the waterfront, **the Quays of the Old Port** reflect the revitalization of what used to be a gloomy wharf. In the summer, harbor cruises and jet-boating call to passersby, while visitors during the cold months can enjoy an ice rink and get drinks from the innovative outdoor **Winter Bar**. At the end of the King George Pier is the **Montréal Science Center**, filled with hands-on science exhibits.

Visible from the port is **La Biosphère**, the geodesic dome pictured at the top of this profile. Perhaps Montréal's most distinctive landmark, it was designed to be a sealed environment but lost its acrylic skin in a 1976 fire and served no purpose until 1995 when an environmental museum was built inside the sphere. Even now, it's interesting but not worth going out of your way to see it.

The similarly named **Biodôme** is an entirely different matter. Adjacent to the **Stade Olympique** built to host the 1976 Olympic Games, it contains four different ecosystems—woodland, aquatic, rain forest, and polar. Each environment is populated with plants and animals appropriate for it and even experiences changing seasons!

Also located near the Olympic Park complex is the **Jardin Botanique**, spanning 185 acres and several cultures. Large greenhouses keep tropical plants safe from the chill of Canadian winters. The largest **Chinese Garden** outside of Asia and a 15-acre **Japanese Garden** with bonsai and a tearoom can be found here.

Wander down **rue Crescent** if you're in the mood for shopping. The downtown area is where you'll find most of the nightlife, though plenty of adorably trashy music spots can be found in the **Quartier Latin**. Last call for drinks is at 3:00 a.m., and most clubs will be open until then.

Sydney
Australia

Australia and the United States were both initially colonized by people unwelcome in Britain—Puritans in the case of America, convicts with regard to Australia. Though each culture has developed in its own way, our histories continue to mimic one another in many ways, making Australia as much a look inward as a trip to another country.

2007 Per Diem Rates: (L) 160 ♦ (M&IE) 130	
Languages: English (official)	
Currency: Australian Dollar (AU$)	**Visa: Yes**

	• Sydney Kingsford-Smith International Airport (SYD) – direct CityRail access
	• Central Railway Station – Rail Australia service; direct CityRail access
	• Coach Terminal, Central Railway Station – Greyhound Pioneer, Firefly Express, McCafferty's, and Murrays Australia service; direct CityRail access
	• Circular Quay – Asia, Pacific, and Oceania itineraries

The "Land Down Under" is a fascinating place of contrasts. It's a continent unto itself, two-thirds the size of the United States and covering nearly three million square miles. Yet, much of that landscape is among the harshest in the world with limited population and home to deadly wildlife like saltwater crocodiles. The major cities, meanwhile, are arrayed along the coastline around the continent and offer some of the finest beaches in the Pacific.

Sydney, on the eastern coast of Australia, is a particularly popular destination for travelers. Consumerism thrives, making the feel of the place familiar for Americans. At the same time, you'll notice differences in both attitude and merchandise (including the McOz sandwich sold at McDonalds).

This is a great place to see, one you'll really enjoy even if you're only able to come for a few days.

JET LAG, AUSTRALIA STYLE

Australia is a long way from the United States—and just about everywhere else, too. A flight from the East Coast will take around 30 hours. To further complicate the trip, you'll cross the International Date Line en route, which moves time ahead by one day on the trip out and back by one day when you return.

This bizarre time effect means that you might leave for Sydney on Thursday evening and arrive Saturday morning—but if your return flight was late Monday morning, you'd be back by early Monday afternoon. Use this to your advantage. Arrive in the early morning, sleep the last eight hours of the flight, and hit the ground running.

Getting Around

It's extremely easy to get around Sydney, thanks to a number of extensive and convenient mass transit systems. CityRail train service is a form of heavy rail, with double-tier cars that move more quietly than you'd expect and can get you around the city as well as from the airport to the downtown main station or Circular Quay. There's also a monorail system that connects portions of Sydney in the Darling Harbour area.

> If you're going to want to see it all, there's a cheap daily pass that gives you unlimited use of the ferry as well as the train. The Monorail isn't included in this ticket.

Staying in Sydney

Backpacking is very popular among Australians. In fact, it's not uncommon for students to take as much as a year off after graduation to travel. You'll easily find a dozen travel hostels just by wandering around, and the rates are very cheap. Given the relatively high price of a plane ticket to Australia (even discounted) the availability of cheap lodging can help to make your stay more affordable. Keep that in mind, because the important thing isn't where you stay but that you come at all.

STUDENTS HAVE IT MADE HERE!

The International Student Identification Card (ISIC) that we covered in Chapter 7 is a huge benefit in Australia, where just about everything has a special student concession rate.

Sightseeing

You can see the entire city from the top of **Sydney Tower**, which is a great way to get your bearings when you first arrive. Catch a ferry from **Circular Quay** to the **Taragona Zoo**, a great place to see native wildlife like koalas and kangaroos along with an impressive array of other animals. Save time and get more great views by taking the **Sky Safari** gondola from the dock to the top of the hill.

To and from the zoo, you'll have a great view of the **Sydney Opera House**, a famous building with rather unusual architecture. Stop by during the day to take a tour, or come back at night and catch a show. As you walk from the Quay toward Harbour Bridge, stop by the **Museum of Contemporary Art**, the only place of its kind in Australia. (Got a backpack? You'll have to carry it in your hand through the museum.)

Want to try something exciting? Sign up for the **Bridgeclimb**, and after you've been briefed, trained, and properly equipped, you'll be part of a group that actually *walks* up the Harbour Bridge. No cameras allowed, but you'll remember the view for years.

On the other side of the bridge is **Darling Harbour**, perfect for souvenir shopping. Walk a bit farther and you'll find the **Aquarium**. Stop in to see the saltwater crocodile, and gaze up at sharks as they cruise overhead in one of the "oceanarium" tunnels. Keep going, and you'll come to the **Chinese Friendship Garden**, an oasis of serenity in an otherwise bustling city. Take an hour, stroll through, then finish up with a trip to the **Paddington Market,** where you can buy clothes, luggage, fresh food, and just about anything else that comes to mind.

Paris
France (Europe)

As you wander the capital of France, you'll find an endless array of sidewalk cafés, specialty boutiques, and photo opportunities. Enjoy fine wines and rich foods, see magnificent architecture and art galleries, and see why Paris has been the talk of the world for over a hundred years.

2007 Per Diem Rates: (L) 285 ♦ (M&IE) 155
Languages: French (official), English (common)

Currency: Euro (€)	**Visa: No, up to 90 days**

- Charles de Gaulle/Roissy Airport (CDG) – direct RER access
- Orly Airport (ORY) – shuttle to RER-C line to Paris

- Gare du Nord – SNCF service to northern France and Britain; direct Métro access
- Gare de l'Est – SNCF service to Luxembourg and central Europe; direct Métro access
- Gare de Lyon –SNCF service to the Riviera, Switzerland and Italy; direct Métro access
- Gare d'Austerlitz – SNCF service to southwest France and Spain; direct Métro access

- Paris-Galliéni International Station, 28, av. Général de Gaulle 93541 Bagnolet – Eurolines and regional coach service; adjacent to Métro

- No cruise ship terminal

Speaking English

For some reason, it's widely believed in the United States that the French are snobs who look down on people who don't speak French. Another common rumor is that Parisians get upset if you try to speak French and don't do it well. Some people feel that way, but they're not the norm.

This is a city used to welcoming tourists. Many (though certainly not all) people do speak English, and an attempt at speaking French is often appreciated. If you've done your homework, put your "travel French" to use whenever you can.

Getting Around

The Paris subway system is technically called the Métropolitain, but everyone refers to it as the Métro. It's run by the RATP, which also operates the RER regional rail network and the Paris bus system. One advantage of that arrangement is that the same fare card can be used on all three systems within central Paris. (You'll need to buy a separate RER ticket to take the regional rail outside of the city.)

PLAN AHEAD AND SAVE MONEY!

Paris Visites passes provide unlimited use of the entire RATP network (Métro, RER, and bus) for up to five days as well as discounts on admission to popular attractions, but there's a catch—you can only buy them online, before you leave for Paris. Check out *www.parisvisite.com* for details.

While you're in Paris, plan to walk as much as possible. Between the Métro and the RER, you can get close to just about everything you'll want to see, and strolling on foot gives you the opportunity to enjoy the ambiance of this beautiful city. It's easy enough to jump on a bus or hail a taxi if the weather changes or you get tired.

Sightseeing

When you think of Paris, a few things come to mind as places you must see. The **Eiffel Tower** is visible from around the city, but you'll want to visit it in person and marvel at its size and magnificence. The **Cathédrale Notre-Dame de Paris** was built more than seven centuries ago—one of the first Gothic cathedrals in Europe—and continues to draw tourists on a daily basis.

Within the corridors of the **Musée du Louvre**, you'll find some of the world's most renowned works of art, including Leonardo de Vinci's **Mona Lisa**. Be warned that a trip to the Louvre can easily consume several days. Spontaneous Tourists who want to see more than the Louvre should be careful about how much time they spend there.

Walk down the **Champs Elysées**, one of Paris' grande avenues. At its western end lies the incredible **Arc d'Triomphe**, commissioned by Napoleon Bonaparte in 1806 to commemorate the victory of his army at Austerlitz. (Use the underground passages that cross under the road to reach the Arc. Trying to run across the unmarked traffic circle that flows around it would be a fatal mistake.)

You'll find the **Colonne de Juillet** in the Place de la Bastille, commemorating the start of the French Revolution in 1789. The nearby **Opera Bastille** is a more recent addition to the city. Completed in 1990, the new home of Paris' leading opera company has 2723 seats, each with an unrestricted view of the stage.

Just a few minutes from the Place de la Nation is the **Cimetière de Picpus**, the only private cemetery in Paris. There, you'll find the grave of the Marquis de Lafayette, who crossed the ocean against the orders of his king to join the Continental Army. The American flag that flies over his grave symbolizes the friendship between our two countries that has existed for centuries.

The Paris Experience

For all the splendor of its monuments and museums, what makes Paris so memorable is the beauty of its avenues, architecture, and cuisine. Start your day with coffee and a pastry from a local patisserie. Wander the city, looking at the intricately carved scrollwork of the buildings.

Have a long lunch at a sidewalk café as you take in the feel of the city. Spend hours reconnecting with a spouse or friend over a leisurely Parisian dinner and fine wine. See what you can, but don't let the sights distract you from enjoying your visit. Paris is more than its tourist attractions.

Singapore
Asia

In general, Americans find traveling to Asia a little harder than going to Europe. Many Asian countries require visas, the trip is longer (and more expensive), and the culture is so different that it can be a little daunting.

Singapore, on the other hand, is very accessible and makes an excellent "intro to Asia" trip. Visas aren't required for short stays (up to 30 days). Most Singaporeans speak Malay or Chinese in social settings, but English is used as the universal business language (though many people speak a dialect popularly called "Singlish").

2007 Per Diem Rates: (L) 163 ♦ (M&IE) 93	
Languages: Malay (official), English (business), Chinese	
Currency: Singapore Dollar (S$)	Visa: No, up to 30 days
	• Changi International Airport (SIN) – direct MRT access
	• Tanjong Pagar Singapore Railway Station at Keppel Rd – KTM Malaysian rail service to Malaysia, Eastern & Orient Rail itineraries; adjacent to MRT
	• Ban San Bus Terminal, Queen and Arab Sts –service to Johor Bahru, Malaysia; adjacent to MRT • Lavender Street Bus Terminal – service to Malaysia south of Kuala Lumpur; adjacent to MRT • Golden Mile Complex, 5001 Beach Rd – service to northern Malaysia and Thailand; adjacent to MRT
	• Singapore Cruise Centre at HarbourFront – Asia, Pacific, and Oceania itineraries • Tanah Merah Ferry Terminal – Ferry service to Indonesia and Malaysia

Another plus is that Singapore is an extremely safe, clean, and orderly place. There is virtually no crime, including things like littering, in the country, so you can wander without much concern. A visit to Singapore is a gentle way to be introduced to Asia and prepare for future trips to other countries.

DO NOT BRING DRUGS TO SINGAPORE

Possession or smuggling of drugs in Singapore is an extremely serious offense. Those responsible for organizing such shipments are likely to receive the death penalty. Be smart and don't try it.

Getting Around

Singapore's light rail system is called the Mass Rapid Transit, or MRT. Like similar systems in other developed nations, the MRT is fast, efficient, reliable, and inexpensive. MRT stations reflect Singapore's high standards of cleanliness.

You'll make use of the MRT to get around Singapore throughout your stay, but there are some places where it doesn't go—the zoo, for instance. In these cases, you'll rely on the Singapore bus network to get you around. You won't love them the way that you'll love the MRT, but Singapore's buses work like every other developed country's buses—they're reliable and cost-effective.

Taxis are readily available throughout the city. Driving is also an option if you're so inclined, but keep in mind that Singapore roads follow the British standard of driving on the left.

Singapore is a beautiful city, carefully planned to include lots of green space, and walking is popular. Unlike some places, you can confidently wander anywhere in the city at any time—crime is rare, and violent crime is almost nonexistent. The biggest threat comes from pickpockets.

THE PERMANENT CARD: IT MAKES SENSE!

The MRT doesn't offer unlimited-use passes, and all fares are debited from plastic smartcards. If you buy a one-way fare, you'll get a card which includes a S$1 deposit. When you finish your trip, you insert the card into a machine and get your deposit back.

The system works, but it's a bit of a hassle, and you can avoid it by getting a permanent card for S$5. Most tourists don't bother, preferring to deal with the rebates. Here's the trick, though: you pay less when your fare is debited from a permanent card than you pay for a one-way fare.

Fares are based on the length of the trip, so specifics vary, but even if you're only in Singapore for two days, you'll save money if you take the MRT ten times or more. You'll also save time by avoiding the deposits, and you'll have a souvenir to take home (or bring back on your next visit).

Sightseeing

Singapore makes its first impression when you leave the plane. **Changi Airport** is an aesthetic marvel, decorated in gentle colors, quiet, with soothing music playing overhead. You'll quickly learn that this is an extremely ordered society, one that used America as a role model and now views Americans as equals.

From the Raffles Place MRT station, head toward the water and you'll find **Merlion Park**. The Merlion is the most popular symbol of Singapore, and tourists often come to get their photo taken beside it. You'll also have an exceptional view of **Esplanade-Theatres on the Bay**, a modern-styled performance complex that is home to the Singapore Symphony Orchestra. In a sense, it is Singapore's response to the famed Sydney Opera House.

In fact, symbols of Singapore's status as an economic power are everywhere. Malls and high-end shopping abound. In Sun-Tec City, you'll even find the aptly-named **Fountain of Wealth**, the world's largest. In a country that has no native freshwater supplies, the fountain is a symbol of triumph. The adjacent **Vivo City** complex, with the nation's largest Cineplex, is another such symbol.

National pride doesn't mean a loss of cultural identity, however. To be Singaporean is in part an acknowledgement of the outside cultures that make up the island's population. Wander the shops of **Chinatown**, then head to the **Tekka Center** in Little India. Stop in to some of the shops along the street for colorful saris or to order tailor-made clothing at attractive prices. Head to **Arab Street** and you'll find Middle Eastern wares as well as the splendor of the **Sultan Mosque**.

From Ang Mo Kio station, you can pick up the bus to the **Singapore Zoo**. Famous for its use of the "open zoo" model where animals are separated from visitors by concealed moats or glass rather than cages, the Singapore Zoo is widely considered one of the world's finest. Here you can see white tigers and elephants as well as the only polar bears living on the Equator.

When the sun goes down, head next door to the adjacent **Night Safari**. Opened in 1994, this exciting park gives you a chance to see nocturnal animals from around the world, including Burmese pythons, Cape giraffes, and Malayan tigers.

315

DINE ON THE WILD SIDE!

One particularly unique option at the Night Safari is to enjoy a lavish three-course dinner while you tour the park in a luxury tram. At S$140 per adult, it's a little pricey, but you'll have a great story to tell. Visit *www.nightsafari.com.sg* for details.

If the hot weather has you wishing for a day at the beach, head to **Sentosa Island**. Amidst the many theme attractions, you'll find three beaches as well as nature trails and **Fort Siloso**, Singapore's only preserved coastal fortress from colonial times.

Switzerland
via Zürich (Europe)

The Swiss have an interesting relationship with the rest of Europe. Switzerland maintains one of the best armies in the world but established and maintained its neutrality through both World Wars. Though surrounded by member nations, the country is not part of the European Union and uses its own currency.

2007 Per Diem Rates: (L) 117–239 ♦ (M&IE) 102–143	
Languages: German (Zurich, Bern), French (Geneva), and Italian (South); English (Common)	
Currency: Swiss Franc (SFr)	**Visa: No, up to 90 days**

 • Zürich-Kloten Flughaven (ZCH) – direct SBB access

 • Zürich Hauptbahnhoff – SBB, ICE, CityNightLine, and regional rail service; adjacent to Züri Linie tram lines

 • Zürich-Sihlquai adjacent to Zürich Hauptbahnhoff – Eurolines and regional coach service

 • No cruise ship terminal

Despite its self-imposed segregation, Switzerland is heavily influenced by its larger neighbors—Germany and Austria on the east, France on the west, Italy to the south. This influence is reflected in architecture, mannerism, and language, with German dominant in Zürich and Bern while French holds sway in western cities like Montreux and Geneva. Italian becomes prevalent closer to the southern border.

To tourists, what it means to be Swiss is a little difficult to identify. That's why the destination is Switzerland itself, rather than an individual city. To get a feel for the place, you've got to move around.

Getting Around

Mass transit in Zürich is provided by the Züri Linie, a combined network of light-rail electric trams and buses. Fares vary, but you can simplify your trip by purchasing a 24-hour *tageskarte* (day pass). There's also a three-day ZürichCARD, which includes travel in all seven zones as well as to and from the airport.

Moving around Switzerland is easy, thanks to the extremely well established mass transit systems, and you'll find convenient local mass transit service in most cities. Even assuming that you have just a few days, it's possible to see quite a bit of this wonderful country.

It's fairly intuitive to find the airport (l'aéroport) in French-speaking areas, but if you don't speak German—which I don't—it's a little tricky in eastern Switzerland.

Knowing that the German word for airport is *flüghaven*, and that *bahnhoff* is station, makes it much easier to get around!

Sightseeing in Zürich

Zürich is Switzerland's largest city and has recently emerged as a hip scene for the arts in addition to its traditional role as a banking center. Expensive stores line **Bahnhoffstrasse**, adjacent to the city's main rail station. You'll find three distinctive famous churches in the city—**Fraumunster, St. Peterskirche**, and **Grossmunster**. Over 2000 animals are on exhibit at the **Zoo Zürich**, widely considered one of Europe's best.

In the evenings, the Swiss head out to party. **Fondue** makes a great meal, or you might enjoy Weiner schnitzel at one of the

German pubs. **Nightclubs** get going around 11:00 p.m. and stay open until close to dawn.

Sightseeing in Geneva

Geneva is in Switzerland, but the birthplace of philosopher Jean-Jacques Rousseau is a world-class city where international bankers, diplomats, and travelers nearly outnumber native Swiss. French is the typical language here, and Parisian-style terrace cafés line the Place du Bourg-de-Four, while cheaper Middle Eastern fare can be found closer to the waterfront.

The famous **Jet d'Eau**, visible from many parts of the city, sprays water 140 meters into the air from Lake Geneva. The European headquarters of the United Nations is at the **Palais des Nations**, and tours are offered daily. You won't want to miss the famed **Flower Clock**, made up of more than 6000 individual blossoms.

Sightseeing in Bern

Arriving in the Swiss capital by train, you're only a few minutes walk from the **Houses of Parliament**, an ornate complex that serves as home to the Swiss Federal Assembly. A number of ornate **fountains** can be found throughout the city, including the **Ogre**, **Messenger**, **Justice**, **Bagpiper**, and **Musketeer**. You'll also want to see the 16th-century astronomical clock at the **Zytglogge** tower.

Sightseeing in Liechtenstein

Nestled on the eastern side of Switzerland, the Principality of Liechtenstein offers a few ski resorts and has a thriving industry making false teeth. You can see this tiny nation in about four hours, counting travel time to and from Zürich.

To get here, take the train to Sargans then switch to the aptly named Liechtenstein Bus, which runs every half hour. It's a short trip to the capital of Vaduz, and when you get off the bus, you're only a few blocks from everything.

Look up to see the **Schloss Vaduz** on top of the cliff. Liechtenstein uses Swiss currency, so cross the street and buy postcards, write them out, then walk next door to buy stamps and mail them. Adjacent is the **Tourism Office**, where you can obtain an official passport stamp for 2 SFr.

Down one block is the **Kunstmuseum Liechtenstein**, the national museum. It takes about an hour to see. When you're finished, have lunch or coffee in a local restaurant. Buy some Liechtenstein wine and pick out a few souvenirs before you head back.

Seville
and Southern Spain (Europe)

Andalusia is the second-largest region of Spain, encompassing its entire southern coastline. For 800 years, it was controlled by Moors from North Africa, who brought with them their own architecture, language, and culture as well as the Islamic faith.

In 1492, the Moorish stronghold of Granada fell to forces under King Fernando and Queen Isabel, unifying Spain under Catholic rule.

2007 Per Diem Rates: (L) 157 ♦ (M&IE) 87	
Languages: Spanish-Castilian (official)	
Currency: Euro (€)	Visa: No, up to 90 days

	• Seville Aeropuerto San Pablo (SVQ) – bus and taxi service
	• Estación de Santa Justa – RENFE express (AVE) and regional service
	• Estación de Autobuses Prado de San Sebastian, Plaza San Sebastian – regional service to eastern Andalusia and Barcelona • Estación de Autobuses Plaza de Armas, Avenida del Cristo de la Expiración – regional service to northwest Spain and Portugal
	• No cruise ship terminal in Seville • Cruise Ship Terminal, Cadíz – Mediterranean itineraries; bus service to Seville

Eight centuries of separation, however, are not as easily replaced as political rulers, and Andalusia has a style of its own. The residents of Andalusia spend their time socializing and partying, enjoying late-night *tapas* alongside their unique *flamenco* form of music and dance. Even bullfighting in its present form began here.

Save cosmopolitan Barcelona or the congestion of Madrid for a later trip. Andalusia is the place to get your first impressions of Spanish culture.

A WESTERN PERSPECTIVE

The whole region is worth seeing, of course, but so is the whole country (and the whole world, for that matter). Spontaneous Tourists don't have weeks to spend, and Andalusia is a very large place.

Western Andalusia, starting with Seville and including the provinces of Cadíz and Huelva as well as offering the possibility of a trip to Gibraltar, gives you a chance to enjoy everything from centuries-old cathedrals to sun-soaked beaches while fitting them into a long weekend. It's also the most frequently overlooked destination by anyone not headed to Portugal.

So, you should come back to Spain when time allows and see more of this lovely country. In the meantime, this is a great place to start.

Getting Around

Seville is in the process of building a subway system, but it won't be finished for a long time. Even once it is, it will supplement the very effective network of buses already in place, which include several different loop routes that help travelers move between neighborhoods. Walking is especially appealing among the small shops of El Centro, and taxis are available throughout the city.

To venture out of Seville and explore the broader region, you can rent a car or rely on mass transit. Most cities in Andalusia can be reached by rail, including the harbor city of Cadíz. Connecting bus service can get you to La Linea de la Concepcion, the crossing point to enter Gibraltar, as well as most other destinations. The challenge, as always, is that taking mass transit forces you to follow a schedule.

You have more freedom when you rent a car, but there are some downsides. Gasoline is much more expensive in Europe than in the United States, often exceeding the equivalent of $5 per gallon. Parking adds to the cost, and the winding streets in some older cities are so narrow that clearance may be just a few inches. Also, automatic transmissions aren't usually available in Spain, so you'll want to be familiar with manual shifting.

Of course, the only wrong decision is that one that keeps you from enjoying your visit. Weigh the pros and cons, and go with whichever choice makes the most sense for you.

SPEAKING CASTILIAN

Castilian, the Spanish dialect most common in Spain, is more formal than the language found throughout Latin America. There are also some pronunciation differences—for instance, the letter "z" is pronounced as "th", so the city of Cadíz is "Ka-deeth" rather than "Ka-deez" as you might expect. It's not that hard to adapt, though.

Sightseeing in Seville

Seville, pronounced in Spanish as "Seh-VEE-ya," is the capital of Andalusia and its largest city, as well as the fourth-largest city in Spain. No surprise that it's also the most expensive, but as you wander the streets enjoying tapas and drinks at the many bars or dance at one of the many clubs that only open at midnight, you'll find your cares slipping away.

The city is built on the Rio Guadalquivir, a mighty river whose unexpected change of course brought fortune to Seville and doom to what had been until that point the thriving Roman city of Italia. (In fact, five miles northwest of Seville are the **ruins** of Italia, which include the remains of one of the largest Roman amphitheatres.)

The foremost attraction in Seville is probably the **Cathedral of Seville**. Built on the site of what had been the city's main mosque while under Moorish control, the Cathedral is one of the largest in the world and includes **Columbus' Tomb** (though it is widely accepted that the remains in the tomb are not those of Christopher Columbus). The nearby **Giralda** was once a minaret of the city mosque but today is home to a massive golden weather vane representing faith, known as **El Giraldillo**.

Across the Plaza del Triunfo from the cathedral is the **Alcázar**, a beautiful complex that has been used over the centuries as a fort, governor's mansion, and royal palace. Today, you can take walking tours through its halls and the elaborate **Alcázar gardens**.

El Centro, the center of the Old City, is an elaborate series of narrow streets interwoven with shops, bars, and restaurants. Bringing a car into El Centro can be a very frustrating experience. On the other hand, you can spend hours happily wandering among the buildings on foot.

El Arenal, the neighborhood along the river, is adjacent to El Centro. Traveling along Paseo del Cristóbal Colón, you can't miss the **Plaza del Toros de la Real Maestranza**. Seville's bullring is one of the most beautiful to be found anywhere in Spain. Tours are held during the morning and early afternoon, while bullfights occur in the late afternoon on days that they're scheduled.

> Spanish bullfights are unique, and if the opportunity presents itself, you should see one while in Spain. Even if you decide you don't like them, you'll know why.

Sightseeing in Cadíz

The bustling port city of Cadíz is famous for its exhibitions of **tall ships** during annual festivals and its enthusiastic celebration of Carnaval. There are also a number of enticing beaches, including the **Playa de la Victoria**, which stretches nearly three miles along the coast.

You'll want to visit the **four Plazas**—San Juan de Dios, de la Catedral, de Topete, and de Mina—which are also useful as navigation landmarks. Flowers and other fresh goods abound at the **Mercado Central**. If you're interested in archeology or art, consider the **Museo de Cadíz**.

Train and bus service connects Cadíz to a number of cities, including Seville. For travelers heading to El Puerto de Santa Mariá, ferries from the **Estación Marítima** offer a convenient and direct alternative.

Sightseeing in El Puerto de Santa María

The town where Christopher Columbus met the man who owned his flagship is famous for its **sherry bodegas**, elaborate houses where the wines are stored, aged, and sold. Most of the bodegas offer tours, but it's best to call ahead.

> Sherry is a dessert wine. Varieties range from dry *fino* to sweet *oloroso*. If you haven't tried it, this town is an excellent place to sample some particularly fine varieties (and tasting is complimentary).

Visiting Gibraltar

Located on the southern coast, Gibraltar is home to an extremely large rock, the only wild primate population in Europe, and a population of around 35,000 people. Set aside a day and you can see the whole thing, but even a half-day provides enough time to make it worthwhile.

Don't forget your passport. Gibraltar is British territory, and as we covered in Chapter 7, Britain didn't sign the Schengen Protocol that eliminated passport control between most European Union member nations.

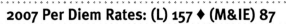

2007 Per Diem Rates: (L) 157 ♦ (M&IE) 87
Languages: English (official)
Currency: Pound Sterling (£) **Visa: No, up to 6 months**

	• Gibraltar-North Front Airport (GIB) – Flights to the U.K. and Spain; walk to Gibraltar or direct bus to the Spanish border
	• No rail service into Gibraltar or to La Linea
	• La Linea de la Concepcion (across the border) – regular bus service to Seville, Cadíz, and other Spanish cities
	• Cruise Ship Terminal, Gibraltar – Mediterranean itineraries

Background and Politics

The territory of Gibraltar is less than three square miles in size, much of it taken up by the massive rock formation that gives it its name. Originally part of Spain, Gibraltar was conquered during the War of Spanish Succession in 1704 and formally ceded to Britain nine years later after a failed attempt to retake the peninsula.

In the decades since, Anglo-Spanish relations have reflected considerable dispute over the future of the territory. In 1967, a popular referendum voted 99% in favor of remaining under British sovereignty, and Spain responded by closing the border. In 1985, however, it was reopened, and relations appear on the mend despite a 2002 referendum in which a new proposal to share sovereignty was defeated by 98.7% of the population.

Gibraltar approved a constitution on November 30, 2006. Today, its status with regard to Britain is similar to that of Puerto Rico's to the United States, emphasizing self-determination and autonomous local government.

On December 16, 2006, Iberian Air made the first flight in history from Madrid to Gibraltar, followed by a British Airways flight to the Spanish capital. A new low-cost carrier, Fly Gibraltar, has announced its intent to establish regular service to the U.K. and Ireland in 2007.

Getting Around

You can walk just about everywhere in Gibraltar, but there's an inexpensive bus system that makes it much easier to get around, especially if you have limited time. (The trek from the border to the cable car station is particularly long on foot.)

Driving is allowed, but it's a bit of a hassle at the border crossing. If you do decide to drive, traffic in Gibraltar follows the continental and American style of driving on the right, not the left-hand approach found in Britain.

Sightseeing in Gibraltar

More than a quarter of a mile high, the **Rock of Gibraltar** is a massive limestone formation that overlooks the Strait of Gibraltar and the entrance to the Mediterranean Sea. The **Upper Rock Nature Preserve** occupies most of what you can see, with a **cable car** at the end of Red Sands Road that can get you to the top in about eight minutes.

The cable car makes a stop halfway up for visitors who want to visit the **Apes' Den**. The number of Barbary macaques that inhabit the island is around 250, and they have their run of the place, but a hundred or more tend to hang out at the Den. You'll find most of the others wandering the Rock.

On a clear day, you'll be able to see **Morocco** across the Strait from the top cable-car station. Walk down from the top toward the Apes' Den to find **St. Michael's Grotto**, a cave now used as a performance space. There's a café outside.

Keep going down, and you'll come to the **Military Heritage Centre**, which features exhibits on the history of Gibraltar in regional conflicts. You can see some of the **Great Siege Tunnels** dug by hand during the eighteenth century, but don't be fooled. Gibraltar is an active military installation, and within the Rock are dozens of miles worth of roads and tunnels that are strictly off-limits to visitors.

You can also see a number of exhibits, including a Neanderthal skull dated to be more than 100,000 years old, at the **Gibraltar Museum**. If you'd rather eat and shop, follow Main Street through **Casemates Square**, once an arsenal and now a gateway to restaurants and shopping. More restaurants can be found along the **Marina**. You'll find a lot of British pub-style food here, including the ever-popular fish and chips.

Bahrain
via Manama (The Middle East)

As you wander the extremely safe streets of the capital city of Manama, you'll enjoy Arabian architecture and encounter very friendly people in traditional as well as Western-style clothing (for men and women). English is almost as widespread as Arabic. Bahrain isn't quite as cosmopolitan as Dubai, and that's part of its appeal. It's modern but still offers a view of the traditional Middle East.

You need a visa to visit Bahrain, but you can get it at the airport when you arrive (5 BD or $15 USD for up to two weeks). Hot day and night, the self-defined party capital of the Middle East is the perfect place for a first visit to this exciting region of the world.

328

2007 Per Diem Rates: (L) 183 ♦ (M&IE) 104
Languages: Arabic and English

Currency: Bahrain Dinar (BD)	Visa: Yes

 • Bahrain International Airport (BAH) – taxi service

 • No rail service to Bahrain

 • SAPTCO service from Saudi Arabia via the King Fahad Causeway

 • Mina Salman – Itineraries via Dubai

Getting Around

There's a public bus system in Manama, but it's not very extensive. Most people drive wherever they go, in part because of the oppressive heat (which can go higher than 120 degrees Fahrenheit during the summer months). You can rent a car, or take one of the many taxis.

> When you take a taxi, insist that the driver use his meter unless you've agreed on a price in advance. Don't accept excuses that it's broken, or you'll end up overpaying.

Another popular option is walking, particularly at night when it's cooler. Before you wonder how smart of an idea this is, put yourself at ease—Manama is an extremely safe city, with virtually no crime (violent or otherwise), and people here are very friendly. You can wander without worry, but if you venture out during the day, bring water.

DO NOT DRINK AND DRIVE IN BAHRAIN!

Drinking and driving is always stupid, but there is no legal limit here: if you've had anything at all to drink and get pulled over, you may be arrested for driving under the influence. Of course, many people drink like crazy in Bahrain, but they take taxis. If you're going to drink, follow their example.

For trips outside of the capital, the best plan is to take one of the tour buses that leave daily from Bab al Bahrain in the central market area.

Sightseeing in Manama

One of the things that makes a trip to Bahrain stand out is the relative lack of must-see sights. You're here to be here, to mingle, and gain perspective. These days, it's more important than ever that Americans see that there are plenty of people in the Middle East who have nothing to do with terrorism, oppression, or religious extremism—and they deserve our friendship and respect.

Bahrain is a place to shop. Choose from a number of high-end malls, or wander **Manama Souq**, the open-air market at the city center near the large gate known as **Bab al Bahrain**, which is also the departure point for the daily tour buses that take travelers to the outlying villages.

> Bahraini merchants expect customers to bargain. Once you get the hang of it, you'll have fun haggling over prices for rugs, furniture, perfume, and much more.

If you're looking for jewelry, **Gold City** is the place for you. Bahrain gets its name—"land of two seas"—from freshwater springs that mix with the ocean around the island, and that water creates some of the most highly prized pearls in the world. You'll also find gold, platinum, and gemstone jewelry.

The **Pearl Monument** isn't far from the city center. As you wander, stop for coffee in one of the cafés that line the streets or grab a bite to eat. Standards of hygiene in Bahrain are good, and you can generally eat food from the markets. You'll also find plenty of restaurants and fast-food shops, including some local options like Shwarma Express.

In the Jafair neighborhood, you'll find the **Ahmad al Fateh Mosque**, also known as the Grand Mosque. Non-Muslims aren't allowed inside during prayer time, but visits may be possible at other times of day. Even from the outside, it's an impressive building. You'll also find the **National Museum** in the same area.

The King Fahad Causeway

Bahrain is connected to Saudi Arabia by a 25km span. You need a visa to actually enter Saudi Arabia, but for 2 BD, you can drive halfway across to enjoy food at a restaurant.

Sightseeing outside of Manama

The Kingdom of Bahrain consists of 36 islands, but most of what you'll see outside of Manama is in or near one of the villages on the main island. You can drive or take a taxi, but it's easier to take a tour bus from Bab al Bahrain (9:30 a.m. and 3:30 p.m. daily).

Near Karbabad Village, you'll find the ruins of the **Bahrain Fort**, often referred to as the Portuguese Fort in acknowledgement of its origins. You'll also find the famed **Tree of Life** about 12km outside of Jebel al Dukhan. A national symbol, the tree has grown in the desert for centuries, and its water source remains a mystery to this day.

331

AND MANY MORE...

There are over 190 countries in the world today, and that number is actually increasing. The destinations featured in this chapter are just a tiny fraction of places that you might go. Have steak in Buenos Aires. Drink coffee in Prague. Climb the Great Wall of China. Play golf in Ireland.

As globalization paves the way into the twenty-first century, it is particularly important for Americans to gain a better appreciation of the world around us. We can't afford to do otherwise, because we have the most to lose if we get it wrong.

Travel takes time and costs money, but it's time and money well spent. Make travel a priority in your life now, not when you retire. Embrace the concept of Spontaneous Tourism and see the world at every opportunity.

Along the way, you'll make mistakes, but that's part of learning. With each trip that you take, you'll be that much better prepared for the next one. Choose your destinations sensibly and always consult State Department advisories for the latest information. Be adventurous, but be safe, and have a lot of fun.

Happy traveling!

Appendix A:

Further Reading and References

AUTHOR'S TRAVEL PORTAL

www.spontaneoustourism.com. Free travel portal with integrated Google search bar, Kayak fare finder, and RSS feeds for daily flight specials and world news. Includes a travel toolbar with organized links to airlines, destination guides, hotels, and more.

ASK THE AUTHOR

Have travel questions? Email *author@spontaneoustourism.com* and get answers from the author!

REFERENCES BY TOPIC

Coded by reference type.
- (B) represents a book
- (M) indicates an article in print media
- (W) refers to a Web site.

General Travel

(B) *Fodor's 1001 Smart Travel Tips.* ISBN 978-1400012381. $9.95/352pg.

(B) *How to Travel Practically Anywhere,* by Susan Stellin. ISBN 978-0618607532. $15.95/336pg.

(B) *Traveler's Tool Kit: How to Travel Absolutely Anywhere,* by Rob Sangster. 3rd ed. ISBN 978-0897323413. $16.95/528pg.

(B) *The Traveler's Handbook: The Insider's Guide to World Travel,* by Ltd. Wexas. 9th ed. ISBN 978-0762740901. $24.95/960pg.

(B) *Tips for the Savvy Traveler,* by Deborah Burns. ISBN 978-0882669717. $12.95/256pg.

Travel Bargains

(B) *Guerrilla Travel Tactics: Hundreds of Simple Strategies Guaranteed to Save Road Warriors Time and Money,* by Jay Conrad Levinson and Theo Brandt-Sarif. ISBN 978-0814471708. $15.00/272pg.

Frequent Travel Programs and Elite Status

(M) Business travelers on airport lounges. (2006, November 14). *USA Today,* 5B.

(M) Hendrix, S. (2006, August 20). 14 days, 5 countries, 1 big bus. *Sunday News Journal,* F6.

(B) *Mileage Pro: The Insider's Guide to Frequent Flyer Programs,* by Randy Petersen and Tim Winship. ISBN 978-0977629503. $19.95/204pg.

(M) Reed, D. (2006, November 14). AirTran, Frontier form alliance. *USA Today,* 6B.

(M) Stroller, G. (2006, August 8). Small airlines set up big rewards. *USA Today,* 10B.

(B) *The Penny Pincher's Passport to Luxury Travel: The Art of Cultivating Preferred Customer Status,* by Joel L. Widzer. ISBN 978-1885211316. $14.95/336pg.

Cruises

(M) Lisagor, K. (2006, August 25–27). Cruise ship confidential. *USA Weekend*, P.6.

(B) *The Essential Little Cruise Book: Secrets from a Cruise Director for a Perfect Cruise Vacation* (3rd Ed.), by Jim West. ISBN 978-0762728282. $7.95/224pg.

Discount Programs

(W) *www.statravel.com*. International Student Identification Card.

(W) *www.narp.org*. National Association of Railroad Passengers.

(W) *www.studentadvantage.com*. Student Advantage.

(W) *www.veteransadvantage.com*. Veterans Advantage.

Lodging

(M) Flynn, S. (2006, July 9). Hostels—yes, hostels—flourish in Europe, flail in U.S. *Sunday News Journal*, F4.

(M) Ruth, E. (2006, July 17). Paradise lost, but not your deposit. *The News Journal*, P.1.

(M) Sisolak, G. A. (2006, November 14). On the road with Elderhostel. *The News Journal: Prime Life*, P.12.

Packing

(B) *Fodor's How to Pack*. 2nd ed. ISBN 978-1400012350. $9.95/192pg.

(B) *Pack It Up: Traveling Safe and Smart in Today's World*, by Anne McAlpin. ISBN 978-0962726316. $14.95/176pg.

(B) *Smart Packing for Today's Travel*, by Susan Foster and Barbara Weiland. ISBN 978-0970219664. $19.95/248pg.

(W) *www.packitup.com*. Anne McAlpin's site, with downloadable packing lists and other tools to help travelers get organized.

Places to See

(B) *1,000 Places to See Before You Die: A Traveler's Life List*, by Patricia Schultz. ISBN 978-0761104841. $19.95/972 pg.

(B)   *Unforgettable Places to See Before You Die,* by Steve Davey and Marc Schlossman. ISBN 978-1552979556. $19.95/256pg.

(B)   *Lonely Planet the Travel Book: A Journey Through Every Country in the World,* by Roz Hopkins. ISBN 978-1741046298. $30.00/444pg.

(B)   *The New Traveler's Atlas: A global guide to the places you must see in your lifetime,* by John Man, Chris Schuler, Mary-Ann Gallagher, Geoffrey Roy, and Nigel Rodgers. ISBN 978-0764160189. $29.99/224pg. (Hardcover)

(B)   *Traveler's Atlas,* by DK Publishing. ISBN 978-0756615291. $30.00/368pg.

Photography

(B)   *Digital Photography Outdoors: A Field Guide for Travel and Adventure Photographers,* by James Martin. ISBN 978-0898869743. $16.95/157pg.

Jet Lag and Health

(M)   Airplane Ear. (2006, October 31). *The News Journal,* F3.

(W)   *www.transmeridiantraveler.com.* Information and a booklet on the stress caused by cross-time zone travel and strategies for staying healthy while traveling.

Appendix B:

Airlines

Links included here are also provided online at
www.spontaneoustourism.com.

DOMESTIC AIRLINES

Nineteen airlines operating within the United States are listed here along with their contact information and the names of their frequent flyer programs. The list is divided into legacy and low-cost carriers. For more information on the domestic airline industry, please refer to Chapter 2.

Contact phone numbers provided are toll-free within the United States and Canada. International customers should refer to the provided Web sites for overseas contact numbers.

Airlines may charge a fee for reservations made over the phone.

Legacy Airlines

All of the legacy airlines operate mileage-based frequent flyer programs and offer tiered status within their elite programs. Each also operates an airport lounge network.

Affiliated airlines allow their members to earn miles on one another's flights and may also offer reciprocal privileges for their lounge members. Refer to each airline's Web site for detailed information.

American Airlines

www.aa.com

Frequent Flyer Program: *AAdvantage®*
Elite Tiers: Gold, Platinum, Executive Platinum

Lounge: Admirals Club

Affiliations: **one**world

Reservations: 1-800-433-7300 (all)

Alaska Airlines / Horizon Air

www.alaskaair.com

Frequent Flyer Program: *Mileage Plan®*
Elite Tiers: MVP, MVP Gold

Lounge: Board Room

Affiliations: American, Continental, Delta, Northwest, and Hawaiian, plus numerous foreign carriers; see Web site for details

Reservations: 1-800-ALASKAAIR (all)

Continental Airlines

www.continental.com

Frequent Flyer Program: *OnePass®*
Elite Tiers: Silver, Gold, Platinum

Lounge: Presidents Club

Affiliations: SkyTeam

Reservations: 1-800-253-FARE (domestic)
 1-800-231-0856 (international)

Delta Airlines

www.delta.com

Frequent Flyer Program: *SkyMiles®*
Elite Tiers: Silver Medallion, Gold, Platinum

Lounge: Crown Room Club

Affiliations: SkyTeam

Reservations: 1-800-221-1212 (all)

Northwest Airlines

www.nwa.com

Frequent Flyer Program: *WorldPerks®*
Elite Tiers: Silver Elite, Gold, Platinum

Lounge: WorldClub

Affiliations: SkyTeam, Midwest

Reservations: 1-800-225-2525 (all)

United Airlines

www.united.com

Frequent Flyer Program: *Mileage Plus®*
Elite Tiers: Premier, Premier Executive, 1K

Lounge: Red Carpet Club

Affiliations: Star Alliance, Aloha

Reservations: 1-800-UNITED1 (domestic)
 1-800-538-2929 (international)

U.S. Airways

www.usairways.com

Frequent Flyer Program: *Dividend Miles®*
Elite Tiers: Silver Preferred, Gold, Platinum, Chairman's

Lounge: U.S. Airways Club

Affiliations: Star Alliance

Reservations: 1-800-428-4322 (domestic)
 1-800-622-1015 (international)

Low-Cost Carriers

While low-cost airlines have a frequent flyer program, some operate on a mileage basis similar to those of the legacy carriers while others use a point system. Several offer elite status, and two operate airport lounge networks.

AirTran Airways

www.airtran.com

Frequent Flyer Program: *A+ Rewards®*
Program Type: Point-based
Elite Tiers: A+ Elite

Affiliations: Frontier

Reservations: 1-800-AIR-TRAN

Aloha Air

www.alohaair.com

Frequent Flyer Program: *AlohaPass®*
Program Type: Mileage-based
Elite Tiers: ali'i Silver, Gold, Diamond

Lounge: ali'i Club

Affiliations: United

Reservations: 1-800-367-5250

ATA Airlines

www.ata.com

Frequent Flyer Program: *Travel Awards®*
Program Type: Point-based
Elite Tiers: ATA Elite

Affiliations: None

Reservations: 1-800-I-FLY-ATA

Frontier Airlines

www.frontierairlines.com

Frequent Flyer Program: *EarlyReturns®*
Program Type: Mileage-based
Elite Tiers: Ascent and Summit

Affiliations: AirTran

Reservations: 1-800-432-1359

go!

www.iflygo.com

Frequent Flyer Program: *go! Miles®*
Program Type: Point-based (called miles)

Affiliations: None

Reservations: 1-888-I-FLY-GO2

Hawaiian Airlines

www.hawaiianair.com

Frequent Flyer Program: *HawaiianMiles®*
Program Type: Mileage-based
Elite Tiers: Pualani Gold, Platinum

Lounge: Premier Club

Affiliations: Alaska, NorthWest, Virgin Atlantic

Reservations: 1-800-367-5320

JetBlue Airways

www.jetblue.com

Frequent Flyer Program: *TrueBlue®*
Program Type: Point-based

Affiliations: None

Reservations: 1-800-JET-BLUE

Midwest Airlines

www.midwestairlines.com

Frequent Flyer Program: *Midwest Miles®*
Program Type: Mileage-based

Affiliations: Northwest, KLM

Reservations: 1-800-452-2022

Southwest Airlines

www.southwest.com

Frequent Flyer Program: *Rapid Rewards®*
Program Type: Point-based

Affiliations: None

Reservations: 1-800-I-FLY-SWA

Spirit Air

www.spiritair.com

Frequent Flyer Program: *Free Spirit®*
Program Type: Mileage-based
Elite Tiers: Elite and VIP (plus additional "ranking" levels within the VIP tier)

Affiliations: None

Reservations: 1-800-772-7117

339

Sun Country
www.suncountry.com
Frequent Flyer Program: *VIP Club®*
Program Type: Unique (discount fares)
Affiliations: None
Reservations: 1-800-359-6786

USA 3000
www.usa3000.com
Frequent Flyer Program: None
Affiliations: None
Reservations: Online only

FOREIGN AIRLINES

Most major foreign airlines are current or former national carriers that belong to one of the three major airline alliances. These airlines are listed in alphabetical order by alliance.

 oneworld
www.oneworld.com
Domestic Member: American

Aer Lingus *
Ireland
www.aerlingus.com

British Airways
United Kingdom
www.ba.com

Cathay Pacific
China (Hong Kong)
www.cathaypacific.com

Dragonair ***
China
www.dragonair.com

Finnair
Scandinavia
www.finnair.com

Iberia
Spain
www.iberia.com

Japan Airlines **
Japan
www.jal.co.jp/en

LAN Argentina **
Argentina
www.lan.com

LAN
Chile
www.lan.com

LAN Ecuador **
Ecuador
www.lan.com

Malév Hungarian Airlines **
Hungaria
www.malev.hu

Qantas
Australia
www.qantas.com

Royal Jordanian Airlines **
Jordan
www.rja.com.jo

* Aer Lingus has announced intent to leave oneworld effective April 1, 2007.
** These airlines are scheduled to join oneworld on April 1, 2007.
*** Dragonair is scheduled to join oneworld in late 2007.

Star Alliance

www.star-alliance.com
Domestic Members: United, U.S. Airways

Air Canada
Canada
www.aircanada.com

Air New Zealand
New Zealand
www.airnewzealand.com

ANA
Japan
www.anaskyweb.com

Asiana Airlines
South Korea
www.flyasiana.com

Austrian
Austria
www.austrian.com

Bmi
United Kingdom
www.flybmi.com

LOT Polish Airlines
Poland
www.lot.com

Lufthansa
Germany
www.lufthansa.com

Scandinavian Airlines
Scandinavia
www.flysas.com

Singapore Airlines
Singapore
www.singaporeair.com

South African Airways
South Africa
www.flysaa.com

Spanair
Spain
www.spanair.com

Swiss
Switzerland
www.swiss.com

TAP Portugal
Portugal
www.flytap.com

Thai Airways
Thailand
www.thaiairways.com

SkyTeam

www.skyteam.com
Domestic Members: Continental, Delta, Northwest

Aeroflot
Russia
www.aeroflot.ru/eng

Aeromexico
Mexico
www.aeromexico.com

Air France
France
www.airfrance.com

KLM
The Netherlands
www.klm.com

Alitalia
Italy
www.alitalia.com

CSA Czech Airlines
Czech Republic
www.czechairlines.com

Korean Air
South Korea
www.koreanair.com

Non-Allied Major Foreign Carriers

In addition to the alliance members, there are a number of major foreign airlines that are not members of one of the three major alliances but provide service to countries that may be of interest to Spontaneous Tourists. Some of them are listed here.

El Al	**Emirates**	**Ethiopian**
Israel	*United Arab Emirates*	*Ethiopia*
www.elal.com	*www.emirates.com*	*www.flyethiopian.com*
Icelandair	**TACA**	**Virgin Atlantic**
Iceland	*Central and South America*	*Worldwide*
www.icelandair.com	*www.taca.com*	*www.virgin-atlantic.com*

Premium-Class Airlines

Recent additions to the airline industry include a number of international airlines operating specially configured planes and offer only premium-class service on specific routes.

A ticket certainly costs more the cheapest available Coach fare on a legacy carrier, but passengers on these flights pay far less than standard Business Class fare and enjoy considerably more amenities. Each also offers a frequent flyer program, and because all seats are premium, there are no status tiers.

Eos
www.eosairlines.com
Route: New York-JFK to London-Stansted
Frequent Flyer Program: *Club 48®*
Lounges: Emirates Lounge (JFK)
          Eos Lounge (Stansted)
Reservations: 1-800-458-1277

L'Avion
www.lavion.com
Route: Newark-Liberty to Paris-Orly
Frequent Flyer Program: *Le Club®*
Lounge: None
Reservations: 1-866-NYC-ORLY

MAXjet
www.maxjet.com
Routes: New York-JFK, Washington-Dulles, and Las Vegas to London-Stansted
Frequent Flyer Program: *MAXflyer®*
Lounge: Departure Lounge
Reservations: 1-888-I-FLY-MAX

Silverjet
www.flysilverjet.com
Route: Newark-Liberty to London-Luton
Frequent Flyer Program: None
Lounge: None
Reservations: 1-877-359-7458

Foreign Low-Cost Carriers

In addition, there are a number of low-cost carriers that have begun operations as regulation has diminished. The list provided here is not complete but includes some of the most popular discount airlines.

> The countries listed reflect the home offices for these airlines, not the extent of the routes they offer.

Europe

easyJet	**Flybe**	**Germanwings**
United Kingdom	*United Kingdom*	*Germany*
www.easyjet.com	www.flybe.com	www.germanwings.com
Iceland Express	**RyanAir**	**SkyEurope**
Iceland	*Ireland*	*Central Europe*
www.icelandexpress.com	www.ryanair.com	www.skyeurope.com
Sterling	**Virgin Express**	**Wizz Air**
Scandinavia	*Western Europe*	*Poland / Hungary*
www.sterlingticket.com	www.virgin-express.com	www.wizzair.com

Asia

JetStar	**SkyNetAsia**	**SpiceJet**
Australia / Singapore	*Japan*	*India*
www.jetstar.com	www.skynetasia.co.jp	www.spicejet.com
Spring Air	**StarFlyer**	**Tiger Airways**
China	*Japan*	*Singapore*
www.china-sss.com	www.starflyer.jp	www.tigerairways.com
Virgin Blue		
Australia / Oceana		
www.virginblue.com.au		

Africa

1time	**Kulula**	**Mango**
South Africa	*South Africa*	*South Africa*
www.1time.aero	www.kulula.com	www.flymango.com

Transcontinental

Condor	**eurofly**	**LTU**
Worldwide	*U.S. – Italy*	*Worldwide*
www.condor.com	*www.euroflyusa.com*	*www.ltu.com*
Martinair	**Oasis Hong Kong**	**Zoom Airlines**
U.S.-Europe-Caribbean	*U.K. – Hong Kong*	*Europe – Canada*
www.martinair.com	*www.oasishongkong.com*	*www.flyzoom.com*

Appendix C:
Hotels and Lodging

Links included here are also provided online at
www.spontaneoustourism.com.

MAJOR CHAINS

Seven major hotel chains are listed here with their associated member brands and rewards programs.

Contact phone numbers provided are toll-free within the United States and Canada. International customers should refer to the provided Web sites for overseas contact numbers or to make reservations online.

Choice Hotels
www.choicehotels.com
Reservations: 1-877-424-6423
Reward Program: *Choice Privileges®*

Cambria Suites
www.cambriasuites.com

Clarion
www.clarionhotels.com

Comfort Inn
www.comfortinn.com

Comfort Suites
www.comfortsuites.com

Econo Lodge
www.econolodge.com

Mainstay Suites
www.mainstaysuites.com

Quality
www.qualityinn.com

Rodeway Inn
www.rodeway.com

Suburban
www.suburbanhotels.com

Intercontinental Hotels Group
www.ichotelsgroup.com
Reservations: 1-877-424-2449
Reward Program: *PriorityClub*®

Candlewood Suites
www.candlewoodsuites.com

Crowne Plaza
www.crowneplaza.com

Intercontinental
www.intercontinental.com

Holiday Inn
www.holidayinn.com

Holiday Inn Express
www.holidayinnexpress.com

Hotel Indigo
www.hotelindigo.com

Staybridge Suites
www.staybridge.com

The Hilton Family
www.hilton.com
Reservations: 1-800-HILTONS
Reward Program: *Hilton Hhonors*®

Conrad Hotels
www.conradhotels.com

Doubletree
www.doubletree.com

Embassy Suites
www.embassysuites.com

Hampton Inn
www.hamptoninn.com

Hilton Garden Inn
www.gardeninn.com

Hilton
www.hilton.com

Homewood Suites by Hilton
www.homewoodsuites.com

Scandic Hotels
www.scandic-hotels.com

The Waldorf-Astoria Collection
www.waldorfastoriacollection.com

Hyatt

www.hyatt.com
Reservations: 1-888-591-1234
Reward Program: *Gold Passport*®

AmeriSuites
www.amerisuites.com

Hawthorn Suites
www.hawthorn.com

Hyatt
www.hyatt.com

Hyatt Place
www.hyattplace.com

Hyatt Summerfield Suites
www.summerfieldsuites.com

Marriott International

www.marriott.com
Reservations: 1-888-236-2427
Reward Program: *Marriott Rewards*®

Marriott
www.marriott.com

J.W. Marriott
www.marriott.com

Renaissance
www.renaissancehotels.com

Courtyard
www.courtyard.com

Residence Inn
www.residenceinn.com

Fairfield Inn
www.fairfieldinn.com

TownePlace Suites
www.towneplace.com

SpringHill Suites
www.springhillsuites.com

Starwood

www.starwoodhotels.com
Reservations: Centralized by individual brand; see below.
Reward Program: *Preferred Guest*®

Sheraton
www.sheraton.com
1-800-325-3535

Four Points by Sheraton
www.fourpoints.com
1- 800-368-7764

W Hotels
www.whotels.com
1-888-625-5144

aloft
www.alofthotels.com
1-888-625-5144 (W Hotels)

347

St. Regis
www.stregis.com
1-800-598-1863

Le Meridien
www.lemeridien.com
1-800-543-4300

Westin
www.westin.com
1-800-578-7878

Element
www.elementhotels.com
1-800-578-7878 (Westin)

Wyndham Worldwide

www.wyndhamworldwide.com
Reservations: Centralized by individual brand; see below.
Reward Program: *TripRewards*®

AmeriHost Inn
www.amerihostinn.com
1-800-434-5800

Baymont Inn and Suites
www.baymontinns.com
1-877-229-6668

Days Inn
www.daysinn.com
1-800-329-7466

Howard Johnson
www.hojo.com
1-800-446-4656

Knights Inn
www.knightsinn.com
1-800-843-5644

Ramada
www.ramada.com
1-800-272-6232

Super 8
www.super8.com
1-800-800-8000

Travelodge
www.travelodge.com
1-800-578-7878

Wingate Inn
www.wingateinns.com
1-800-228-1000

Wyndham
www.wyndham.com
1-800-996-3426

HOSTELS

Hostels offer local flavor, low prices, and a chance to meet other travelers from around the world. Several good sources for finding hostels are included below.

Hostel World
www.hostelworld.com
Online reservations, SMS confirmation, and over 900,000 reviews of hostels around the globe.

Hostels.com
www.hostels.com
More than 10,000 hostels worldwide, searchable by region and with reservations accepted online.

BOUTIQUE HOTELS

Independent boutique hotels operate around the world in virtually every country. Here are two sources that may be useful in finding local boutique hotels for your trips. Internet searches are also useful in identifying boutique properties.

Preferred Boutique

www.preferred-boutique.com

Reservations: 1-877-474-7500

A premier collection of boutique hotels that offer superior ambience and local flavor in locations around the world.

Design Hotels

www.designhotels.com

Reservations: 1-800-337-4685

Over 140 hotels located throughout the world united by progressive design.

CAMPGROUNDS

Camping is available in many places around the world, including most national and state parks within the United States and other countries. There are also several private campground organizations, including those listed here.

Go Camping America

www.gocampingamerica.com

Information on camping locations throughout the United States national and state park systems.

KarmaBum

www.karmabum.com

Information on camping and budget travel in Europe, including RV rental and sites accessible by train.

KOA (Kampgrounds of America)

www.koa.com

Information: (406) 248-7444

Campgrounds and facilities throughout the United States and Canada.

349

Appendix D:

Rental Car Companies

Links included here are also provided online at
www.spontaneoustourism.com.

WORLDWIDE COMPANIES

Nine worldwide rental car companies are listed here along with the names of their elite programs where applicable.

Contact phone numbers provided are toll-free within the United States and Canada. International customers should refer to the companies' Web sites for appropriate contact numbers.

Alamo
www.alamo.com
Reservations: 1-800-GO-ALAMO (all)
Elite Program: *Quicksilver*

Avis
www.avis.com
Reservations: 1-800-331-1212 (all)
Elite Program: *Preferred Service*

Budget
www.budget.com
Reservations: 1-800-527-0700 (domestic)
1-800-472-3325 (international)
Elite Program: *FastBreak*

Dollar
www.dollar.com
Reservations: 1-800-800-3665 (all)
Elite Program: *DOLLAR Express*

Enterprise
www.enterprise.com
Reservations: 1-800-261-7331 (all)
Elite Program: None

Europcar
www.europcar.com
Reservations: 1-877-940-6900 (all)
Elite Program: *Privilege*

Hertz
www.hertz.com
Reservations: 1-800-654-3131 (domestic)
1-800-654-3001 (international)
Elite Program: *#1 Gold*

National
www.nationalcar.com
Reservations: 1-800-CAR-RENT (all)
Elite Program: *Emerald Club*

Thrifty
www.thrifty.com
Reservations: 1-800-THRIFTY (all)
Elite Program: *Blue Chip*

ECO-FRIENDLY OPTIONS

Bio-Beetle
Los Angeles, CA and Maui, HI
www.bio-beetle.com
Reservations: 1-877-873-6121

EV Rental
Arizona, California, and Nevada
www.evrental.com
Reservations: Online

Appendix E:

Major Currencies of the World

Links to currency converters are provided online at
www.spontaneoustourism.com.

Every country in the world has the sovereign right to print (or coin) its own money. Many do so, while others prefer to use established currencies of other nations to avoid the cost involved in managing a money supply.

Some of the most common currencies are listed below by region.

North, Central, and South America

United States Dollar (USD)	Canadian Dollar (CAN)	Mexican Peso (MXN)	Costa Rican Colon (CRC)
Columbian Peso (COP)	Venezuelan Bolivar (VEB)	Brazilian Real (BRL)	Argentine Peso (ARS)
Chilean Peso (CLP)	Peruvian New Sol (PEN)		

Europe

British Pound (Sterling) (GBP)	Euro (EUR)	Swiss Franc (CHF)	Danish Krone (KNE)
Swedish Krona (SEK)	Norwegian Krone (NOK)	Polish Zloty (PLN)	Hungarian Forint (HUF)
Czech K oruna (CZK)	Slovakian Koruna (SKK)	Russian Ruble (RUB)	New Turkish Lira (TRY)

Asia

Japanese Yen (JPY) ¥	South Korean Won (KRW)	Chinese Yuan (Renminbi) (CNY)	Hong Kong Dollar (HKD)
New Taiwanese Dollar (TWD)	Singapore Dollar (SGD) S$	Indonesian Rupiah (IDR)	Thai Baht (THB)
Malaysian Ringgit (MYR)	Vietnamese Dong (VND)	Indian Rupee (INR)	Pakistani Rupee (PKR)

Australia and Oceana Region

Australian Dollar (AUD)	New Zealand Dollar (NZD)	Philippine Peso (PHP)

The Middle East

New Israeli Shekel (ILS)	Saudi Riyal (SAR)	Jordanian Dinar (JOD)	Bahraini Dinar (BHD)
Egyptian Pound (EGP)	Iranian Rial (IRR)	Kuwaiti Dinar (KWD)	U.A.E. Dirham (AED)

Africa

South African Rand (ZAR)	Zimbabwe Dollar (ZWD)	Moroccan Dirham (MAD)	Kenyan Shilling (KES)

Appendix F:

Packing List

Links to packing tips are also provided online at
www.spontaneoustourism.com.

Clothing

__ Long-Sleeve Shirts	__ Underwear
__ Short-Sleeve Shirts	__ T-Shirts
__ Casual Pants (Jeans)	__ Socks
__ Shorts or Skirt	__ Belt
__ Walking Shoes	__ Money Belt

Electronics

__ Digital Camera	__ Extra Batteries
__ Cellular Phone	__ Phone Charger
__ Plug Adapter Kit	__ Flashlight
__ Laptop Computer	__ Power Supply

Climate-Specific

Tropical (Beach)

__ Bathing Suit	__ Beach Towel
__ DEET Bug Repellant	__ Blanket or Mat

Arid (Desert)

__ Loose-Fitting, Light-Colored Clothes

__ Hat   __ Water Bottle

Cold Weather

__ Long Underwear   __ Coat

__ Knit Cap   __ Sweater

__ Gloves   __ Scarf

Wet Weather

__ Raincoat or Poncho   __ Pack Cover

__ Umbrella

Documents and Currency

__ Drivers License   __ Lodging Confirmation

__ Passport and visas (if needed)   __ Rental Car Confirmation

__ Credit or Debit Card   __ Travel Itinerary

__ Cash (not more than $200)   __ Health Insurance Card

First Aid and Medical

__ Painkillers   __ Bandages

__ Allergy Medicine   __ Antibiotic Ointment

__ Anti-Diarrhea   __ Prescriptions

__ Antacid   __ Contraceptives (optional)

__ Lip Balm   __ Sunscreen

Personal Hygiene

__ Toothbrush   __ Soap or Shower Gel

__ Toothpaste   __ Shampoo

__ Mouthwash   __ Conditioner (optional)

__ Dental Floss   __ Lotion (optional)

__ Razor   __ Towel

__ Shaving Cream   __ Feminine Hygiene Items

Note: All gels and liquids must be 3 oz. or less and packed into a single quart-size zip-top plastic bag to be taken through security in a carry-on bag. For more information, visit *www.tsatraveltips.us*.

Miscellaneous

__ Pen or Pencil   __ Travel Log or Notebook

__ Phone Calling Card   __ Guidebook

__ Water Purification   __ Maps

Index

375

377

Notes

CrystalOrb LLC

An Independent Publishing Company

POB 100188
Arlington, VA 22210
http://www.crystalorbllc.com

Book Order Form

Please make your check or money order payable to "CrystalOrb LLC" and mail it along with this form to the above address.

	Quantity		Price/Each		Subtotal
Trade Paperback					
ISBN 978-0-9791897-0-8					
6 x 9 Trim / Perfect Binding	_____	x	$14.95	=	$_____
Large Print Edition					
ISBN 978-0-9791897-1-5					
8.25 x 11 Trim / Perfect Binding	_____	x	$19.95	=	$_____
Shipping					
U.S. Postal Service Media Mail	_____	x	$2.49	=	$_____
			TOTAL ENCLOSED:		$_____

Shipping Information

Name: _____

Address: _____

_____

City: _____ State: _____ Zip: _____

Signature: _____

Do you have a Promotional Code?	Code: _____